"I was underwater in Seoul, humiliated. I couldn't stay under there
forever, so I came up and started swimming to the side of the pool.
Looking out into the crowd, I could tell that everyone was shocked
and concerned. They could probably tell that I was upset, too. My
first reaction was to get angry with myself for hitting the board—
my first reaction is always to be angry with myself. But the anger
passed quickly, because I was terrified about something that I'm
sure never crossed the mind of anyone in that hall. . . . *What if I
cut my scalp? What if I'm bleeding? What if I get blood on someone?*"

Everyone's life has moments that shine like gold in memory and
others that are painful to relive. Greg Louganis's life has had many
more than most. In this awesomely candid book, he relives them
all—the highs and lows—to emerge from an ocean of publicity
and sea of controversy, not as an icon of athletic excellence but
as a living, loving, hurting, hoping human being.

GREG LOUGANIS is a four-time Olympic gold-medal diving
champion. He lives in Malibu, California. ERIC MARCUS is an
author whose books include *Making History: The Struggle for Gay
and Lesbian Equal Rights, 1945 to 1990; Is It a Choice?;* and *And
Why Suicide?*

P9-DWK-366

Darcy,
Believe in yourself!

BREAKING
THE
SURFACE

GREG LOUGANIS

with

Eric Marcus

with a New Epilogue by
Greg Louganis

Greg Louganis

Ⓟ
A PLUME BOOK

PLUME
Published by the Penguin Group
Penguin Books USA Inc., 375 Hudson Street,
New York, New York 10014, U.S.A.
Penguin Books Ltd, 27 Wrights Lane,
London W8 5TZ, England
Penguin Books Australia Ltd, Ringwood,
Victoria, Australia
Penguin Books Canada Ltd, 10 Alcorn Avenue,
Toronto, Ontario, Canada M4V 3B2
Penguin Books (N.Z.) Ltd, 182–190 Wairau Road,
Auckland 10, New Zealand

Penguin Books Ltd, Registered Offices:
Harmondsworth, Middlesex, England

Published by Plume, an imprint of Dutton Signet, a division of
Penguin Books USA Inc.
This is an authorized reprint of a hardcover edition published by Random House,
Inc. Published by arrangement with Random House, Inc. For information address
Random House, 201 East 50th Street, New York, N.Y. 10022.

First Plume Printing, March, 1996
10 9 8 7 6 5 4 3 2 1

Ⓟ   REGISTERED TRADEMARK—MARCA REGISTRADA

ISBN 0–452–27590–3
CIP data is available.

DEDICATION PAGE PHOTO: Greg Louganis with Jeanne and
Ryan White at the 1987 Pan American Games, Indianapolis.
Courtesy of the Ryan White Foundation.

Grateful acknowledgment is made to the following for permission to reprint
previously published material:
The New York Times: Excerpt from "Backtalk; Louganis Approaches the Edge of
the Stage, and Leaps," by Robert Lipsyte (September 19, 1993). Copyright © 1993
by The New York Times Company. Reprinted by permission.
Warner Bros. Publications Inc.: Excerpts from "If You Believe," words and music by
Charlie Smalls. Copyright © 1974 by Warner-Tamerlane Publishing Corp. All
rights reserved. Made in USA. Reprinted by permission of Warner Bros.
Publications Inc., Miami, FL 33014.

Printed in the United States of America

BOOKS ARE AVAILABLE AT QUANTITY DISCOUNTS WHEN USED TO PROMOTE PRODUCTS
OR SERVICES. FOR INFORMATION PLEASE WRITE TO PREMIUM MARKETING DIVISION,
PENGUIN BOOKS USA INC., 375 HUDSON STREET, NEW YORK, NEW YORK 10014.

To Ryan White,

my inspiration and guardian angel

and to Dr. Stan Ziegler,

my strength

Believe in yourself right from the start
Believe in the magic that's inside your heart
Believe all these things
Not because I told you to
But believe in yourself
If you believe in yourself
Just believe in yourself
As I believe in you

—"If You Believe," from the musical *The Wiz,*
    words and music by Charlie Smalls

CONTENTS

INTRODUCTION

Lots of people think I'm shy and quiet. That's because I've held so much inside my entire life. Now I want to say everything all at once. As I went through the process of writing this book, there were times when I tripped over my own words and thoughts, trying to explain everything in one paragraph.

It may sound odd that I have so much to say. After all, I've been a public person for much of my life, with plenty of opportunities to say whatever I wanted. But for many reasons, I couldn't. And the more I grew in public stature over the course of my Olympic career, the less I felt I could say. By the time I started this book, I had so many secrets that I couldn't keep track of them anymore. For me, this book means no more secrets.

For years the press has described me as "reticent," "shy," "quiet," a "mystery," an "enigma" even. I've had a reputation for never discussing my personal life, although there's always been plenty to read between the lines of newspaper and magazine profiles.

What has been known about me, the basic facts, can fit in a paragraph: I was born in 1960 to a Samoan father and Northern European mother. Nine months later, I was adopted by a Greek father and a Texas farm-girl mother. I was reared in the San Diego suburbs and started diving at age nine. When I was sixteen, I won a silver medal at the 1976 Olympics in Montreal for 10-meter platform diving, and I won two gold medals at the 1984 Olympics in Los Angeles, one for 10-meter platform and the other for 3-meter springboard. When I was twenty-eight, I gashed my head on a diving board at the 1988 Olympics in Seoul and still won two more gold medals. I got into a little trouble with drugs and alcohol along the way. I also did some acting, endorsed a handful of products, and appeared in several ads. When I was twenty-nine, I had to get a restraining order against my live-in "manager." Then I disappeared for a few years, only to turn up in an off-Broadway play about gay dating in the nineties as a chorus boy who dies of AIDS. Most recently, I finally confirmed what's been rumored for years—that I'm gay—and then I entered the fray over the scheduling of the 1996 Olympic volleyball preliminary competition in Cobb County, Georgia, a place where some people think that the best way to deal with gay men and women is to pass legislation against us. I'm very proud that I helped get that venue changed.

I could have left it at that. I could have chosen never to talk about being gay. Most high-profile athletes who are gay never do, and for good reason. Instead, I've chosen to talk about my life—a life that sometimes I can't believe I've lived.

A lot of people think they know who I am, especially parents who bring their kids to meet me at public appearances. They say they want their kids to grow up to be just like me. My reaction to that has always been, Would they feel that way if they *really* knew me? My second thought has always been, I wouldn't wish my life on anyone. Now, I want people to know who I really am and what I went through. Then, if someone still wants his or her kids to grow up like me, I won't have to wonder, What if they knew?

I also want to set the record straight about who I am, because my secrets have become overwhelming. I want to start living my life the way normal people do, without having to watch every word, without having to remember what I've shared with whom. I want never again to feel compelled to hide out in my house in the California hills, avoiding situations in which I have to edit what I say and lie about my life.

I hope my story will help anyone who has to face adversity, young people in particular—especially those who face challenges like the ones I've had. I also hope to dispel myths about gay people, some of which I have struggled with for most of my life. Maybe I can prevent one teenager from being infected with HIV. And maybe I can give hope to people who are in abusive relationships: You can get out and start over again. You've got to.

I'm not writing this book because I want anyone to feel sorry for me. It's not my intention to shock anyone, but looking objectively at some of what I've lived through, even I find parts of my life shocking, and I was there to live it. All in all, I've had an extraordinary life. I was given a remarkable gift and wonderful opportunities that I made the most of. I've been lucky to have the unwavering love of my mother, supportive friends, and enthusiastic fans. But telling my story frightens me. For one thing, I'm a diver—I'm accustomed to speaking with my body. I've never been comfortable expressing myself in words, and I've generally avoided it. I'm frightened that people won't accept me for who I am or that they'll focus only on the personal aspects of my life and forget what I accomplished as a diver. I worry that I'll hurt some of the people who have protected me for so long by keeping my secrets and supporting me in my desire to remain a private person. They worry that I'll be hurt by criticisms of who I am and some of the things I've done. My mom worries that I won't be able to make a living, that I'll lose the house I worked so hard to buy. Others fear that by stepping forward I'll be closing the door on future professional opportunities. My friend Megan worries for my personal safety.

Fear has ruled my life for too long, and I'm grateful to my family and the friends who helped protect me, but I don't need that kind of support anymore. To my friends and family, who already know much of what you're going to read about my life, I have a simple request: Don't protect me anymore. Don't keep my secrets anymore. Help me live my life openly and honestly.

Breaking the Surface is the story of a lonely boy who struggled with dyslexia and discrimination yet discovered he had a great gift for acrobatics and diving. It's about a shy kid who battled low self-esteem, bouts of depression, and conflicts over his sexuality yet still went on to become one of the most accomplished divers of all time. It's about a man who had a world of opportunities yet lost his way when those opportunities ended. And it's the story of a man who is learning to live with HIV.

Many people have asked me why I've chosen to tell my story now. Some wonder why I didn't write it years ago. Others have asked me why I didn't wait until I'm older. I didn't do it years ago because I wasn't ready to risk telling the truth. I'm doing it now because I want to tell my story in my own words while I still have the chance. I'm finally ready to share my story. I hope you're ready to hear it.

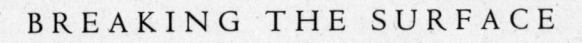

BREAKING THE SURFACE

I

~~~~~~

T H E

N I N T H

D I V E

THE PRELIMINARIES WERE going off almost as well at the '88 Olympics as they had in 1984: Thirty-five divers from around the world were competing for one of twelve spots, and after eight dives, I was leading. Only three more dives and I'd be on my way to the finals and a chance at my third gold medal.

Several thousand people were packed into Seoul's Chamshil Pool, and the atmosphere was electric. As I waited at the bottom of the ladder for my turn, I went through the dive in my mind, visualizing each step and playing music in my head to the beat of the dive. Most of the time I dove to "If You Believe," from *The Wiz*, because of its message: "If you believe within your heart you'll know / That no one can change the path that you must go. Believe what you feel, and know you're right / Because the time will come around when you'll say it's yours."

Once the diver ahead of me was in the air, I climbed up the ladder to the 3-meter board. My next dive, the ninth, was a reverse two-and-a-half pike, usually one of my best dives. The crowd was still cheering the previous diver as I walked out onto the board and set the fulcrum, the movable bar you adjust to give the board more or less spring.

My dive was announced, and I walked to my starting point on the springboard, got into place, took a deep breath, and told myself to relax. I took the first step, the second step, the third step, and the fourth step, all to the beat of the music from *The Wiz* that only I could hear. On the fifth step, I swung my arms in a smooth arc and started bending into the hurdle, pushing the board down. As I pushed into the hurdle, I inhaled, reaching up with my arms straight over my head, bringing my right knee up toward my chest, and extending my left leg down toward the board. I listened to hear the board bounce once against the fulcrum, then a second time, and then came down on the board with both feet. I pushed down on the board with the full weight of my body, bending into the board in preparation for the takeoff.

To take off from the board, I reached up with my arms and pushed off with my legs at the same time, allowing the board to kick me into the air. As I pulled my shoulders back a bit and pushed my hips up and out, I could feel right away that my weight was back in the direction of the board, which meant I was going to be close. When that happens, you worry about hitting your hands on the board, so my concern as I went through the dive was to get my hands out of the way.

Ron O'Brien, my coach, was standing at the side of the pool far-thest from the board. From the moment I pushed off, he later said, he could feel in his stomach that I was going to hit, but he didn't know whether I was going to tick my head, hit my head, tick my hand, or break my hand. He said he hoped I was going to slide by the board like I'd done in the past when I was close. I'm usually able to make split-second adjustments to get out of the way of the board when I know I'm going to be close.

So, as I brought my legs up into the pike position to initiate the somersault, I exhaled and held my breath. Spinning through the somersaults, I saw the water once, then a second time, and then I came out of the pike position with my arms wide so I wouldn't hit my hands on the board. I thought I'd cleared it, but I heard this big hollow thud and felt myself landing in the water in a really strange way.

I was underwater before I realized that I'd hit my head. Once I did, the first emotion I felt was embarrassment: This was the Olympics, I was a gold medalist, and here I'd gone and hit my damn head on the board. I'd had accidents before, but never at the Olympics.

While I was still underwater, I tried to figure out how to get out of the pool without anybody seeing me. I guess I was in shock. Ron ran to the side of the pool where the diving board was, watching to see if I was coming up. If I wasn't coming up, he was going in after me. Ron's wife, Mary Jane, was up in the stands holding her breath. She knew better than most people how bad that thud could be. She also knew that a springboard is pretty forgiving compared to a 10-meter platform. Nine years before, I'd hit my head on a platform in Tbilisi, in the former Soviet Union, and was knocked out for twenty minutes: They had to pull me out of the water. I had a concussion and had to drop out of the competition, but I was lucky I wasn't killed.

So there I was underwater in Seoul, humiliated. I couldn't stay under there forever, so I came up and started swimming to the side of the pool. Looking out into the crowd and at the people standing on the deck, I could tell that everyone was shocked and concerned. They could probably tell that I was upset, too. My first reaction was to get angry with myself for hitting the board—my first reaction is always to get angry with myself. But the anger passed quickly, because I was terrified about something that I'm sure never crossed the mind of anyone in that hall.

As I swam toward the side of the pool, all kinds of thoughts raced through my head: What if I cut my scalp? What if I'm bleeding? Is there blood in the pool? What happens if I get blood on someone? In normal circumstances that wouldn't have been such a big deal, but these were anything but normal circumstances. I was in a total panic that I might cause someone else harm. It was sheer terror. I didn't even pause to think that I might be badly injured. But whatever was going through my mind, I had to get out of the pool.

As I climbed onto the deck, I felt around my scalp to see if I was bleeding. Ron was coming toward me, but before he got to me, one of the other coaches, Jan Snick, started digging through my hair to see if I had a cut. I held up my hand to get him to back off and to keep everyone else away. I was angry at Jan for trying to help, but he wasn't doing anything unusual. He just didn't know that he was dealing with HIV. I didn't want anyone to touch me—except Ron, who knew the whole story.

Several months before, I'd finally gotten my courage up to go for an HIV test. My lover of six years had already been diagnosed with AIDS; it wasn't surprising that I was HIV-positive. But hitting my head on the diving board was a complete shock. I know it must seem irresponsible now, but I hadn't considered the possibility that I could injure myself in that way. Since my diagnosis, I'd focused entirely on my training for the Olympics and was in almost complete denial about my HIV status. Now, having hit my head, there was no denying the terrifying truth.

Ron got to me, and he put his arm around me and walked me out of the pool area toward a waiting room just beyond the pool. He asked me how I felt, if I was okay, trying to see if I was alert or not. I told him how embarrassed I was, and then, just as we were walking past where most of the divers and coaches were sitting in the stands, Ron saw a trickle of blood coming down the back of my neck. He used his hand to push it back up under my hairline and out of sight. Ron didn't want anyone to see it because he thought it would upset people even more if they saw I was bleeding. But there was also another reason: The Chinese divers and coaches, who were very competitive with me, were standing right there, and he was sure they were thinking, Here's our chance now. Ron always wanted the Chinese to think I had ice water in my veins.

We got to the waiting room and the team doctor, Jim Puffer, met us there. I sat down on the edge of a massage table, and Dr. Puffer started digging around, trying to find the wound.

So many things went through my mind. One stream of thought was: Did I get any blood in the pool? Is the filtration system working? Did they allow ample time before the next diver dove? Did any blood spill on the pool deck? Could I have infected Ron? Then I worried about Dr. Puffer, who wasn't wearing gloves. Was I putting Dr. Puffer in danger?

I was too panicked in that moment to think clearly, but eventually I had a chance to think it through, and then later I talked with Dr. Anthony Fauci, who is the director of the National Institute of Allergy and Infectious Diseases and one of the nation's foremost experts on HIV and AIDS. Dr. Fauci explained: "Even if you started bleeding before you got out of the pool, there would have been an extraordinarily low risk of infecting anyone who used the pool following your accident. There are two reasons for this. First, there's the profound dilutional effect—at most, there may have been a minuscule amount of blood in a pool filled with tens of thousands of gallons of water. Second, the chlorine in the pool would have killed the virus." I was relieved to learn that I hadn't put any of the other divers at risk.

The only people who were at any risk, it turns out, were those who came in direct contact with my blood, and according to Dr. Fauci, the risk was extremely small. He explained: "Even if Dr. Puffer had a syringe that contained some of your blood and accidentally injected himself beneath the skin, there would still only be a 0.3 percent chance of infection. In this case, Dr. Puffer was not using a syringe, but a [solid] needle, to stitch the wound, so if he had punctured his own skin, the risk would have been much lower than 0.3 percent. As far as Ron O'Brien and Dr. Puffer both coming in direct contact with your blood, the risk was also extremely low, but how low depends on a number of factors. If they got the blood on intact skin—in other words, they had no abrasions or cuts on their hands—then the risk was very, very low. In fact, there are no well-documented cases existing of somebody becoming infected from having HIV-infected blood splashed on intact skin. If there were an abrasion or a nick or a cut, that would increase the risk, but it would still be a small risk." Since 1988, both Ron and Dr. Puffer have been tested for HIV and both are negative.

Before we left for the '88 Olympics, I had debated telling Dr. Puffer about my HIV status. I realize that it was irresponsible for me not to inform him, but I didn't want him to have the burden of keeping such a difficult secret. We knew a lot of the same people, and I was afraid it might put him in a position to have to lie to somebody. I had entrusted only a handful of people with that information—Ron, my coach, and Tom, my lover, were the only two people at the Olympics who knew. And now I wanted to warn Dr. Puffer, but I was paralyzed.

Ron was standing beside the table where I was sitting, and I looked at him, and I broke down. I wanted to say something about the HIV, but all I could do was cry. Everything was all so mixed up at that point: the HIV, the shock and embarrassment of hitting my head, and an awful feeling that it was all over. The Olympics, I thought, were over for me.

Ron held me as I cried and said, "Greg, you have a wonderful career to look back on. You don't have to do this. You don't have to do anything. No matter what you decide, I'm behind you a hundred percent." Between sobs, I managed to say, "I got halves and zeros on that dive. I can't still be in the contest."

Ron knew I wasn't out of the running, and he was just trying to figure out if I was physically and emotionally up to going on. Actually, I had a strong enough lead when I hit the board to make it into the finals as long as I did reasonably well on the last two dives. Ron went out to check my standings and came back with the news that I was in fifth place. The top twelve divers make the finals. So it wasn't over as long as I had the strength to compete. Ron asked me what I wanted to do.

It was easier for me to focus on diving than it was to think about the possibility of having put Dr. Puffer in danger of contracting HIV. Diving had always been my refuge, and once again it gave me something to focus on in a moment of crisis: It was my way of escaping, just as it had always been.

Once I knew I was still in the running, I never considered giving up. I thought about my friend Ryan White, the teenager from Indiana who had become a national spokesman on the AIDS epidemic. I knew Ryan would never give up, and that gave me the extra push I needed. So I said to Ron, "We've worked too long and hard to get here. I'm not going to give up now." Ron checked his watch. We had about twelve minutes until I had to do the next dive. He asked Dr. Puffer how many stitches it would take to close the gash in my scalp. Dr. Puffer said it would take three or four, and Ron told him to get going. There was no time for anesthetic, so they put me facedown on the table and Dr. Puffer sewed up my scalp and put on a waterproof patch. By then, we had six or seven minutes to go.

Lots of people were standing around the room, and Ron thought we should go for a little walk before I went back for my next dive. We went out the door and walked down a long hallway to the 50-meter pool that was used for water-polo practice. No one was there. Ron told me to jump in the water, to get moving again and get my energy back up. I got in for a minute and got out.

On our way back to the main pool, Ron reminded me that what had happened was a fluke, that I should forget about it. We talked about what I had to do next: Get back up on that board and do my last two dives, which were even more difficult than the one I'd just done.

The next dive, the tenth, was a reverse one-and-a-half with three and a half twists, and the final dive, the eleventh, was a reverse three-and-a-half tuck. They're both tough dives, and they're also executed by turning in the same direction as the dive that cost me the four stitches in my scalp. To reassure me, Ron said, "Well, hockey players get hit in the face with a puck and get fifty stitches and then come out and play the rest of the game. You only have four stitches, and you only have to do two dives." We both laughed. Neither of us mentioned the HIV.

As I went to the ladder to get back on the board, Ron said, "Greg, you've done this a thousand times in practice. Just do it like you do it."

I knew I had to jump it out, put a little more space between me and the diving board. It was never my nature to play it safe, to hold back. You don't win gold medals by playing it safe. My instinct was to stand it up, stay close to the board, so I was fighting with myself. I had to turn my head off, or I wasn't going to be able to do it. Ron's "just do it like you do it" helped me stop obsessing over what I was about to do and how I should do it.

I walked over to the base of the ladder and waited for the diver before me to go. I probably wasn't there more than half a minute, but that's always a dangerous time. You're out there all by yourself, with thousands of people in the stands watching, and if your confidence goes, you're in trouble. As I waited to get on the board, I kept repeating to myself, "Breathe, relax," which was how I got focused.

When the diver ahead of me left the board, I climbed the ladder. I walked out on the board and set the fulcrum. Then I tossed my chamois down onto the deck. Your chamois is essential equipment, like your bathing suit. It's a rectangular, absorbent cloth about the size of a large napkin, and you use it to dry yourself after each dive. My chamois was also sort of a security blanket, and I was never without it at a diving meet.

As I stood on the board shaking out my legs and arms, they announced my name. To my complete surprise, there was thunderous applause. Then, when they announced the dive, it got eerily quiet. You could feel the tension in the hall, and I was already terrified. I still hadn't figured out what I'd done wrong in the last dive, and here I was about to do a dive that again would put my head within inches of the board. I didn't want to embarrass myself in front of all those people. Millions of people around the world were watching on television. And what if I hit the board again?

In preparation for the dive, I rubbed my right hand through the back of my wet hair to get some water on it. Then I rubbed my hands together to get them equally damp—that was one of my diving rituals—and for a moment I stood there trying to get focused. Then I took a really deep breath and patted my chest so that everyone in the hall could see that my heart felt like it was pounding outside my chest. Then I smiled, and everybody started laughing, and I laughed along with them. The tension broke when they saw that I was more nervous and scared than they were. Their laughter helped me relax. It also made me realize how much support I had. I realized that the audience *wanted* me to do a good dive.

Once everyone quieted down, I went through the dive one more time in my mind. Then I just did it. I approached the end of the board, propelled myself into the air, executed the dive, and broke the surface of the water.

I still remember how quiet it was under the water, completely silent. I remember that I had a moment to enjoy the relief of having done the dive without hitting my head again. I knew it was a pretty good dive. As I swam up toward the surface of the water, I started to hear the crowd. I could tell that they were cheering for me. But as I neared the side of the pool and the water drained from my ears, the cheers got louder and louder, until they sounded like a roar. I couldn't help but smile. I had never felt that kind of approval before, and it was all a little unreal.

I didn't get a perfect score, but I did get 87.12 points, the highest score for any dive in the prelims. Ron thinks it was the best dive of the Olympics, even though I was still a little too close. He reminded me that I had one more dive to go, and it was my most difficult. Before I went to the ladder to get back on the board for my last dive, Ron said, "Jump it out a little bit, okay?" Then he told me to believe in myself.

The final dive was just fine, and it was such a relief to be through. I wound up coming in third in the preliminaries. All this just for a chance to compete for the gold.

I sometimes can't believe what I had to go through to get to that point. And it wasn't just the bump on my head, not just the HIV diagnosis, but a lifetime of fear and pain and always feeling that the next dive would make it all right. I'd survived once again, but that ninth dive changed everything.

Ron was in a hurry to get my wound properly cleaned up and re-stitched. On our way out of the building, reporters, waiting to ask questions, stopped us. One of them yelled, "What happened?" So I said, "I hit my head on the board." But then she asked, "*How* did it happen?" So I looked at her and said, very matter-of-factly, "Well, I guess I was too close to the diving board." All the reporters laughed, including the one who had asked the question. Someone else called out, "Did it hurt?" I smiled, and said, "What do you think?"

There was an official van waiting for us outside, and I was driven to the Olympic Village, where I went to see Dr. Puffer. He redid the stitches, but again didn't use gloves. I should have told Dr. Puffer that I was HIV-positive so he could take the proper medical precautions. He never asked me about my HIV status, but AIDS wasn't something people in sports talked about in 1988. They just figured we were all perfectly healthy. It's no excuse, but I wasn't the only one in denial about AIDS in 1988. The whole world was still in denial then, as many people still are in 1995.

After Dr. Puffer was done, Ron walked me back through the Olympic Village courtyard to my room. We talked about going up there the next day and doing the same thing, except that this time I wasn't going to hit my head. Neither of us considered dropping out.

Besides worrying about me, Ron had his own worries. His mother had been very ill with a rare neurological disorder. She had taken a turn for the worse just after we got to Korea, and Ron had thought of leaving before the competition began, but the doctor said she was in a coma and that there was nothing he could do. Still, he was tempted to go home, but he said that his mother would have wanted him to be at the Olympics. Just before the springboard preliminaries got under way, Ron got the news that she'd passed away. He didn't tell me about it until after the Games were over.

In some ways, getting through those last two dives after I hit my head was easier than getting through the night and preparing for the next day's competition. I really didn't have a lot of time to think about those final dives, but I had all night to think about what I'd done wrong: what I'd done wrong on the dive and what I'd done wrong in life. Had I put someone else in danger, and what had I done to deserve HIV? Was AIDS a punishment? What would happen tomorrow? I tried to figure it all out, and for the life of me I couldn't figure out any of it. So I focused on the ninth dive, and kept playing it over and over in my mind, trying to get my body to understand what had gone wrong. Ron had told me what I'd done wrong mechanically, but I couldn't see it in my mind's eye. I couldn't get my body to feel it. Usually, if I could see it and feel it, I could make the correction. This time I couldn't. I couldn't correct any of it.

Even worse, I couldn't relax enough to mentally go over my list of dives for the next day. Normally, the night before a major competition, I'd run through my dives in my head, imagining them in the pool that I was competing in, complete with the visual surroundings. That always helped me get to sleep. But that night I couldn't sleep. And as I tossed and turned, every once in a while I'd hit my head on the headboard. It hurt—a lot.

I finally fell asleep for a while, but my alarm went off in the middle of the night. I was taking AZT to keep the HIV in check, and I had to take it every four hours, around the clock. In the months since I'd been diagnosed, no matter how hard I tried to pretend that everything was normal, I always had my AZT alarm to remind me every four hours that my life was changed forever.

I hardly slept at all, just stayed in bed until around six in the morning, time for practice. The final round of the springboard competition was only five hours away. I had no idea how I was going to get through it, but I knew deep down that I had to. I couldn't give up now.

2

‘‘ I

C A N

D O

T H A T ’ ’

BY THE 1988 Olympics in Seoul, I'd been diving for nearly twenty years. When I was nine, my parents had a swimming pool built in our backyard, and I very quickly began practicing my gymnastics stunts off the diving board. I had a lot of fun, but I landed on my back a lot. If you looked at our old family home movies, you might wonder why I didn't give up after the first couple of times.

Long before I became a competitive diver, gymnastics and acrobatics were my real loves. By age nine, I was already a seasoned performer on the local talent-show and convalescent-home circuit. I've heard my mother tell the story of how I got started so many times that it feels like *my* memory. It also sounds like the song "I Can Do That" from *A Chorus Line*.

My sister, Despina, was taking dance and acrobatics classes at the Hallik and Vaughn Dance Studio, and my mother would take me along when it was time to pick her up. We'd get there early, and I'd struggle to get out of my mother's lap and go into the rehearsal room. I could hear the music, and I could hear the teacher calling out instructions, and I wanted to see what was going on. Sometimes my mother would let me sneak into the back of the room to watch. But I didn't want to just watch, I wanted to jump right in there.

The teacher found it hard to ignore an eighteen-month-old kid in diapers doing acrobatics, so after a couple of classes she talked to my mother about putting me in the class. My mother had some reservations because I was so young, but the teacher pointed out that I was a quick learner and that I seemed to be having fun. So Mom signed me up for the three-days-a-week class. The only problem was that I learned everything so quickly that my sister and the other kids in the class had a hard time keeping up with me. Most of the time I could outdo everyone. My mom was very proud, because the other parents kept telling her how good I was. Years later, in newspaper stories about me, reporters always said that I got into gymnastics when I was diagnosed with asthma. I was already pretty active in gymnastics by the time I developed asthma, but the doctor simply said that I should keep doing it because the exercise would be good for me. Eventually, I outgrew the asthma.

I was three when I was first paired with Eleanor Smith, a very pretty blond-haired girl who was usually an inch or two taller than I was during the nine years we performed as a pair. We were more than partners—we were also friends. We went to dance and gymnastics classes together and did hundreds of routines together: somersaults, back handsprings, and jazz choreography, all set to music.

Eleanor and I worked very hard. We always competed with each other, but it was always fun. We each had to learn the same things: I would learn a trick and then Eleanor would have to learn it. Then she would learn one and I would have to learn it. We constantly pushed each other with a bit of one-upsmanship, and as the years went by, we learned more complicated routines.

I didn't know it at the time, but Eleanor's mother had arranged for her to take private classes so that Eleanor would be able to keep up with me. I only learned this years later from my mom. There was one time when I got to the dance studio early and saw Eleanor working on something new with the instructor, but I just thought they had gotten started without me. I had no inkling that Eleanor needed extra lessons to keep up with me.

I always got along better with Eleanor than I did with my own sister. We never fought, even though we spent an awful lot of time together in class, at each other's houses, and performing. We performed all over the San Diego area. The dance studio we belonged to made the arrangements, and we performed everywhere from convalescent homes to the local naval base. I loved the people at the nursing homes—some of them reminded me of my grandmother, and they'd say nice things about how wonderful we were to come and entertain them. It was difficult when they'd wheel in someone who wasn't conscious or when someone would have to be suctioned during the show to keep from choking. Sometimes the homes weren't particularly clean and the floors were sticky and smelled of vomit. Sometimes it was depressing.

What was more disturbing was performing in homes where there were mentally handicapped people. I saw myself in those kids, and sometimes I thought that's where I belonged. At school my classmates were always calling me a "retard," because I had trouble reading. I'd look in the faces of the kids in the homes, most of whom were older than I was, and the reflection of myself that I saw scared the hell out of me. When the kids would rush up to us after a performance to give us hugs, I'd just freeze. My mom knew I hated to perform at these homes, but I never told her why. I'm glad now that I did the performances, but it was tough.

What I loved best about acrobatics were the talent contests. I loved winning trophies. Eleanor and I often won first place. One of the most exciting competitions was the 1970 sweepstakes at Grossmont High School in La Mesa, which was for people from dance studios all over San Diego County. The performances went on for two days. The competition was broken down into jazz, tap, acrobatics, and music. There was even a Tahitian dance category. Eleanor and I competed in Pee Wee Jazz, Pee Wee Acrobatics, and Pee Wee Tap. The ten highest-scoring acts performed in the final round, and we were one of the ten.

While the judges were tallying the final scores, they had the previous year's winning act perform its routine for everyone, but I couldn't wait for the judges to announce the final results. When they announced that we'd won, Eleanor started crying—so I started crying, too, because it seemed like the right thing to do. They gave us a trophy that was about three feet high. Winning that trophy was great, but then you always want more.

Even as a kid I was a perfectionist. I practiced my routines over and over again until I got them perfect. When I was three, my dance instructor suggested I play the performance music at home and do the routine in my head. Instinctively, I understood: I would do every step over and over in my head until I visualized getting it right. That was how I memorized the whole routine.

One of my biggest fears was always being out onstage and forgetting what I was supposed to do next. By practicing over and over in my head, I stopped worrying about going blank. I had the routine so deeply memorized that I could feel it. Dancers call it kinetic memory. I memorized each routine so well that my body could do it without my even thinking about it.

I've thought a lot recently about why it was so important to me that I do everything perfectly: I wasn't very good at school, particularly in reading, and this was one way to prove that I wasn't retarded. I may have brought home D's from school, but I could go out onstage and get applause and win first prize at competitions. I found the one thing I was good at, but being good at something wasn't enough—I had to be the best at it.

≈

MY MOM AND Eleanor's mom put a lot of effort into making us look great. With the help of our teacher, they made all our costumes, which wasn't easy because the costumes had to be functional. Eleanor and I were little contortionists, doing splits and handstands and touching our feet to our heads. Everything had to stretch. We wore a lot of leotard-type outfits, mostly decorated with sequins.

Mom bought the fabric for my costumes out of her grocery money. I often went with her when she bought material, and she always said, "Don't tell your dad." She was afraid that Dad would get angry with her if he knew she was spending so much money on our costumes. I don't know where he thought the money for the material was coming from, but I knew never to say anything.

It's embarrassing to look at some of the pictures, because our home-made costumes fit the styles of the times. We had one jazz costume that consisted of a short shirt that tied in front, huge bell-bottom stretch pants, and a multicolored headband. We would have fit right in with *The Partridge Family* TV show. We had another outfit that was all pink, including a pink sequin-covered cummerbund, a sequined V decorating the shirt, and a line of pink sequins down the side of the stretch pants. It was a tuxedo-type design. It was very . . . pink.

But my favorite costume was a little tuxedo. The entire thing, from top hat to tails, was midnight-blue glitter, and my mother had to stitch it by hand because the fabric kept breaking the sewing-machine needle. I was only three, but I knew it was fabulous.

My mom was great. Besides making my costumes, she also took me to my classes and never missed a performance. Unlike a lot of the other moms, she was not a backstage mother. There were plenty of them, hovering over their kids, constantly fixing their hair, getting angry if they made a mistake, telling them: "Bite your lip"; "Pinch your cheeks"; "Point your toes." The pinching and the biting were to bring blood to the lips and cheeks, for color. But my mom wasn't like them at all. Her attitude was, You can't always win, but you can always do your best. Her only comment to me before a performance was, "Have fun," which always brought a smile to my face.

Eleanor's mother, however, was a bit of a stage mom, and very competitive. I was lucky Eleanor and I were on the same team because otherwise I might have been in trouble. But she was a great sport and, together, she and my mom were right in there setting up the props and ladders for us to tumble from.

My dad hardly ever came to any of my performances. He paid for my classes, which was supportive financially, but his main concern was that it shouldn't interfere with what my mom was supposed to do around the house. It was worst for her on the weekends, when we had our performances, because Dad didn't like her to go out when he was home.

A lot of times we skipped performances because she was afraid that my father would be angry. On weekends, she'd cook dinner in the morning before she took us to a competition, so all she would have to do when she got home was heat it up. During the week, she'd make dinner while we were at school so she could take us to practice in the afternoon and not be late with dinner.

But diving sparked my dad's interest, even though it was Mom who enrolled me in classes. She was afraid I'd hurt myself trying gymnastics stunts off the diving board, so she asked about diving lessons at the La Mesa pool, which was right next to the recreation center where Eleanor and I took gymnastics. It wasn't that my mother had a vision of me being a great diver or anything—she just didn't want me to break my neck.

I hated my first diving coach. He was a big, dark, hairy guy who was always yelling at us. He was so awful that I thought of quitting all the time, but I stuck with it as soon as I discovered that I was good at it. It was my dad who found me my next coach.

John Anders, a local police officer, often came by to watch us practice. One afternoon, Dad struck up a conversation with him, and it turned out that John used to be a diver and did some coaching on the side. My father later called him up and asked him if he'd consider coaching our team. I wasn't the only one who wanted to quit; all the divers were unhappy.

John was wonderful, encouraging in a way that made us all want to do well. He took the time to explain things to us and presented diving in a way that made a lot of sense to me, like the dance instructor who had taught me to visualize. John said that he once had a coach who told him that diving should be like poetry, each movement flowing into the next. He also taught us to "ride the board." He said that when you push off into your hurdle, you should hear the board bounce twice against the fulcrum before you land on it. So I started listening for the board, and pretty soon I learned how to ride it. That's the first step toward doing a good dive.

John was a very soft-spoken family man. I was impressed with the way he went camping and hiking with his sons. I envied John's sons, because he was the kind of father I wanted. They spent a lot of time doing the things fathers and sons do together. My father always made me feel like I was putting him out, that I was a bother, that he'd rather be doing other things than spending time with me. The only time he did something special with me was when he took me camping with the Y Indian Guides. It was the first and last time. He made it clear that he was fulfilling an obligation, and he had a contemptuous attitude toward the people there, as if he was somehow better than everyone else. I was very sensitive to my dad's unspoken words. So to make sure we didn't go again, I told him I had a miserable time and asked if it was okay if we didn't do this again.

Coach Anders, on the other hand, always gave us the sense that he cared, that he wanted to be there with us, and that he wanted us to do our best. At the same time, as long as we did our best, it didn't matter to John whether or not we won. He made us feel good about getting second or third place. No matter how we placed, he would concentrate on the best dive we had done in that competition and praise us for doing it so well. Of course, for me, that really made me want to win so I could please him even more. Because he made me feel good about myself, I looked forward to practice, even when it was cold and I didn't feel much like diving. If every coach and gym teacher had those values, we'd see a lot fewer problems with young athletes.

I was about ten years old when I started with Coach Anders. It was a very important time for me, because I really flourished. A year later, in 1971, he got me to the national Junior Olympics at the Air Force Academy in Colorado Springs. I made it all the way through local and regional 1-meter springboard competitions, and I qualified. This was my first national competition, the biggest meet I'd ever been to. There were divers from Florida, New York, Arkansas, Washington—all over.

It was the most exciting competition I'd ever been in, but also the hardest.

I don't know if it was the pressure of my first national event or what, but I wasn't diving as well as I knew I could. There were about thirty divers, and each time they cut, I was the last one to make it. So when they cut to the top sixteen, I was sixteenth. When they cut to the top twelve, I was twelfth. My parents, who were there with me, knew something was wrong, especially when John took me over to see them before we finished the second round and I wouldn't say anything. My father told my mother to take me outside and talk to me.

I didn't want to talk to anyone, not even my mom. I'd done so well before I got to Colorado that I couldn't understand what was wrong. I just clammed up. Mom walked me to the restaurant next to the pool building and asked me what was up. Suddenly I started crying. I told her I was afraid of disappointing her and my father and, worst of all, Coach Anders. She told me that it didn't matter to her what happened, because I was always going to be her son and that, no matter what, she would always love me. She told me that however I did, it was okay. I don't know why, but this came as a surprise to me. She's told me the same thing all my life, and it's one of the things that I've always counted on.

Mom walked me back to the pool, and I did my last three dives better than everybody else. From twelfth place, I moved up to tie for second. Number two was okay because I knew my mom loved me and that John was proud of me. And I had something to work toward: number one. Even then, winning was a way of making sure they loved me.

For the first two years I dove, my father took me to the pool for practice after school three days a week; in summer we trained every day. He didn't just drop me off and then come get me after the workout, like the other parents did. Most of the time he sat on a bench outside the pool area and watched every single dive. I would have been happy that he took such a great interest, except that on the way home he would repeat every word that my coach had said to me during practice. That was especially tough on bad workout days, because I already felt bad, and there was my father telling me all over again what I'd done wrong.

It wasn't only that my dad repeated the criticisms; it was also that he showed so much interest in my diving after having showed no interest in my acrobatics, gymnastics, and especially my dance. He rarely came to any of my performances with Eleanor, but he was there for every one of my diving meets. Looking back, I realize now that my father might have had more time when I was diving because by then he was more established financially. But at the time I just thought it was because he didn't think that dancing and acrobatics were the kind of thing he wanted his son doing. He was saying that these things I loved weren't worth doing. So when the kids at school started calling me "sissy" and "faggot," I thought my father was saying the same thing by not coming to my performances, and maybe he was. His interest in my diving was the other extreme—it felt like my father was *too* involved, like it was more about him than it was about me. When I was eleven, I finally asked him not to come to my workout sessions anymore.

One day I was supposed to learn a back one-and-a-half pike on the 1-meter springboard. It was a new dive, and I couldn't get myself to do it. I was physically prepared, but mentally I couldn't do it. Actually, I was scared. Learning new dives is terrifying, because you don't know yet what to expect. You don't know what you're going to see as you go through the dive, and you don't know exactly how to execute it. It's the fear that you're going to crash and burn. Besides, it was a very cold day. So I just stood on the board, freezing and frozen. No matter how many times John urged me to just do it, I couldn't. I can be pretty stubborn, so the more he pushed, the more stubborn I got. Finally, he gave up and said, "Let's try tomorrow."

Dad watched the whole thing, and on the way home he didn't say a word, but I knew he was angry. When we got home, he said, "Get your suit on." I looked at him and asked what he was talking about. He said, "You're going to do that back one-and-a-half pike." He wanted me to do it on the board in our pool, and I said, "Dad, it's not a regulation springboard." He said that he didn't care, and he took off his belt and told me not to talk back. You didn't argue with my father. There was one way to do things—the logical way, his way.

Mom tried to stop him, telling him to give me time, but he got mad at her. He didn't like when she contradicted him. I can't remember if he hit me with the belt then or waited until I had my suit on, but he hit me across my backside and legs until it burned. That I can't forget. I didn't want to give my father the satisfaction of seeing me cry, so I held it in.

I got into my suit and put on a short-sleeved wet-suit jacket and went down the stairs to the pool. That's when I started crying—I was still afraid I'd crash and burn on the new dive. He made me do four or five back one-and-a-half pikes. To punish him, I would land flat, purposely trying to hurt myself. Fortunately, the wet suit took some of the sting out of hitting the water flat, but each time, it knocked the wind out of me. I wanted my father to feel bad that he was forcing me to go out on such a cold day in an unheated pool using a substandard board. I was furious with him and felt really hurt. He didn't understand me at all. So I tried to punish him by hurting myself.

My mother didn't come down to the pool. She stayed up at the house and watched from there, crying. There was nothing she could do but watch.

So, what were my father's reasons? Had I embarrassed him by not doing the dive? Was he punishing me for failing? Part of me thought I deserved it, and in an awful way, his punishment helped motivate me. But I never wanted him to do it again.

That evening I had a conversation with my mom. I told her, "He's going to tell me that he has to take me to workouts because you have to cook dinner and keep the house clean." She agreed to offer to take me to my workouts in addition to cooking and cleaning, but she insisted that I talk to him myself.

The next day I talked to my dad and told him that I didn't want him coming to my workouts any longer. My heart was pounding as I said this, and I'm sure my voice was shaking. I told him that I still wanted him to come to my competitions, that I still needed his support. From then on, Mom would drop me off at practice and then go run errands. She was interested in my diving, but it was different. She never pressured me. What was most important to her was that I be happy with whatever I was doing.

I'm sure my father realized that what he had done was wrong. In retrospect, that experience taught me how to stand up to my father. He pushed me to stand up to him, and that made me much stronger. I'd love to know how he felt about what happened that day, but we never talked about it before he died.

3

~~~~~~

SISSY,

NIGGER,

RETARD

THANK GOODNESS FOR the acrobatics and the diving. Without them, I'm not sure how I would have gotten through what turned out to be a challenging and lonely childhood. Between my doubts over whether my adoptive mother and father truly loved me, getting taunted and beaten up by kids at school, and fighting off my own terrible moods, there were times when I wanted to give up. But then I'd go to a talent contest and win first prize or do well in diving practice, and everything would be okay—for a while at least.

My mother tells me that I was very easygoing as a child, very easy to please, and that all you had to do to keep me happy was give me a toy and I played with it. I slept from six o'clock in the evening and waited in my crib until my mother got up at six or seven in the morning, eager to please even in the crib. Sometimes, though, I could have a stubborn streak, and there were times when I wasn't so easy.

The first time my parents saw me, I was nine months old. They'd gotten a call from the Children's Home Society that a Polynesian baby was available for adoption. They asked my mother if she knew what that meant, because most people didn't want anything but a blond, blue-eyed baby. But Mom comes from a family of light-skinned blonds—she's Scotch-Irish—and she specifically wanted dark-skinned, black-haired children, which she told them. My parents had already adopted my sister, Despina, two years earlier, in 1958, and like me, Despina had dark skin, black hair, and brownish-hazel eyes. She's a mix of Native American, French, and English-Scots.

Another thing about me that appealed to my parents was the fact that I was nine months old. They'd adopted Despina at birth, and she was a handful. At nine months, I could sit up by myself. But Mom said that what really cinched the deal was my smile. Once she saw that, she didn't want to look at any other babies.

For my first nine months I lived with a foster family. The adoption agency was having a tough time placing me because of my coloring. The family that took care of me called me Timmy, which might have been the name my natural parents had given me. My natural father was Samoan, and my natural mother was Northern European, blond and blue-eyed, like my adoptive mother. Obviously, I didn't get her coloring. Both of them were teenagers when I was born, and they weren't married.

I don't ever remember asking Mom if I was adopted. It was something I always knew. I remember her saying that she couldn't have children, so adoption gave her the chance to have kids, which made perfect sense to me. It was also the perfect way to tell us we were adopted.

My adoptive mother, Frances Louganis, was born in 1927, in Mount Pleasant, Texas, a farming community of about eight thousand. Her parents were farmers, and grew everything from sugarcane and cotton to corn and potatoes. She and her sister and four brothers worked on the farm, which my mother hated, and as soon as she graduated from high school, she moved to Dallas and got a job with a loan company.

Despite Mom's experience, I have fond memories of the farm and her parents, especially my grandfather, from my visits with them when I was very young. I would sit with Granddad in his rocking chair all afternoon. He always had a bottle of beer in his hand and we'd sip beer together. Before very long, I'd be a happy, giggling little four-year-old. Given that my grandfather was an alcoholic, I'm sure he didn't think twice about getting his grandson started on alcohol at such a young age.

My favorite thing to do with Granddad was to go fishing. We'd spend hours sitting by the pond, not saying anything, and usually not catching anything either.

Granny wasn't fun like Granddad was. She liked to bark out directions: "Get the table set!" "Get the napkins out!" "Get the silverware!" "Put out the plates!" And I did exactly what she told me to do.

Mom left Texas in 1948 and moved to San Diego, where she eventually landed a job with General Dynamics doing statistical typing. And in 1952 she met my father, Pete Louganis, who was working as a bookkeeper for the tuna fleet. One of the things Mom says she liked best about my dad when they met was that he loved to go out and have a good time. Unfortunately, the minute they got married, that stopped. Dad wanted to save money to buy a house, and after a year and half of saving, they put a down payment on a house in Lemon Grove, California, just outside San Diego. It was a three-bedroom, with a bath and a half and a large L-shaped living room with a dining area. At some point, Dad built a family room with a fireplace, but he forgot to put insulation in the walls, so it was too hot for us to use for much of the year.

My parents had a very traditional marriage. Dad worked, and he expected Mom to keep a clean house, iron his clothes, and to have dinner on the table when he got home. When it came to raising the children, that was to be Mom's responsibility.

Dad originally wanted four children, and they started trying to have kids shortly after they married. It turned out that Mom couldn't have kids, so they decided to adopt. They started with Despina and me, but after Mom saw how Dad was with us, she put her foot down and said that two was enough. I can't blame her. Dad never helped take care of us, and he always liked things quiet. He couldn't stand when we cried, so when Despina and I were young, most of the time Mom had to put us to bed before he got home from work.

Dad was born into a traditional Greek family in Boston in 1922. His mother died when he was nine months old, and his grandmother moved in to help rear him and his two older sisters, Mary and Virginia. Dad's father had a crippling heart attack shortly after that, so my father's grandmother wound up taking care of all of them on her own. After high school, Dad went to a professional school to become an accountant and then moved to California.

My father was not a handsome man, but he made a definite impression. He was about five feet eleven inches, with a medium build, a rather long face, and a very Roman nose. His hair was salt-and-pepper, and he had a receding hairline. Mom says that Dad was born an angry old man. He was a real authoritarian, but growing up, I don't remember him being around much, because he spent a lot of time at the fueling dock where he worked.

Dad wasn't the type of father who would give you a hug and say that he loved you. He was stoic and, except for anger, not very good at expressing his emotions. Mom was more affectionate. I could run to her side and put my arm around her or massage her neck. She would fuss with my hair or put her arm around me or take my arm. When I was a kid, she always tucked me in and kissed me good night.

From a very early age, I loved playing practical jokes on Mom. She still likes to tell people about the time, when I was three or four, that I tricked her while she was folding the laundry. I knew she would be putting the towels away soon, so I crawled into the cabinet where she kept the linens and hid. When she started putting the towels away, I grabbed her hand and scared her. She jumped back, and all the towels fell down. As soon as she realized it was me, she said my full first name and my middle name very sternly. I knew I was in trouble when she said, "Gregory Efthimios!" Needless to say, she made me refold all the towels, but she laughed.

You didn't play practical jokes on my father, ever. The best way to deal with him was to steer clear. It was like we were always walking on eggshells at home because of Dad, and even then, he'd fly off the handle, especially when he was drinking, and he drank every night. It was pretty typical for him to come home after work and have two or three martinis before dinner. Despina and I would prepare them for him, or my mother would.

Mom would usually have only one martini, but Dad kept right on drinking through dinner. Sometimes when he was drunk, he could be very nice, and that was the time to ask for a new bicycle. But more often than not, he would get angry and we knew to leave him alone. We'd make ourselves scarce and let him fall asleep in front of the television.

Because of Dad, Mom got very withdrawn, and over the years she and Dad said less and less to each other. It wasn't an overnight thing, but by the time I was twelve or thirteen, it wasn't out of character for all of us to sit through dinner in silence. That was our time together every day as a family, but we rarely said anything to one another. I figured Dad must be preoccupied with his work and that whatever I was doing wasn't important to him.

I don't remember a lot of specific incidents when Dad got angry, but one time that really stands out was when my mother was in the hospital for a few days having a benign lump removed from her breast. Without Mom, it was just the three of us at home. I was on the phone talking to my girlfriend at the time. After a while, Dad came in and said that I'd been on the phone long enough and that it was time to get off. I said okay, but of course we stayed on the line. We were kids.

Dad came in a second time to tell me to get off the phone. Eventually I hung up, and I went into the kitchen to tell him that I was off the phone. I did it in a snotty way, which angered him. He said, "You get over here," and started chasing me. I ran into the bathroom and locked the door. He started kicking it in. I'd seen his temper fly before, and I wasn't sticking around to find out how angry he was, so I crawled out the window. Typically, he took out his temper on my sister or my mom. But I knew he'd been drinking, so I was afraid he was going to beat me up. Most of the time I wasn't afraid of that, but this time was different. He was out of control.

I climbed out the window and ran down the street to a canyon I often went to when I wanted to be alone. I sat there for a while watching the stars. Eventually I went home, but before I went inside, I looked in the window to see where Dad was. He'd fallen asleep in front of the television, so I figured I was safe. I crawled back through the bathroom window, unlocked the door, and sneaked into my bedroom and went to sleep. I knew he'd wake up at some point and find me sleeping in my bed and not worry that I'd run away. The next day, it was like nothing had ever happened.

Another time, Despina stole money from Dad's wallet. I took the blame for it, but he somehow found out that I was covering for her. He started screaming at her and grabbed her. He was about to start hitting her when my mother came running in, yelling, "You turn her loose, and when you're drinking don't you lay a hand on her." She was really mad. He pulled away, and Mom told me firmly to take my sister next door to the neighbors.

Despina and I were too embarrassed to go next door, because that would have meant answering questions. So we just went to the canyon and talked about running away because we were so scared of our father. I don't know what was going on with him then, but he seemed to be drinking more.

Despite his temper, Dad never hit my mother or threw things at her. If Dad got mad, she usually just shut up. She said she didn't want to give him any excuse to do anything. Mom learned from being with her dad that you don't talk back to a drunk. That's how she learned to keep the peace. Unfortunately, that's how I learned, too.

The way I saw it growing up, Mom had three primary jobs: to take care of Dad and the house, to make ends meet, and to protect us from my father. Mom got an allowance every month for groceries, but it was never enough, especially once she started spending some of that money on costumes for me and Despina, who was also performing in talent contests. It made us feel special that our mom was saving her grocery money for our costumes, and we did what we could to help out around the house. I had my chores, like taking out the garbage, and sometimes I'd vacuum. When I was older, I helped in the kitchen.

It seemed like Mom was always broke by the last week of every month, trying to stretch her allowance. Mom made tuna casserole a lot, but we never went hungry. What she didn't know at the time was that Dad made more than enough money, so when he came home one day and said they were buying a new house, she was shocked. She had no idea they could afford it.

The payments on the new house were nearly three times higher than those on the old one, which made Mom very nervous. But it was a much bigger house in a much nicer neighborhood. We moved to a typical suburban street, with ranch houses and deep lawns. It was very hilly, and there were lots of places for kids to play hide-and-seek and great places for a moody teenager to go when he wanted to get away from everyone. Ours was one of the first houses built on the street, so there was plenty of open land around us.

The house had double front doors, four bedrooms, two baths, a two-car garage, a circular driveway, and a palm tree in front. It was set on a very deep one-acre lot, which was sloped steeply in the back. You had to go down a flight of stairs to get to the pool, which Dad had built a few years after we moved in.

Nothing really changed once we moved to the new house except that we had more room and now I had some great places to explore in the hills. Mom still struggled to make ends meet, and she had to work even harder at maintaining the peace. She tried her best to protect us from Dad. If I wasn't home at a time I was supposed to be home and Dad asked where I was, Mom would say I was in my room taking a nap, just so he wouldn't get mad. It really wasn't until Despina and I were out of the house that Mom started standing up for herself.

≋

SCHOOL WAS HARDLY a refuge from what was going on at home. As soon as Despina started school, I couldn't wait to go. She brought home books, and she had new friends. I thought it would be a lot of fun, like my acrobatics classes. Well, it wasn't. From almost the first day at Chase Elementary School the other kids started calling me names. At first they teased me because I stuttered, and they called me "nigger" because my Samoan complexion got very dark in the San Diego sun. Almost all the kids at my school were white.

At the time, I didn't know *what* I was. I knew my natural father was from Samoa, but I didn't know where Samoa was. For all I knew, I *was* from Africa, so it made odd sense to me why they were calling me that. It didn't occur to me to ask my parents or to look in the atlas to see where Samoa was. It wasn't until much later that I discovered I was a Pacific Islander. This was not a time when people celebrated ethnic diversity, and you can see why I think it's so necessary.

There was only one other kid at school whose skin was dark. He was from India, so no one knew what to make of him. He wasn't very popular, and I didn't go out of my way to be his friend. I was afraid, because I thought my classmates would say, "Oh look, the niggers stick together."

Because of my stutter, I was put in a speech-therapy class. Most of the kids in that class were mentally impaired in addition to having speech impediments. I didn't feel like I belonged there, but I had this problem, so I thought that I must be like them, that I must be retarded too. After I got put into a special reading class, the other kids started calling me "retard." From the start, I had trouble reading, but it got really bad once we got past single words and simple sentences. Unfortunately, the special class didn't help. I got frustrated and withdrew into my shell and wouldn't talk. After school, I went to my room and closed the door.

My teachers sent me home with books for Mom to read with me, and she tried to help me. But that was even more frustrating, because she tried to show me how to read the way she read, the way most people read. What I couldn't explain—and what I didn't realize—was that I was dyslexic. I couldn't explain that I read a sentence forward, then backward, then forward again before I can get the letters and the words in order, so I can figure out what the sentence means. It never occurred to me to say anything about the way I read, because I just thought I was a little slower than other people. I thought this until my dyslexia was diagnosed in college.

One time my Aunt Geri—who's not really an aunt but my god-mother—tried to help me. She bragged to my mother that she could have me reading in an hour. So she took me into my room, but before the hour was out, she said to Mom, "Don't ever ask me to do that again."

My mother could not understand what the problem was. When I was first learning, I could read books where there were single words, like *ball* or *dog*. I could even read three-word sentences. It was easy for me to unscramble small words and sentences like "The dog barked." But any more words than that took me a long time to unscramble, which I couldn't explain to my mother. All my mom could do was blame my teachers.

I didn't complain about the name-calling until everyone found out that I did acrobatics. That was when they started calling me "sissy." I went to my teacher and told her it made me feel "red hot" when the kids called me names. I told her which names they called me, and she said, "They could have called you a lot worse." I took her remark to mean that I deserved what I was getting and that I was worse than what they were calling me. I never said a word about any of this to my mother, and she had no idea why I always seemed so unhappy, beyond the fact I was having trouble reading.

For me, unlike for most of the other "sissies," the bright spot was athletics. At first, I was one of the last ones picked for team sports because I was small, but once the other kids began to realize that I was athletically gifted, I was often chosen as team captain in volleyball, kickball, and softball. Despite my athletic abilities, there was always a part of me that wanted to hide, a part that felt inadequate. No matter how well I did, I'd look at the other kids and think, I wish I could be like everybody else.

The most important lesson I learned during my years at Chase Elementary School was how to make sure I wasn't called on to read. I did my best to be nice to my teachers, even the one who told me that I could have been called worse. At first I sat in the back of the class and tried not to be noticed, but that made her make a point of calling on

me. So I volunteered to erase the blackboard and became the good little boy in very visible ways. That worked—I didn't get called on as
much.

After I finished third grade, the school district zones changed and I
was transferred to Fuerte Elementary School. I looked forward to going
there because I no longer had to go to special-ed class or speech therapy. No one at the new school would know I was a retard. I still needed
help with my reading and speech, but no one had to know that I'd had
those classes at Chase, and I wasn't about to say anything.

Unfortunately, some other kids also transferred from Chase to
Fuerte, and the name-calling followed me. This time I started getting
beat up a lot, mostly by the tough kids at the bus stop. If I didn't fork
over my lunch money to some bully or if I happened to bump into one
of those kids in the lunch line, they'd pick a fight. I usually told them
that I didn't want a fight. I would say, "I know you can kick my ass, so
why bother?" Then they would call me a "sissy-boy faggot." They'd say,
"See, we knew you were retarded." That would really get me going. I
would want to fight back, and of course I'd get my ass kicked.

Generally, I didn't tell Mom what was going on. If my shirt was
torn or I had grass stains on my knees, I'd tell her that I'd been playing
on the jungle gym and had fallen or that I had been running and
tripped. I would make up pretty believable stories. I didn't want my
mother to know what was going on, because I thought she might be
ashamed of me. I already thought that I was a disappointment to her
because I couldn't keep up academically. My teachers never called
Mom about the name-calling or the fights. I was on my own, especially
because I didn't have any close friends at school. Most of the other
kids had a best friend, but I never did.

I got beat up often enough that it seemed like a lot to me. The boys
picked the fights, and some of the girls cheered them on. I internalized
all of it. I always thought that right prevailed, so since I got my butt
kicked, I figured I must be wrong. They must be right to call me names
and beat me up. Since I got my butt kicked, it had to be true that I was
a sissy. Since I got beat up, I must be a bad person. Since I was a bad
person, I must deserve it. If I didn't deserve it, I would have won the

fights. Such convoluted logic, but it made sense to me then, and it still makes sense to too many kids today.

The worst time I got my butt kicked was when I was ten. It was by this older blond kid, Charlie Brown (his real name). I have no idea why he wanted to fight me, but he told me to meet him at the bus stop one day after school. The way I remember it, we were there alone, and he punched me and slammed my head into the asphalt until I bled. I was embarrassed to go home because I was a mess and my shirt was torn.

I recently talked to Mom about my childhood, and one of the things we talked about was that fight. She said that she remembered it very clearly, because she was there watching. I was shocked to hear this, because I was sure it was just Charlie and me alone.

As my mother explained it to me, she had heard from someone in the neighborhood that there was going to be a fight down at the bus stop after school and that I was going to get beat up. By the time she got there, a crowd had already gathered to watch. It was mostly kids from school, but in the crowd, Mom spotted my father and my cousin. She ran home crying because she knew there was nothing she could do to stop it, and she couldn't bear to stand there and see me get hurt.

When Mom told me this, it explained some things that I'd found very confusing about my memory of this fight. During the fight, I remember it felt like my father was the one throwing the punches. For years after, I had this awful feeling that Dad thought I deserved to get beat up, that he thought I was a sissy, and that he agreed with all the things the kids at school said about me.

Those feelings made perfect sense when I realized that my father was there watching. I remember now that he let it happen and that I knew at the time that he was there. He might as well have been the one throwing the punches. That he could be there and not help me was so terrible that I blocked it from my memory. All I remembered was the fight itself and feeling that my father thought I deserved what I got.

Why didn't my dad at least put his arm around my shoulder, walk me home, and explain to me that I'd have been worse off if he'd interfered? I'll never forget feeling so humiliated walking home by myself after the fight. Mom tells me that my dad and cousin came in a few minutes before I did. She was angry at them for not breaking up the fight, but she didn't say anything because she was afraid. No one contradicted my father.

Over the years, I've thought a lot about those kids who taunted me and beat me up, especially during the 1988 Olympic trials, which happened to coincide with my tenth high school reunion. Most of the kids from elementary school had gone on to the same high school I went to. I wanted to be there and see them. I wanted to say to them, "Yes, I am that sissy boy, but look what I've done." Maybe I will if I'm still around for my twentieth.

I recently looked at some of my class pictures from elementary school. All I saw was just little kids, pictures of little kids. Little kids whose words and fists hurt.

Being beat up at elementary school—like being beaten by my dad—proved to be a big motivator. The name-calling and the humiliation pushed me to strive to be better than everyone. It made me angry, and I learned to focus most of that angry energy on my acrobatics and diving.

Unfortunately, I turned some of that angry energy on myself, which made my usual up-and-down moods even worse. As I approached my teens and my outlook on life got more and more bleak, I started thinking about killing myself.

4

SUICIDE

BY THE TIME I was twelve, I was one miserable kid, even though most of the time I managed to hide it, at least at school. If you asked the kids I went to school with what I was like, most of my classmates would probably describe me as happy-go-lucky. I got involved in things, like the student council in grammar school. When I ran for vice-president, at the end of my election speech, I said, "If you vote for me, I'll flip for you." Then I did a back flip, and although I felt that many of my classmates didn't like me, I won the election.

Still, my self-perception was terrible. When I looked in the mirror, I saw an ugly kid who had a hard time reading. I felt terribly isolated and depressed, and was convinced that nobody could or would want to understand me. I played negative messages over and over again in my head: My natural parents didn't want me; my adoptive parents don't love me; I'm retarded; I'm ugly.

I got really caught up in feeling unloved, especially because I rarely saw my father. Even when he was around, he wasn't interested in either of his children, and he absolutely didn't understand me. My mom was really withdrawn herself, so she couldn't help me. Sometimes, when I was particularly sullen, she'd ask me what was going on, but I couldn't answer her, which made her crazy, because she and my dad weren't talking, either. I felt like I could confide in no one.

The depression wasn't consistent. It was like a roller coaster, but more often than not at that age, I was down in the dumps. A real low point came when I was twelve, right after I'd been having trouble with my knees and my mom took me to the doctor. He told me that I'd have to quit gymnastics, acrobatics, and dance because my knees couldn't take the constant pounding. Many of the exhibitions Eleanor and I gave were in places that had concrete floors, which is how I'd damaged my knees. He'd allow me to continue diving because, unlike a hard surface, the diving board gives.

Even without the knee injury, it was getting to be more and more difficult doing both diving and gymnastics. With gymnastics, you're supposed to land on your feet. With diving, you're supposed to land on your head. After doing both sports for a while, I started having trouble landing right side up in my gymnastics routines. One of my tumbling runs was a front handspring/front somersault, and I kept landing on my face. I didn't intend to dive into the mat face first, but after a couple of years on the diving board, my brain was geared to my landing on my head. I came away from that workout with a bloody nose.

So after more than ten years of classes and performances and competitions, I gave up acrobatics, gymnastics, and dance. I'd hoped to compete in gymnastics at the Olympics one day, but now that dream was gone. At twelve years old, I decided that I would kill myself. I went into my parents' medicine cabinet and took a bunch of different pills, mostly aspirin and Ex-Lax. Then I took a razor blade out of the cabinet and started playing with it over my wrist. I started to bleed, but I didn't go deep enough to cut any veins or arteries. It also turned out that I didn't take enough of anything from the medicine cabinet to cause myself harm. I never told my parents about the suicide attempt, and they didn't notice the missing medicine or the scratches on my wrists. Afterward, I was even more angry and depressed, because I didn't see any way out.

I'm sure part of the problem with my moods was from the drugs I had started taking in junior high school, starting with marijuana in seventh grade. The kids I wanted to fit in with smoked pot, and some of them were also smart. I didn't think I had the brains to keep up with them, but I could be a part of their group when I got high.

One of my sister's friends got me into selling drugs for him, mostly pot. The other kids knew I could get it for them, so they'd ask me, and I'd tell them how much it cost. I'd bring the pot to school, and they paid me for it. Then I'd bring the money home to my sister's friend. All I got was some extra pot here and there, which I didn't really care about, since my favorite drug was speed. I wasn't comfortable buying it from my sister's friend, so I used my allowance money to buy pills from other kids at school. It wasn't expensive, and I didn't take it every day, just once a week or once every other week. If I had a book report due and I'd put it off for too long, then I might do speed for a few days in a row, but generally I was pretty good at pacing myself. At least I thought I was.

The more depressed I got, the more I pushed my parents. I guess I was testing them to see if they loved me, and one way to do it was to defy my curfew. All my parents knew was that they had a stubborn, defiant, and combative twelve-year-old making them crazy. They suspected I was on drugs, but they never found anything in the house.

One time, when my dad said something about me being up past my curfew, I said something back to him and he slapped me. Without thinking, I punched him in the stomach. I think I was more stunned than he was, but we were both very angry. He tried to put me over his knee to spank me, and it turned into a wrestling match. We were struggling on the floor, both out of breath. Mom was horrified.

But a short time later I got into a fight with my mom. I got up early on a Saturday morning and decided to go for a walk. I left a note saying, "I'm going for a walk if you care." I tossed it on the kitchen table, left for a while, and then came back and went to my room. Mom came in and asked me what the note meant. I said it meant just what it said.

She asked me, "Do you think we don't care? Why would you write something like this?" She told me that she loved me, but I didn't believe her. Mom came toward me, and I assumed she was going to slap me, so I reared back on my bed and kicked her in the chest. She stumbled back and fell against my closet doors, but she stayed on her feet. Mom was in shock and left my room without saying anything. I was surprised myself, because I'd never done anything to my mother like that before.

Once my mom left my room, I pulled the covers over my head and went to sleep. Next thing I knew, there were two police officers in my bedroom waking me up. They started asking me if I'd taken anything and if I had any drugs in the house. I said no. I can't remember for sure, but I may have been on speed the day before.

When they were done questioning me, the policemen handcuffed me and walked me out of the house to the patrol car. All the neighbors were out on the street watching. My parents stood there the whole time.

It turned out that after I went to sleep, Mom called my father at work and told him what had happened. She said that they had to do something about me because I wasn't in my right mind. I'd never done anything like that before, and it scared her. Dad came home and called John Anders to see what he thought they should do. They didn't know if I was smoking pot or taking other drugs. Mom didn't smell liquor, so she knew I hadn't been drinking, but because of my mood changes, she knew I was doing something. They felt that they couldn't control me, and they had to do something.

When we got to juvenile hall, I was checked in, strip-searched, and forced to take a shower, and they issued me jeans and a T-shirt. The whole thing was more humiliating than frightening. I was angry at my parents for doing this to me.

They put me in a room with a kid younger than I was, probably eight or nine, who was there with his older brother for robbery. Another kid at juvenile hall, in for grand theft auto for hot-wiring cars and joy-riding, was a repeat offender. During the three days I was in there, his parents never visited him, but mine were there every day.

Their daily presence made me start to believe that my adoptive parents loved me, that they cared about me, that they were indeed my parents. Of course, the first time they came to see me, I was still angry at them and said I didn't want to see them. I was forced to meet with them and a counselor the day after I was taken there. The counselor did most of the talking, and most of the time he talked to my dad; he never asked Mom anything. When he asked me questions, all I would say was "yes" and "no," but I wouldn't elaborate on anything.

The counselor asked my parents if they wanted to take me home. Dad said yes, but Mom said no. She told them that I was no different from when they brought me in the day before, that I was still sulky and I wouldn't talk. She said that she didn't know what she'd do with me when she got me home.

We met again with the counselor the next day, and I started talking. One of the things that came out during the counseling session was that I wanted to find out more about my natural parents. My parents agreed that I could go to the adoption agency and ask whatever questions I wanted to about my natural parents.

My parents also talked privately with the counselor and arranged the terms under which I would be released. I was allowed to go home if I agreed to go straight home from school for the rest of the school year, to help my mother around the house with whatever needed to be done, and to not hang out with my friends.

During the six months after my stay in juvenile hall, my mother and I got much closer. I know she was happy about the change, because she told me that I'd gone back to being her "sweet, lovable, handsome boy."

Until recently, I didn't know that my mother had to have surgery on her breast because of that kick, which apparently aggravated a problem she'd been having with cystic mastitis. I felt awful, especially since I was so caught up in my own world that I didn't know anything about it.

Every day after school, I'd come home and we'd sit at the kitchen table and talk for an hour or so. Sometimes we talked about diving. Sometimes we talked about school. Our relationship really turned around. She didn't judge me. She made me feel it was okay to feel and think whatever I was thinking or feeling at the time.

One of the things we talked about when I came back from juvenile hall was drugs. At one point she told me to bring home a joint and we'd get stoned together, so she could see what I was talking about. But I didn't like getting high on pot, so we never did it.

My relationship with my dad remained pretty much the same, but we talked more. The most meaningful conversations we had were about diving. It was the one thing about my life he could talk about in any depth. He was interested in my trips, my schedule, and my training. And it was something I felt comfortable talking about with him. After I got out of juvenile hall, he got me a dog and a color television, trying to make up for having me put in juvenile hall. It seemed odd that I was being rewarded for having done something bad.

As promised, after I got out of juvenile hall, we made a trip to the adoption agency that had handled my case. I found out what my biological dad looked like and that he was interested in sports. I didn't find out much more about my mother than I already knew, except that she was living in San Diego. I didn't know where my father was. My father had apparently wanted to keep me, and his parents had wanted to raise me as his brother. That alone was enough to convince me that my natural parents cared about me. That's what I needed to hear the most: that I was wanted. But I also found out that my natural mother didn't want me raised by my father's family because, the adoption agency said, she wanted me to have more opportunities in life than they could offer.

It was comforting to know that thought went into the decision to put me up for adoption. I had always assumed that my biological parents didn't love me. There were so many blank spots in the story, and I had chosen to fill them in as negatively as I could imagine, a pattern I repeated often in my life. I assumed that my biological parents had simply wanted to unload me. I never thought of two teenagers knowing they wouldn't be able to provide the opportunities they wanted me to have. I never thought that giving me up might have been a difficult decision for them.

≈

AT THAT POINT my curiosity was satisfied. I knew I had
been loved by my natural parents, and I realized that the Louganises
were my family. My natural parents may have been the two fifteen-
year-olds who had me, but Peter and Frances Louganis would always be
my real parents. That realization really helped turn things around for
me. But the emotional damage had already been done, and I've struggled throughout my life with trusting whether anyone genuinely cared
for me.

5

~~~~~~

OLYMPIC

DREAMS

WHEN I STARTED taking diving lessons in 1969, training for the 1976 Olympics never crossed my mind. I didn't have any long-term goals other than doing my best in competitions and learning the most I could from my coaches. The two biggest challenges during the years leading up to the Olympics were finding a place to dive and getting enough consistent time with my coaches. With Coach Anders, we traveled to wherever we could find a pool that had the proper facilities, which was especially tough once I started training on the 3-meter springboard and the 10-meter platform. Platform facilities were nonexistent in San Diego, and the 3-meter facilities were terrible. We spent more time driving than diving.

Despite these frustrations, the three years I dove with Coach Anders were very exciting, because I began competing in regional and national meets, I had the chance to go the Junior Olympics in Colorado Springs, and in the summer of 1973, I got to compete in Europe for the first time in the World Age Group Championships. My dad's friend Joe Madruga sponsored me, covering the cost of my travel to New York, where I met up with the U.S. team for the trip to Luxembourg. Joe also paid for all the required uniforms: a travel uniform, a parade uniform, and sweats. Almost every Olympic athlete has a similar story about someone who helped finance supplies and travel. People like Joe Madruga are true Olympic heroes.

The trip to Europe was a blast. We were all kids, so you can imagine what it was like, many of us away from home for the first time. The youngest of the group was Bruce Kimball, who was later one of my major competitors. He was only eight years old, and before we left for Europe, his dad asked me if I would keep an eye on him.

Some of the things we did were pretty typical: shaving-cream fights, water balloons tossed out the hotel window, romping through the streets, stopping traffic with backflips. We were kids, but we were athletic.

After my first couple of years training with John Anders, he began telling me that I needed to find another coach. He could only take me so far. So in the summer of 1974, at his recommendation, I went to live with a family in Tucson, Arizona, to work with a new coach, Charlie Silber, who lived near a training center that had a diving platform. Then after I came home in the fall, I started working part-time with Dr. Sammy Lee, an Olympic diving coach.

A year after I stopped working with John Anders, my mom came into my bedroom one morning and threw a newspaper on my bed, very upset. I started going through the paper and there was a picture of Coach Anders. He had died of a heart attack. I was lucky to have had so much time with him. He taught me many of the fundamental diving skills I've used throughout my career. But more important than that, he was one of the few people who taught me to value myself. If only I had learned that lesson better.

≈

DR. SAMMY LEE was going to be the coach to take me to the next stage in my diving career. He himself had won two gold medals in men's 10-meter platform, at the '48 and '52 Olympics, and one of the divers he coached, Robert Webster, had gone on to win gold medals in the '60 and '64 Olympics in men's platform. Dr. Lee had a medical practice, so we only worked together on Wednesdays and weekends.

I first met Dr. Lee at the Junior Olympics in 1971. It was the first time he saw me dive, and he later told me how impressed he was with this little eleven-year-old diver. From the time I started training with him, he thought I had a shot at making the 1976 Olympic team. No one had ever thought that of me before. Even though I hadn't yet come close to diving at that level, I didn't question him. Dr. Lee was my coach. His goals were my goals, and that's what we worked toward.

Diving with Dr. Lee, however, was not fun. He was hard-nosed and inflexible, and like with my father, it was his way or no way. His approach was very aggressive: Go for it; get killed; get up; go for it again; get killed again. I had thought of myself as aggressive before, but not in the way Dr. Lee was. When I dove, I tried to do my best, competing against myself and not thinking about the other divers. What mattered to me was how I did in comparison to my own record. Dr. Lee wanted me out there competing with the other divers, beating everybody else at any cost. I didn't appreciate that valuable lesson at the time, but it was one I would call on years later. All competitive athletes have to balance doing their best with outdoing their competitors.

Dr. Lee told me that I didn't have a killer instinct, that it wasn't in my nature to fight. By his measure I was not a fighter. Part of his training was to toughen me up, which I needed. He taught me to dive in all kinds of weather and to dive whether I felt like it or not, even if it was raining and cold and I didn't feel good. He taught me to push through those difficult workouts when all I wanted to do was crawl into bed and pull the sheets over my head. Despite his telling me I wasn't a fighter, however, Dr. Lee often expressed how much faith he had in me, which gave me the confidence I needed to compete. I'm grateful to him for that.

One of the ideas Dr. Lee introduced me to was the importance of being a proper role model. It was part of his image of me as an Olympic diver. He'd say, "You're a role model, and you have to live an exemplary life." Up until then, I hadn't exactly been leading an exemplary life. At fourteen, I drank too much, and I'd been smoking since I was nine. At first I'd just sneak a few cigarettes out of the house, but by the time I was eleven or twelve, I was stealing whole packs of cigarettes from my parents, both of whom smoked. Dr. Lee had a very strict rule about not coaching a smoker. If I got caught, that would have been it. So I cut way back on my smoking to five cigarettes a day.

During those years, diving was still pretty much seasonal for me, and summer was the time when I had the opportunity to do concentrated full-time training. So the summer after I started training with Dr. Lee, in 1975, I went to Ron O'Brien's diving camp in Decatur, Alabama. By then I knew that Ron was one of the top coaches in the country.

I was only supposed to go to diving camp for one week, but I stayed for three. I kept calling home and asking if I could stay a little longer. Ron gave me the technical help I needed at that stage of my training. He got me on the trampoline and helped me straighten out my twisters, which are dives where you're somersaulting and twisting—sort of rotating like a top—at the same time. He started working with me on how to "spot." Spotting is being able to spin and see where you are in your spin by picking out a point, like dancers do in pirouettes. The spot for a diver is usually the surface of the pool.

I also learned to do both back and reverse two-and-a-halfs on the platform, which was a real breakthrough for me. At the time, I needed to know these dives to remain competitive on a national and world-class level. With a back two-and-a-half, you stand at the edge of the platform with your back to the water. You have the balls of your feet on the edge of the platform, with your heels hanging over the edge. You jump into the air and do a somersault, then another somersault, and then you kick up toward the platform and look for the water. With the reverse, you face the water, and when you jump up in the air, you do a somersault in reverse, spinning back toward the platform. That's supposed to be a more difficult dive, but for me it was easier than the back two-and-a-half.

Ron really understood me. He knew that I needed help with both the technical and the mental aspects of my diving. I wasn't the kind of diver who did a dive because I wanted to be a daredevil. I had to be physically and mentally prepared to do it. I had to be able to see it in my head. Each new dive had to be a part of my overall goals. If I thought that I needed the dive to do better in competitions, that would give me the motivation to overcome my fear and do the dive. Ron helped me with all of that.

I returned home after diving camp and went back to training part-time with Dr. Sammy Lee. In January 1976, I moved in with him and his family. Dr. Lee lived closer to good diving facilities. From the day I moved in, I trained every day, no matter what the conditions.

Dr. Lee's family was very good to me, and I was only a few hours north of where my parents lived. I talked to them twice a week and saw them on holidays. Dr. Lee had a daughter, who was already in college, and a son my age. I loved Mrs. Lee, who welcomed me with open arms. I spent a lot of time helping her with the chores and cooking, and we really enjoyed each other's company.

During the time I lived with the Lees, I'd go to school, and afterward we'd train in Dr. Lee's backyard pool on his 1-meter springboard and 1-meter platform. Sometimes we'd train at Santa Ana College, which had a 3-meter springboard, or at the Los Coyotes Country Club, where there was an outdoor 10-meter platform. We would also use the indoor facility at Belmont Plaza in Long Beach, but the swim team was usually doing laps, so we had to dive in between the swimmers. It was frustrating, because we were constantly driving around trying to find a place for me to dive. There was no one place where I could train indoors on both the 3-meter springboard and 10-meter platform without having to dodge swimmers. Fortunately, I was pretty good at dodging.

≈

AS THE MONTHS passed, I got more and more excited about the possibility of making the Olympic team. I knew I had a shot at qualifying for the team on 10-meter platform, because I'd come in second at the most recent nationals. That meant I'd get to compete for a spot on the three-man Olympic team at the Olympic trials. During the year leading up to the Olympic trials, I was always the top American diver on platform in any international competition. So it looked good for the Olympics.

Dr. Lee was not only sure that I'd make the Olympic team in platform diving, he was sure I'd win a gold. He was sure, but I wasn't. That meant beating Klaus Dibiasi of Italy, who was favored to win his third gold in a row on platform. What made it even more complicated was that Dr. Lee himself had won two consecutive golds for platform diving. He was depending on me to keep Dibiasi from breaking that record. At the time, I didn't put in perspective what a difficult goal that was. Just two years before, I'd failed to make the nationals and wasn't even in the picture.

In addition to qualifying to compete in platform at the Olympic trials, I qualified in 3-meter springboard, but only because of a calculating error at the nationals, which I was responsible for. Before the competition, I had to prepare a list of my dives for the people who tabulated the scores. On that list, you also put the degree of difficulty for each dive. A dive is assigned a degree of difficulty based on how hard it is to do—the harder the dive, the higher the degree of difficulty and the higher the final score. The way they tabulated your final score at that time was to take the scores given by the five judges, throw out the high and low scores, add the remaining three numbers, and multiply the total by the degree of difficulty. In 1976, the highest degree of difficulty was a 3.0, with most of my dives ranging from 1.6 to 2.8.

For one of my dives, an inward dive layout, I accidentally wrote down the wrong degree of difficulty, increasing it by one tenth of a point. Because of that extra tenth of a point, I made it into a round that I shouldn't have, and wound up making it through the following rounds, which allowed me to qualify for the Olympic trials. They discovered the error only after I had qualified for the finals, which was too late to disqualify me. The whole mix-up left me feeling less than confident going into the Olympic trials.

The trials were held in Knoxville, Tennessee, and it was both exciting and frightening for me. My parents and Aunt Geri came to watch and cheer me on the whole time. I was glad they were there.

The first competition was in springboard, which Dr. Lee had told me to think of as a warm-up for 10-meter platform. Given what was at stake, he saw platform as the real event. Besides which, no one expected me to make the team on springboard, because the competition was stiff and I wasn't as well prepared as I was on platform. Well, I shocked everyone, because not only did I make the team in springboard, I came in first.

It was no surprise when I made the team in 10-meter platform, but it *was* a surprise when I came in first again. I was now the top American qualifier going into the Olympics, which was exciting and scary. Everyone's expectations were raised now, especially my own.

During the month between the Olympic trials and the Olympics themselves, Dr. Lee boasted to the press. When Steve Bisheff, a reporter for the *Evening Tribune* in San Diego, asked him about my being "America's diver of the future," Dr. Lee said, "To hell with that. I might not be here in 1980. Greg's going to do it now."

All the hype put more pressure on me. The fact was, I was sixteen years old, I'd never been to an Olympics before, and here I was expected to win one gold, if not two. Yes, I could dive well, and maybe I could win a gold, but I was still young and inconsistent. I was capable of scoring 10's, but I was just as capable of scoring 2's. The worst part was that Dr. Lee was losing sight of the fact that this was about a young diver competing to the best of his ability: He wanted me to win a gold medal to protect his own record.

And I, of course, like always, was convinced that if I didn't win that medal, I would be a complete failure.

6

~~~~~~

MONTREAL

1976

ONE MONTH AFTER the trials, we were on our way to Montreal for the Olympics. I was incredibly excited, awestruck, and frightened, all at the same time.

I packed all kinds of things for the Olympics, because it was going to be a two-week event, but when we arrived in Montreal, I discovered that I could have shown up with nothing: The U.S. Olympic Committee gave us parade uniforms, casual clothes, everyday sweats, warm-up sweats, around-the-Village sweats, award-ceremony sweats, and six kinds of footwear, from tennis shoes to dress shoes. They also gave us hair dryers, toothbrushes, toothpaste, shaving cream, razors, and cameras.

When we got to the Olympic Village, there were representatives from various companies giving away running shoes, T-shirts, and more sweats. You name it, we got it.

The first day of practice, I got into a really bad mood and my confidence went right out the window. Generally, in any competition, you have one diving board that's really good, and everybody wants to use that one. It's important during practice to spend time on the diving board you plan to use in the competition, because every board is a little different, and you adjust your dives accordingly. So whichever one you practice on is the one you use for the competition.

In Montreal, I wanted to use the good board, too, but I was intimidated and didn't want to get in anybody's way. This was a world-class competition, and I felt like I was just a kid. All these other divers who had a lot more experience at international competitions wanted to use the board, and I was reluctant to compete with them for it.

I probably could have gotten enough time on the good diving board if I'd tried, but I thought I needed extra time in order to feel really prepared. So it was just easier to use one of the boards that no one else wanted to use. Unfortunately, when it came to the actual competition, I was stuck using that board, because it was the one I'd gotten used to. That didn't help my performance.

There was another reason I didn't want to get in anyone's way. Some of the other divers were mumbling that I was too young and inexperienced to have made the team on springboard. They said I had just gotten lucky. Given that I'd qualified to compete in the Olympic trials because of that calculating error, I tried to be as invisible as I could.

Then I discovered that Dr. Lee wasn't allowed to come down to the pool deck to coach me, and that pushed me over the edge. Dr. Lee may have been tough on me, but I really needed him there to coach me. But Dr. Lee wasn't one of the team coaches, so he wasn't allowed onto the pool deck. I was left on my own.

Ron O'Brien, whose diving camp I had attended, was the head coach there, but he had his own four divers to coach. There were two other coaches, but they too were coaching their own divers. I got so frustrated that I walked over to the side of the pool deck and started crying. The team manager stepped in to help, but it wasn't enough. I needed fine-tuning, and no one was helping me.

The preliminary round in springboard didn't go well. I barely made the cut. Eight divers made it into the final round (after 1980, twelve divers made it to the finals), and I placed sixth. That night, I really needed my sleep, but between being upset about how I'd done in the preliminaries and worrying about how I'd do in the final round, I couldn't sleep.

The U.S. diving team had a strict curfew. At the world championships, divers had been out partying until three and four in the morning. Ron was determined to prevent that from happening in Montreal, so he set a curfew of 10:30 P.M., but people sneaked out after Ron checked us in and wandered in at all hours.

One of my roommates stumbled in drunk at three in the morning. I was already tossing and turning, and his stumbling around just made things worse. I was trying my best to follow the rules, but no one else seemed to care.

As we were getting ready for the springboard finals, one of my teammates wished me luck and said, "Whatever you do, don't take the gold away from me." I'm sure now that he meant it as a compliment, but at the time it upset me. I thought he was acting as if the gold were already his, and that I'd better not steal it from him. I thought we were supposed to be teammates, which to me meant that we were supposed to be encouraging each other to do our best.

One of the toughest lessons for me at the 1976 Olympics was that it was each man for himself, just the opposite of the Olympic ideal. There was a shocking lack of camaraderie on the U.S. team. I shouldn't have expected any different, because in general there was never any kind of team spirit among the divers. Individual sports are very competitive. Some of the divers didn't make a big deal of the rivalries, but others did. I usually kept my mouth shut and let my diving speak for me.

The final round of springboard was a big disappointment. I placed sixth and was so embarrassed that I went straight to the lockers without saying a word to my parents, who were waiting for me by the side of the pool. I didn't want to see them. I went back to the Olympic Village in shame and went to bed. I didn't want to talk to anyone or see anyone.

The preliminary round for 10-meter platform was even worse. I developed an awful toothache, and it felt like my head was going to explode every time I did a dive. Still, I managed to win the preliminaries, and as soon as I could get out of the pool, I went to the dentist in the Olympic Village, who found a hairline fracture in one of my molars and did some drilling to try to relieve some of the pressure I was feeling. By the next day, the pain was gone, just in time for the final round.

The diver to beat was two-time gold medalist Klaus Dibiasi, the twenty-eight-year-old Blond Angel, as he was sometimes called. He was seventeen when he went to his first Olympics, so in some ways we'd had the same beginning. This was now his fourth Olympics and my first. We had competed once before, at an international competition several months earlier, where I came in a close second to him. I'd already beaten Klaus in the platform preliminaries, so I was feeling confident that I could do it again in the final round.

It must have been exciting for the audience watching the final round, because Klaus and I were matching each other dive for dive, right through the eighth dive. I was more terrified than excited. We had only two more dives to go, and as long as I didn't blow a dive, I stood a chance of beating Klaus for the gold.

My ninth dive was a front three-and-a-half pike. Not a lot of divers had been doing that one yet, and I still wasn't that consistent with it. Sure enough, I made the same mistake I'd made before: For some reason, as I was stretching for the water, I kept my head down, so it washed over—I went past vertical. I got between 4's and 6's on the dive, which effectively knocked me out of the competition for the gold.

Even before I came up from under the water, I knew I'd done a bad dive. As I got out of the pool, Dr. Lee was there to let me know just how bad. We were on the side of the pool, and even though there were people around us, Dr. Lee was cursing at me. He called me *dummkopf*, saying, "Goddamnit, you're so stupid. How could you do that?" All I could do was stare at the ground, with my arms folded across my chest.

I was humiliated. Dr. Lee was saying that I'd let him down. In typical fashion, I wasn't mad at him; I was mad at myself. All I could think was that he'd put so much work into getting me to the Olympics, he'd made so many sacrifices, and I had failed him. He had cut back on his medical practice to train me, and he had lost money. I didn't say anything to him. I just yelled at myself in my own head. I beat myself up pretty bad, telling myself how stupid I was and how I was a failure at diving. I let all my self-doubts about being retarded drag me down, and I felt worthless. It makes me sad now when I think of how hard I was on myself. I was only a kid. This was my first Olympics, and I'd won a silver medal. That was a lot to be proud of. Unfortunately, I had so little self-confidence that I couldn't see it, and there was no way I could defend myself against Dr. Lee's outburst. I counted on his approval in the same way I had counted on the approval of my past coaches and my parents. And when I got just the opposite, I thought I had only myself to blame. It never occurred to me then that Dr. Lee was out of line.

When Dr. Lee was done yelling at me, I went off to a little waiting area near the pool to get ready for my final dive. I thought that at some point he would come back to see me, but he didn't. I interpreted that to mean that he was so angry with me that he didn't want to see me. I tried to stay focused and said to myself over and over again, One more dive, and it's all over.

Just before I got up to walk over to the platform for my last dive, Dr. Lee came up to me and said that even though the gold was out of reach, I should show them what I was made of. He said, "Go out and nail your last dive." I heard it, but it didn't sink in. At that point, I was too hurt to really hear anything Dr. Lee had to say.

The last dive was a front triple-twisting one-and-a-half, one of my more consistent dives. I could always find vertical, no matter what was going on around me or in my own head. So I climbed the ladder to the platform, shut everything out—the audience, my competitors, the judges, Dr. Lee, and my doubts—and executed the dive. Beyond knowing that it was an adequate dive, I had no idea how it went.

After I finished my dive, I went to get dressed for the awards ceremony. Then I walked with the other two winners to the waiting area where we stood before they announced us. Klaus came over to me and put his arm around me and said, "Next time, Moscow 1980, I see you win two gold medals." That felt wonderful. It was like the passing of the torch from one of the greatest divers in the world. It meant a lot to me, especially because Klaus had won a silver medal in Tokyo when he was seventeen, and now he'd won his third Olympic gold medal. Given all the competitiveness and lack of good sportsmanship I saw at the Olympics, it was surprising and wonderful to see such a gracious winner.

As soon as the ceremony ended, my mom came down from the stands to meet me on the deck. We hugged, and both of us cried. She was crying because she was thrilled: I'd won the silver. I was still crying because I'd let everyone down. I thought everyone, from Dr. Lee to the people in the stands, expected me to win the gold medal. So I was still feeling ashamed for having lost. I didn't think of myself as a winner, although with the exception of Dr. Lee, everyone else did, including my father. He was there with Mom, and he put his arm around me and whispered in my ear, "I'm very proud of you." It didn't make sense to me, and I thought he was just trying to be nice.

Before we left the pool hall, an American official came up to me and thanked me for my ninth dive, which confused me even more. He said, "I thought we'd have to protest the scores." He and the other American officials felt the judges had been scoring me low and Klaus high since the start of the platform finals. So even if I'd nailed my ninth dive, he believed I wouldn't have scored high enough overall to win the gold.

The scoring of dives is subjective, and judges are not immune to human emotion. I was the young newcomer with no Olympic record. Klaus had an established record. He was a favorite, who had proven himself over and over again. It made sense that he got the benefit of the doubt. It would be the same situation in 1988, when I was the old-timer being challenged by a young upstart and I would get the benefit of the doubt.

I had no way of knowing if the judges were scoring me low at the Olympics. I had nothing to compare it to, and since I missed my ninth dive, it didn't make a difference. But even if they'd scored me low, it wouldn't have surprised me.

≈

THERE WAS SOMETHING else that happened, however, that had surprised me. A judge had approached me before the platform competition and said, "I understand you want to win the gold medal. We need to get together and talk." This was in the pool area, and I'd been standing off by myself. The judge, who was not American, suggested that I come to his room to talk about it.

I was naive—I was sixteen—but I wasn't stupid. It was as clear as day to me that he was propositioning me. Here was a man who was older than my father, a man who was supposed to be judging my dives, and he wanted to get me to his room. The whole thing was surreal. I was shocked. I knew the judging was often political, but did divers actually sleep with a judge to get a higher score? And since they throw out the high and low scores, how much of a difference could one judge make, anyway?

I was offended by the whole thing, but I managed to say no as graciously as I could. I have no idea if that affected my scores, because I never thought to go back and check the record to see if he scored me low. That was the one and only time a judge ever propositioned me, but I doubt I'm the only Olympic athlete who has ever had that experience.

≈

FOLLOWING THE AWARDS ceremony, there was a team dinner. All the divers were seated at a head table. I was so stunned from the competition that the evening was a blur. I remember Dr. Lee getting up and talking about how I was like a son to him, how he was so proud of me, how I'd come so far. I know now that he was genuinely proud of me, although at the time I was deeply confused. I was still hurt from the dressing down he'd given me for failing to win the gold. It was his way of apologizing, but I still felt guilty that I had let him down. His praising me in public only made me feel worse.

I *was* like a son to Dr. Lee. And he was like my father. Both were stoic, stern, often unbending and uncompromising. I always wished Dr.

Lee had been more like John Anders, more like the fantasy father I wished I'd had.

It would be many years and another two trips to the Olympics before I could hold that silver medal in my hand and feel anything other than revulsion. And it would be many more years before I would understand that I should have been angry at Dr. Lee for making me feel that winning the silver was a defeat.

7

~~~~~~

FAME

ON THE TRIP home to California from Montreal, we had to change planes in Chicago. As we were walking through the airport to our gate, a guy in a business suit kept staring at me. I turned to my mom and asked if we knew him; she said that we didn't. I looked down to see if my fly was open, but it wasn't. Finally, he approached me and asked, "Are you Greg Louganis?" He told me that he'd watched me on television at the Olympics and wanted to congratulate me. It hadn't occurred to me that people might actually have been watching the event. Even if they had, why would they remember me?

Recently, I came across a letter my mom wrote to her sister after that trip, which captures what happened pretty clearly.

I've never had a celebrity in the house before. It couldn't have been any worse if he had won a "gold."

We came in last Thursday night and the pilot on the plane

announced Greg was aboard. Well, for four hours we were enter-
tained aboard—free drinks and the bits. Then when we landed,
that was something else. All the TV stations and newspaper people were there. Greg walked down the ramp and all of a sudden
the lights came on. Pete walked around one side and I the other.
There were people inside the airport with signs. It took us an hour
just to get out and on the way home.

When we turned the corner to home there were people everywhere with streamers and signs welcoming Greg home. I don't
know how many people were in the house. All I know is they
went through twelve quarts of champagne. I stayed in the kitchen
and got loaded on martinis. The TV people were in the house,
too, and stayed taking pictures for an hour.

Then Friday, his fan mail started. Greg asked me to take care
of it for him. Well I figured a couple of days was all, but it has
turned into a nightmare. Three hours each day is spent on his
mail. He has received over two hundred letters and telegrams, two
from President Ford, one inviting Greg for a tour and reception. I
called the White House and told them why he couldn't come and
the next telegram was congratulating Greg on his achievement in
winning a silver medal. . . .

When the pilot announced that I was on the plane, I still felt embarrassed because I was only a silver medalist.

My sister was one of the first people to reach me when I got off the
plane, and Despina stayed right by my side and helped clear a path for
me through the crowd. She also helped me move along as people
stopped me to talk to me.

At one point, the mayor of El Cajon stepped up to me and introduced himself. I had no idea how big a deal the Olympics were, that
they meant so much. I thought diving was such a minor event. I had no
perspective on what I'd done, so the crowds of people and all the press
attention didn't make any sense. Also, it wasn't as if I had gone around
telling everyone I was a diver. I knew that in the minds of a lot of people diving was a sissy sport, like dancing and acrobatics. But now everyone wanted to talk to me because I'd won a medal.

Finally we got home. But as we turned onto the street before ours, there were people holding banners and waving. Then we turned onto our street and it was filled with people. My dad suggested I get out of the car and greet people, which I did. People congratulated me, but all I could manage to say was "thank you" over and over again, to everyone. After a few minutes, Dad told me to get back into the car and we drove down the block and into the driveway.

Inside the house there were more people, and in the middle of the living room there was a big cake, with a platform on it and a little diver. There were people everywhere drinking champagne.

There was even one guy who crashed the party. My dad had been tending bar, and this guy went up to him and told him he'd tend bar. He told my father to go enjoy himself. After the camera crews left and it was just close friends and family, my dad asked me if he was one of my friends. I said I thought he was one of Despina's friends. But Dad had already asked Despina. Dad asked him if he knew anyone at the party and he said, "Oh no. I just saw Greg on TV and wanted to welcome him home. I'm just helping out." Dad asked him to help himself out the door.

I found out later that even before I came home, the local television station had gone to my Aunt Geri's house to tape her reaction as she watched my diving events. She even had champagne on ice in case I won a medal.

Everyone seemed to be in on all the excitement. Everyone except for me.

I got lots of phone calls that night congratulating me. One of the calls was from a reporter asking about Sergei Nemsonov, a Soviet diver who had defected in Canada earlier that day. I had been involved in helping to make it happen. Toward the end of the Olympics, word had gotten out to the Soviet team's handlers that one of the male divers was going to defect. So all of them were restricted to their room, even having their meals delivered to them.

Sergei went to a diver from the Canadian team, Scott Cranham, to ask him to help him defect. Scott came to me to ask me to help figure out a way to get the Soviet divers out of their room for a little while, long enough for Sergei to slip away. Scott asked me because I was the one person he knew who had easy access to the Soviets. I had been hanging out with them, so it was perfectly natural for me to be seen by the Soviet coaches and the Soviet officials. Also, I was sixteen and looked innocent, so Scott figured that no one would guess I was in on anything.

I didn't think twice about agreeing to help. I simply thought if Sergei wanted to live in Canada or the United States, why should his government try to stop him? Most of Sergei's teammates agreed.

The plan was for me to use the excuse of leaving for home to get the Soviet divers to join me for my last meal in the Village. So I came down to their room with my bags and asked them if they would come down to the cafeteria with me for a goodbye meal. Their coaches were busy saying goodbye to people, too, so they weren't paying that much attention.

In the cafeteria, we met up with Scott and some of the other Canadian and American divers. We had a quick lunch, and then it was time for me to leave. I thought I could just leave and have the Soviets see me off, but there was a complicated checkout procedure at the Olympic Village. Finally, we got out of there, and the Soviets helped me get my bags through security and out to the sidewalk, where I was meeting my father for the ride to the airport.

The Soviets' goodbyes were very emotional. Not only were they saying goodbye to me, they were saying goodbye to Sergei as well. Then I left with my dad to meet my mother at the airport.

During the goodbyes, Scott and some of the other divers took Sergei to an office under the Olympic Village that was a "neutral zone" where athletes could seek asylum from their governments. It wasn't until I returned to San Diego and got the call from the reporter that I knew Sergei had been successful. The reporter said that I must have known about it because I was friends with Sergei. I told her that I was friends with the entire Soviet team and didn't know anything about it. That was the end of the conversation.

Sergei didn't stay in Canada for very long. Life was a lot more complicated in the West, and he was overwhelmed by all the choices and by all the decisions he had to make, so he decided to go back to his family in the Soviet Union.

Despite how things turned out, I was proud of myself for having helped Sergei defect. To take on that much responsibility made me feel like a grown-up.

≈

I WAS SORRY that I couldn't accept President Ford's invitation to the White House, but I was only home for a short time before leaving for Japan and Hawaii on a month-long tour with Dr. Lee and Jane Ward, another diver he coached. In Japan we gave exhibitions and clinics, and I competed in the Japanese nationals. Japan was one of a number of countries that allowed foreigners to compete in its nationals. We were also wined and dined for the two weeks we were there, and then we went to Hawaii for two weeks, mostly for R & R.

When I got back home in October, El Cajon declared a Greg Louganis Day, and I was invited to speak before the chamber of commerce. They also made me the marshal of the Mother Goose Parade, which is held in El Cajon every November. It's one of the biggest parades in Southern California. I'd performed in the parade before as an acrobat, but now I was in the parade as the guest marshal. It's a little awkward to sit in a car filled with giant cartoon characters and maintain any dignity. But it's all part of the job, and besides, waving is a lot easier than diving.

Things were getting crazy with all the phone calls from reporters and people we didn't know, and we had to get the first of our unlisted phone numbers. Even with unlisted numbers, the crazies still got through occasionally.

One time, not long after I got back from the Japan tour, I answered a call on my sister's line, which was still listed. I said hello, and the guy on the other end of the line asked, "Is this Greg?" I said it was, and he said, "I just wanted to ask your permission to masturbate to your picture." I thought about what I could say, but all I said was, "Yeah, I guess so," and hung up. I didn't know whether to be embarrassed for me or for him. That was when my sister got an unlisted number too.

That caller was one of the more extreme, but after the Olympics, I discovered that lots of people found me desirable, both men and women. More than a few girls I didn't know called to ask me for dates, and a couple of girls called to ask me if I'd take them to their senior prom. At various diving events, I'd be surrounded by girls wanting my autograph. The *Evening Tribune* described the scene at the Valhalla High School swimming pool where I was practicing my dives shortly after the Olympics: "The young girls with sun-bleached hair sit together in the bleachers and ogle him as if he were Fonzie or Paul McCartney or someone. . . . Louganis seems embarrassed and uncomfortable amid all the attention and does his best to concentrate on the task at hand. . . . 'Ohhhhh, Greg,' coos a pretty blonde with a camera. 'Could you come over here so I could take your picture?' Greg goes over, poses, chats for a while and then walks away, blushing slightly and shaking his head." I always got the impression the reporters wanted to be in my shoes, surrounded by pretty girls who desired them. But it had more to do with them than with me.

The sexually charged attention made no sense to me. I didn't see myself the way other people saw me. To them I was this sexy Olympic icon, an image the newspapers seemed to encourage when they described me as having a "muscular, brown, supple body." I may have been all those things to others, but at sixteen, when I looked in the mirror I didn't see anyone different from the skinny, dark-skinned sissy I'd been before I went to the Olympics. That would prove to be an ongoing problem for me. No matter how many nice things people would say about my looks, no matter how many times I would be photographed for magazine spreads, no matter how many men and women would make passes at me, I could never accept that I was attractive, let alone a sex object. Only now, in my mid-thirties, am I beginning to explore with a professional counselor why I've always had a bad self-image.

Although I didn't win the gold at Montreal, it was clear that life wasn't going to be the same anymore. It wasn't. Nobody at school ever called me a sissy again—at least to my face—and I got more recognition on the local sports pages than even the football players did.

My life wasn't the same, but I was.

8

COMING

OUT

PARTICIPATING IN THE Olympics was a major rite of passage for me, and not only as an athlete. Montreal was where I remember telling someone for the first time that I was gay, where I fell in love for the first time.

I don't really know how I knew what a gay person was, but by the time I got to the Olympics, I had no doubt that I was one. I really wanted to talk to someone about what I was feeling, because I was having trouble dealing with it. When I met Scott Cranham, the Canadian diver who helped Sergei defect, I thought he might be the person I could confide in. For one thing, I thought he too was gay. He was studying psychology in college, so I hoped that even if he wasn't gay, he would be a sympathetic ear.

We had been hanging out together occasionally since we had both arrived in Montreal, and one afternoon, walking in the Olympic Village, I took him aside and told him I thought I was gay. My heart was pounding because I had never told that to anyone before, and I was afraid of how he might react. I explained to him that there was no one else I could talk to about it.

Well, Scott couldn't handle it. After that day he came near me only if there were lots of other people around. He avoided any situation where there might be the opportunity to talk one-on-one. I was very disappointed and sad and angry. When you're sixteen and you reach out, you're taking a huge risk. I felt totally vulnerable and totally alone.

What made it even worse was that I didn't just like Scott, I had a crush on him. But what I felt for Scott was nothing compared to the crush I developed on one of the Soviet divers: I fell for him like a boulder off the 10-meter platform.

The first time I saw Yuri (not his real name) was at an international competition in 1976, a few months before the Olympics. He was older than I was and absolutely beautiful, and I was instantly attracted, with a breathless, overwhelming desire you read about only in romance novels. I'd never experienced anything like it before.

I spoke no Russian and he didn't speak a whole lot of English, but all I knew was that I wanted to be with him.

I spent a lot of time with the Soviets in Montreal because several of them were around my age. Yuri and I were introduced to each other by one of the other Soviet divers whom I already knew. It was more fun for me to be with the younger Soviet divers than with the American divers, but the fact that Yuri was there probably had something to do with it.

It didn't go unnoticed among my American teammates that I was spending a lot of time with the Soviet divers. I was doing things with the Soviets and having meals with them. This was still during the period when the Russians were supposed to be our enemies. But I didn't really care about politics. They were athletes, no different from any of us. Unfortunately, most of my teammates had a knee-jerk negative attitude toward the Russians because of all the propaganda. One of them started calling me a Commie fag.

It was right after I'd told Scott Cranham that I was gay that I got called a Commie fag. I assumed he'd broken my confidence and I was mad at him for years, although I never asked him about it until I visited with him recently in Canada. Scott told me that the only other person he told was his girlfriend and that she didn't tell anyone. He also told me that the reason he ran away from me was that he couldn't accept the fact that he himself was gay. It terrified him when I first went to him to talk about being gay. It was the last thing he wanted to deal with. Scott's been out of the closet for years now, and he said it was okay to mention it in my book.

Of all the Soviets, Sergei Nemsonov spoke the most English. He didn't do much translating for me, but I'd hear the word *cinema* in a conversation and I'd chime in, "Oh yeah, let's go to the cinema." Or I'd hear the word *disco* and say, "Yeah, let's go to the disco." I listened very carefully, but generally I didn't know what the hell they were saying. I suppose they could have been saying, "Let's go blow up the disco," and then I would have been guilty of espionage, but generally athletes come to the Olympics to compete in their sport, to meet fellow athletes from around the world, and to have a good time. That's the true Olympic spirit.

At some point, my Russian friends tried to fix me up with Tatyana, one of the female divers. I wasn't interested—I just wanted to be near Yuri—but it gave me another excuse to hang out with them. Tatyana must have figured that American boys were just shy.

One time I got to spend a few hours alone with Yuri. After the team dinner at which Dr. Lee said I was like a son, I went back to the Soviets' room to hang out. The diving events were all over, and it was time to party. They'd brought cases of vodka, cognac, champagne, and caviar to Montreal, so for three days we stayed up late, drinking, carrying on, and crying on one another's shoulders about not doing as well as we were supposed to. A lot of the Soviets didn't come close to doing as well as they were supposed to, so there were plenty of sorrows to drown.

Yuri had been openly affectionate with me during the Olympics. He'd give me big hugs to greet me and say goodbye, and he thought nothing of putting his arm around me, which to me was wonderful.

On the last night of the marathon party, I stayed down in the Soviets' room well past midnight, just to be near Yuri. By the time everyone passed out it was very early in the morning, and only Yuri and I were still awake. I had my head in Yuri's lap and I had my arms around him and he was holding me. We had most of our clothes off and we cuddled.

Being with Yuri was wonderful. It felt wonderful to be held by him and to caress him. It wasn't bad or sinful. It was the most natural thing in the world, and I felt no guilt. He wasn't repelled by me and it felt great to know that he found me attractive. I wanted to stay there forever.

Not only was I sexually attracted to Yuri, but also I felt protected and taken care of by him, like with an older brother. It was easier to think that I was simply looking for a big brother to put his arm around me and protect me from the world than to think of myself as gay. But of course I was, and my feelings for Yuri were both emotional and physical.

That night was the only sustained physical contact I ever had with Yuri. After that, we saw each other periodically at competitions and he always greeted me with a big hug and a kiss. I found the Russians, in general, to be affectionate, but the affection from Yuri was new to me.

Yuri was my first crush, but he was not the only man to catch my eye at the 1976 Olympics. During the opening ceremonies, I wanted to sneak a cigarette. The only other smoker I knew of, Robert Cragg, was talking to this other American. I didn't know who the other American was, but as I took some drags off Rob's cigarette, I thought, "God, what a hunk!" I found out later that the handsome hunk was Bruce Jenner. I must have been the only person in the world who didn't know who Bruce Jenner was.

Long before I met Yuri, I can remember being attracted to men, as far back as age seven or eight. I didn't understand what it meant, but I knew what my feelings were. At that age, I just assumed that's how everyone felt.

I remember being very attracted to one of my older cousins and doing everything I could to spend time with him. He was in his teens, with an athletic physique and brown hair. He was taller than I was, but everybody was taller than I was.

I was in acrobatics at that time and I was pretty agile. My cousin would toss me around and hold me up in an arm stand while he was underneath me. It wasn't as if I was sexually active at that age or even thinking in those terms, but I loved the physical attention and I wanted to be with him as much as possible.

By that age, I was already being called sissy and faggot, but I didn't associate those names with being attracted to men. All I knew at first was that being a faggot was a bad thing and that there was some type of shame in being one. At some point I asked one of my classmates what a faggot was, and he told me that it was a man who walked and talked like a woman and dressed up in women's clothing. By the sneering way the words were said, you knew it had to be bad. But sissy and fag were just two of the many sneering things I was called. They all blended together to make me feel that I was truly worthless and had no right to live.

When I was around twelve or thirteen, I began to understand that sissy and fag meant homosexual. I don't remember how I came to know that, but I knew immediately that it was something to be ashamed of. I don't remember hearing anything about it from my parents or in church or on television, but I must have, because I knew what it was and I knew it was bad. Now I feared that I was one, but I couldn't accept it and tried not to think about it.

Before that night with Yuri, I had a few adolescent experiences of playing around with other teenagers, the kind of thing that happens when boys stay over at each other's houses. I didn't think anything of it, and neither did the guys I played around with. Most of them are married now, with kids. At the time, I didn't think of it as sexual, because it was just kind of wrestling and rolling around with our clothes off. It was exploration and experimentation. But I was definitely intrigued and excited by the whole thing. I never told anyone and barely acknowledged to myself what I was doing. If I had, I wouldn't have been able to dismiss it as just playing around. I wasn't emotionally prepared at fourteen or fifteen to acknowledge what my real feelings were and what they meant.

However, there was one guy, when I was in my mid-teens, with whom it was definitely more than just playing around. We were both curious and we both enjoyed it, and things got sexual. I'm sure it was a lot more significant to me than it was to him, and for a long time I worried that I "made him" gay. I also introduced him to cigarettes and pot, so I didn't think of myself as a good influence.

But at that age, I assumed that these feelings were something I'd outgrow, that this was the kind of thing all teenage boys went through. I tried hard to believe that, because I didn't want to believe that I was gay.

What made things even more confusing was that I found girls attractive. I thought that if you were gay, girls were supposed to repulse you, but that wasn't the case. I was sexually involved with one girl from a very early age. We began to have sex in junior high school, and she'd kill me if I used her real name, so I'll call her April Jordan.

We were both twelve years old when we began. We liked to go to the movies, hang out in the canyons, hike, and catch lizards together. There were a lot of houses under construction in the area, and we liked to explore foundations and basements. One day, April found a book called 101 Positions for Sex. She suggested that we try them, starting with number one. I was still too young to ejaculate but not too young to have intercourse. Also, I was still taking acrobatics at that point, so I could do just about anything. We'd look at the positions and say, "Oh, let's try this." I think we got through about ninety of the positions before we lost interest.

It was just something to do after school, something that was a lot more fun than reading. We'd do it just about anywhere we could: in her house, in my house, in the canyon, in the basements of the unfinished houses. This went on for about two years, and the only time my parents almost caught us was in my dad's office, when we didn't hear them pull up in the driveway. Fortunately, we were already getting dressed when we heard them walk in the house. We just pretended that we were sitting in my father's office talking. From then on, we were careful to listen for the car pulling up in the driveway.

To us, sex wasn't really a big deal. I don't think we ever thought of it as lovemaking, although we were wonderful friends. It was like play-ing duck-duck-goose. It was physical activity, so it was fun, and it had a certain danger, because we knew we weren't supposed to be doing it. This was for grown-ups. But we didn't realize the significance of what we were doing. We only knew that we shouldn't tell anyone about it.

Later, when the heterosexual boys at school began talking about doing it, I came to find out that I was probably the first one to begin "doing it."

April was the only girl I ever had an extended sexual relationship with, but there were a few other women I had relationships with as I tried to sort out my sexuality. Even when I didn't have a girlfriend, the sports reporters who wrote about me often made it seem like I did. When I came home from the Olympics, the local newspaper published a big story about my arrival back in El Cajon, including a picture of a friend of mine, whom they identified in the caption as my girlfriend. She and I used to ride horses together and sometimes we kissed, but that was as far as it went. This friend had made it very clear that she was going to wait until she was married. Generally, we had fun doing things together, and eventually I asked her to go steady. I thought that was what I was supposed to do. We went on dates but never had sex, so perhaps we *were* boyfriend and girlfriend, after all.

The only other girl that reporters seemed to speculate about was Megan Neyer, a diver who remains one of my closest friends to this day. We were on the same team, and every four years, in '80, '84, and '88, the sports reporters were suggesting that Megan and I were having a torrid affair. They'd publish photos of us together, with Megan rubbing my shoulders. It was never reported that we were an item, but it was implied, and we didn't try to discourage the speculation. Megan always thought it was good for my image, and we laughed about the whole thing. But the truth was, Megan and I were incredibly good friends and we did spend a lot of our free time together. It's just that we spent a lot of time talking together about the guys we were both interested in.

Megan and I also joked about getting married. We talked a lot about how it might hurt me if I came out publicly. She thought it would be a lot better for my image if we got married, but I didn't think it would fool anyone. Anyway, it was never more than talk, but our kids would have been great divers.

≈

NOT LONG AFTER I got back from the Olympics, I got involved in a relationship with a man for the first time. I was still con- fused about my attraction to men, but after my experience with Yuri, I longed to be held by a man again. The problem was, I had no idea where to meet other gay people. There wasn't exactly a gay teen center in El Cajon in 1976. There was no place I could meet other gay kids like me, no place to sort out my conflicts over my sexuality, and no way to start going out on dates with boys my age.

So, because I couldn't find other gay people, someone found *me*. During the fall semester of high school in 1976, my classes ended shortly after noon, and I'd gather up my books and drive to the beach. I told myself I was going to do my schoolwork there, but I rarely opened a book.

One afternoon a few weeks into the semester, this guy at the beach kept staring at me. He looked very similar to a guy who worked at the pool, rather attractive, in his late thirties, with brown hair and a stocky build. He looked similar enough to the guy I knew that I went over to talk to him. He told me his name, which I didn't recognize, and then he asked if I wanted to get a drink at his place, a Coke or an iced tea. I told myself that he was just being nice, but I thought he was attractive and in the back of my mind I hoped that something *would* happen, so I went. At that point, I still couldn't admit to myself that this was what I wanted. I couldn't deal with what that would mean about me.

He wanted me to go with him in his car, but I suggested that I follow him in my car to his house. I was smart enough to know that I'd better take my own car, smart enough not to get myself into a situation where I might be stranded.

During the drive there, my mind was racing with different thoughts: Should I really do this? Is this proper? What if I'm caught? What does he really want? Is he just being nice, or is he a murderer?

Nevertheless, I was intrigued and curious and attracted, and I was not turning back.

We got to his place, a nice two-story town house, and we went in and sat down in his living room. We talked for a while and he got me something to drink. At some point he said, "Let me show you around the place," and eventually we ended up in his bedroom. He put his arms around me and kissed me. I really liked being held, and I was thrilled that this guy found me attractive.

While it was happening, I enjoyed what we were doing, but afterward, I felt guilty and ashamed for having had sex with a man. On the one hand, it felt right, I was attracted to men, I wanted to be held, and I enjoyed being physical with a man. But on the other hand, it felt wrong; sex between two men was a sin according to my church. It upset me that he was so much older, not because I felt molested or anything—I had been a more-than-willing participant—but the difference in our ages somehow made the experience even more shameful. But where could I go to meet gay people my own age?

Before I left, he gave me his phone number. Of course, I didn't give him mine. I told him that I lived with my parents and that it would be a very bad situation for me if they found out. It didn't occur to me that it also might be a bad situation for him, given my age. On the drive home I could smell his scent on me. I worried that my mother would know I had been with a man. As soon as I got home, I jumped in the shower and scrubbed myself clean.

Over the next six months, we got together maybe a dozen times. I'd stop on my way to the beach and call him and ask if I could come by. If he wasn't home, I'd go to the beach and sometimes I'd run into him there. At some point he told me he was concerned about seeing me because I was under eighteen. Apparently, he'd been jailed in the past for picking up minors.

I thought that over time I'd feel less ashamed about what I was doing, but it only got worse. The age difference bothered me more, and he couldn't exactly be a part of my life. I felt stupid telling him what I was doing at school, and I couldn't introduce him to any of my classmates. I hated the separateness and the secrecy, but I kept going back for the affection, the holding, the cuddling—more those than the sex. I was starved for affection, and he was happy to give it to me.

I know that plenty of gay men and lesbians can tell stories about having had similar experiences with older men and women when they were teenagers. Most will tell you that they were willing participants. But age of consent is nonetheless a volatile issue among gay people, just as it is among heterosexuals, especially because of the persistent myth that gay men are by definition child molesters. The truth, of course, is that the vast majority of child molesters are the male heterosexual members of a child's family.

Given a choice, I would have preferred to meet and date someone close to me in age. But as for most gay and lesbian teenagers, even today, there were no places for me to meet my peers. If there were more opportunities for gay and lesbian teens to meet one another, perhaps fewer of them would find themselves seeking refuge in the arms of adult lovers. That said, I don't regret the affection I exchanged with this man.

I don't regret any affection I exchanged, ever.

9

~~~~~~

DIVING

GOING BACK HOME and returning to Valhalla High School in the fall of 1976 was a big adjustment for me. I'd been at Santa Ana High School for the spring semester, living with Dr. Lee and his family, training for the Olympics. Now I was home again, and there was no way to go back to the way things had been. I had left Valhalla an invisible person and I returned a hero. Now everyone wanted to be my friend, but I didn't know whom to trust. Sure, I wanted friends, but not the kind who wanted to be around me only because I'd won a medal. From that point on, I could never tell if someone liked me for myself or for who they thought I was.

I'm also shy, and it seemed easier to keep to myself. My parents had gotten me a car when I went to live with Dr. Lee, so now as soon as classes were over, I would hightail it out to the beach. Some people at school thought I was snobbish, that I thought I was too good for them, but that wasn't it. The new attention was more than I could handle, and I needed to get away.

Nevertheless, I still got involved in school activities and managed to have a pretty good time. I began coaching the men's and women's diving team, and I also helped coach women's gymnastics. Despite what I may have thought of myself, and despite what they may have thought of me, my classmates voted me best dressed, best dancer, as well as best physique. I liked the attention, but it was more than a little embarrassing. And it always felt like they admired someone else, that if they knew the real me, they'd take it all back.

I continued training with Dr. Lee and going to diving competitions, but I began to have trouble with my back. Shortly after I started diving again that fall, I was doing a routine dive—an arm stand, cut-through reverse one-and-a-half—and I came up short of vertical, which meant I was going to enter the water on an angle. That would have cost me points, so I tried to pull it in, and the combination of being out of alignment and the impact of the water compressed my back and threw it into a spasm. For the rest of the year, there were days when I could dive and others when the pain was too much. There were even some weeks when I couldn't get in the pool at all. Not being able to dive got me really down.

By the summer of 1977 most of the pain was gone and I was finally getting into a normal training routine, but I reinjured my back at a diving exhibition in Greenwich, Connecticut. We were on our way to Europe for competitions in Sweden, Austria, and Italy. To give my back a rest, I didn't compete in Sweden, but after that I had to dive through the pain.

By that point in my career, diving with pain was nothing new, certainly not a reason not to dive. For every athlete who competes at a world-class level, pain just goes along with the territory. A back problem is a different story, because there were times when I simply couldn't move the way I needed to and I had to rest.

Over the years I have had plenty of painful injuries, from badly gashing my shin and severely spraining my wrists to dislocating my shoulder and, of course, hitting my head on both the 3-meter spring-

A reverse dive layout, 1970. Not bad for a ten-year-old. (*Collection of the author*)

Mom said that when she saw my smile, she knew I was the one she wanted. (*Courtesy Frances Louganis*)

At Dad's fuel dock in San Diego with my sister, Despina, April 1963. (*Courtesy Frances Louganis*)

At Aunt Mary's house in Van Nuys, California, with Tina. I loved dogs from the very beginning. (*Courtesy Frances Louganis*)

Who is that masked man? I think it's me. (*Courtesy Frances Louganis*)

A month after I was adopted, with my god-parents, "Aunt" Geri and "Uncle" Bill Louganis. (*Courtesy Frances Louganis*)

My first Christmas with my new family. (*Courtesy Frances Louganis*)

At Dad's fuel dock with Dad, Mom, and Despina. (*Courtesy Frances Louganis*)

Five and a half years old. Taken at Florence's Art Studio, La Mesa, California. (*Courtesy Frances Louganis*)

My favorite tux. Thanks to Mom, it was fabulous. (*Courtesy Frances Louganis*)

My stage debut at age three, with my teacher following me with the microphone so I could be heard. (*Courtesy Frances Louganis*)

I loved acrobatics.
(*Courtesy Frances Louganis*)

Too cute?
(*Courtesy Frances Louganis*)

"All That Jazz." Mom was inspired.
(*Courtesy Frances Louganis*)

With my performance partner, Eleanor
Smith. (*Courtesy Frances Louganis*)

Recital with Eleanor for Merlin's School of
Dance, December 1969.
(*Courtesy Frances Louganis*)

I was Denise Christiansen's date at her senior prom in 1977 in Tucson, Arizona. Denise was also a diver and I was living with her family at the time and training with Charlie Silber. Where did I get that tie? (*Collection of the author*)

I couldn't believe the crowds of people at the airport who welcomed me home from the 1976 Olympics. That's Despina in the background, at center. (*Collection of the author*)

Coaching the women's diving team at Valhalla High School in El Cajon, 1977. (*Collection of the author*)

Mom and Dad at the Junior Olympics in Seattle, Washington, in 1972.
Mom was so proud of how I did that I gave her my gold medal to wear.
(*Collection of the author*)

With Mom and Dad in the 1970s, just after I
got an award. My parents were always very
proud. (*Collection of the author*)

With Dad after a competition in the mid-
1980s. (*Collection of the author*)

At the 1976 Olympic trials. Mom was thrilled that I made the team, and so was I. (*Collection of the author*)

Thanksgiving dinner, 1992, with Mom at home in Malibu just before the guests arrived. I cooked everything by myself. (*Collection of the author*)

Dancing with Mom at the International Swimming Hall of Fame induction dinner, May 1993. (*Courtesy Mary Jane O'Brien*)

With Mom at the International Swimming Hall of Fame induction. (*Courtesy Mary Jane O'Brien*)

With Mom and my first coach at the International Swimming Hall of Fame in Fort Lauderdale, Florida, for a competition in 1969. (*Collection of the author*)

At the Nationals in Mission Viejo, with Dr. Sammy Lee, my most demanding coach. (*Collection of the author*)

At the team dinner with Ron O'Brien during the 1976 Olympics in Montreal, before I started coaching with him. (*Courtesy Mary Jane O'Brien*)

With Ron and Dad at Mission Bay in Boca Raton, Florida. (*Photo by Bob Taylor,* THE DIVER *magazine*)

My induction into the International Swimming Hall of Fame, Fort Lauderdale, Florida, May 1993, with Ron, Mom, and Mary Jane O'Brien. Don't we look smashing.
(*Courtesy Mary Jane O'Brien*)

My cousin, Dr. John Christakis, and Mom.
(*Courtesy John Christakis*)

At the Great Wall of China in 1980 with Megan Neyer
during a tour of Japan and China with the Olympic team.
(*Courtesy Megan Neyer*)

Megan and I went all over the world, and
even to Thunder Basin.
(*Courtesy Megan Neyer*)

Megan and fellow diver and friend Kent
Ferguson at my thirty-third birthday party.
(*Courtesy Mary Jane O'Brien*)

The U.S. team for the 1973 World Age Group Championships, Belgium—my first trip to Europe. That's Bruce Kimball in the front row, second from the left.
(*Collection of the author*)

The 1976 U.S. Olympic team.
(*Collection of the author*)

The 1984 U.S. Olympic team.
(*Courtesy Mary Jane O'Brien*)

The 1988 U.S. Olympic team.
(*Courtesy Mary Jane O'Brien*)

IF THE ELECTION WERE HELD TOMORROW... WHO WOULD YOU VOTE FOR?
GREG LOUGANIS.
POLLS
THE PITTSBURGH PRESS
UNITED FEATURE SYNDICATE

board and the 10-meter platform. Routine injuries are no big deal, but diving can be an unforgiving sport.

Probably the scariest thing for a diver is getting lost in your dive. That's when you lose sight of your spots and you don't know where you are as you're spinning in the air. When that happens, you don't know if you're going to land on your head, your back, or your face.

I only got lost in a dive a few times, but one time I remember really well was at Belmont Plaza in Long Beach. I was doing a front three-and-a-half. As I came out of the dive, I stretched for what I thought was the water, but it turned out that as I was spinning, I'd confused a wall of windows for the surface of the pool. So instead of hitting the water hands first, I landed flat on my face and stomach.

When I landed, it didn't just hurt, it was a shock, because I wasn't expecting it. It's very disorienting, because you think you know where you are, but you don't, and the only way you find out is when you slam into the water.

Another time, in New Zealand, I was doing an inward three-and-a-half. I came out of the dive, and instead of stretching for the water, again I stretched for the windows on the far side of the pool. I went a quarter of a turn too far, to a perfect three and *three quarters*, and I landed flat on my back. I couldn't breathe and all I could see were stars—just like in the cartoons.

Getting lost in your dive is always scary and painful, but the injuries from doing a back flop off a 10-meter platform are usually just a few welts, some split skin, and a bruised ego. But two experiences I had with the 10-meter platform really drove home the point how unforgiving diving could be.

In 1979 I was at a U.S./U.S.S.R. dual meet in Tbilisi. I was doing a reverse dive pike on the 10-meter platform, and I don't know if it was the soft cushioning on the platform that I wasn't used to or I was just trying a little too hard to do a perfect dive, but I jumped off the platform, brought my legs up and touched my toes, and saw the sun through my legs. That's the last thing I remember. Apparently, I hit the back of my head solidly on the platform and was knocked unconscious.

I landed flat on my back in the water. Megan saw the whole thing, and at first she thought I was dead. If not for the soft cushioning covering the concrete platform, I probably would have been dead. They had to go into the pool and get me out.

Megan watched from the side of the pool as they pulled me out, and she said I was lucky I hadn't broken my neck, because they weren't careful getting me out of the pool. These days, with that kind of injury, the procedure is to keep the diver in the water until you've got a backboard under him and have secured his head, just in case he's broken his neck.

I was knocked out for twenty minutes, and when I came to, I was on a stretcher in a waiting room adjacent to the pool. I thought I was watching cartoons running backward, because I couldn't understand what anyone was saying. Actually I couldn't, because everyone was speaking Russian. I thought for sure that my mom was there, shaking me and offering me some peanut butter cookies. I smelled something that smelled exactly like my mom's peanut butter cookies.

When the fog cleared a bit, I realized that Mom wasn't there. It was a Russian nurse, stroking my forehead. I looked around and saw other nurses, but I couldn't understand what they were doing there. When I heard somebody announce Bruce Kimball's next dive, I realized where I was: in the middle of the competition. Naturally, I tried to get up and get ready for my next dive. The nurses gently pushed me down and told me to relax. Jane Ward, one of the American divers there with me, calmly told me that I was finished for the day and that I was lucky I wasn't finished for life. If I'd been doing a reverse two-and-a-half or three-and-a-half, dives with tremendous momentum, I could have been killed.

The nurses tried to give me a sedative. They handed me a little cup with a liquid in it and told me to drink it, that it would make me calm, but I thought, No way—not in Russia. It was only then that I started to understand what had happened: I was out of the competition. I'd already won in 3-meter springboard, after our coach, Dick Kimball, had told us that a foreigner would never win in Russia. Like many Americans, he believed that Soviet judges would favor the Russian divers.

I could have won on platform—I was in the lead—but there was no way they were going to let me get back on the platform after that. For all they knew, I might have fractured my skull.

Once I was conscious, they took me on the stretcher in an ambulance to a hospital. Jane Ward, who had a nursing background, and Dick Kimball came with me. There was no team doctor or trainer with us in Russia.

The Soviet X-ray equipment was so old that it looked like something out of a Frankenstein movie. They X-rayed my skull and didn't find a fracture, but there was a big bump on the back of my head from where I'd hit the platform. The doctors were sure that I had a concussion, but they weren't sure how serious. So they wanted to keep me in the hospital for observation, in case there were any complications, like convulsions. Jane objected to their keeping me overnight, so I was taken back to the hotel. Several people, including Megan, stayed with me all night. For most of that time, we talked and played cards.

My head didn't really hurt, but my back was sore from hitting the water, covered with welts that swelled and split, like having razor cuts all over your back. Megan rubbed lotion on me to keep the skin from splitting even more. That was when Megan and I got very close. I made it through the night okay, and we left for home a day or two later.

Although my doctor had told me to take it easy for at least a month, I didn't. Three days later, after returning to the University of Miami, which I was attending at the time, I was back on the platform. I did only three dives the first day, because they made me dizzy. But within a few more days I was back doing my regular routine. I had to—I needed to get ready for the World FINA Cup, which was less than two weeks away. I won.

Hitting my head on the platform was a pretty bad experience, but I was knocked out, so I don't remember it. It was much more terrifying for my friend Megan, who saw it happen. I witnessed something four years later, in July 1983, at the World University Games in Edmonton, Canada, that was even more horrifying, and it's something I'll never forget.

There were thirteen divers competing on 10-meter platform, and I was standing on the 7.5-meter platform, waiting my turn along with a young Canadian diver who was diving ahead of me. A Russian diver, Sergei Shalibashvili, above us on the 10-meter platform, was about to dive. I saw the dive number 307C on the scoreboard across the pool, so I knew he was about to do a reverse three-and-a-half, a very difficult dive. I was the person who had started using the dive in international competition, and my doing it pushed the other divers to try to do it even if they weren't fully prepared. Sergei and I were the only two divers attempting the reverse three-and-a-half at the World University Games.

In previous dives, Sergei had been coming very close to the platform, and we were all worried. In fact, one of the American coaches approached a Soviet coach to express his concern about how dangerously close some of his dives had been. The Soviet coaches didn't know that Sergei also wasn't feeling well, but some of the American divers did. He'd been having severe diarrhea and was pretty weak, which added to the possibility of his having an accident. I didn't think Sergei should have been diving, but it wasn't up to me. If it had been me, I would have done the same thing and hidden the fact that I was sick. You do some stupid things just to compete. Every athlete does, and most of the time you get away with it, but it isn't worth the risk. Coaches need to help athletes understand that winning isn't everything—life is.

I had an awful feeling that he was going to hit, so when they announced his dive, I turned around and looked away from the pool. I plugged my ears with my fingers and started humming lightly to myself. I didn't want to see or hear him hit the platform.

I didn't see it or hear it, but I felt it. There was a jolt, and the whole tower shook. I unplugged my ears and looked toward the deck where the coaches were standing and scanned the audience to see their reaction. Everybody was out of their seats and people were yelling, "Get a stretcher! Get a backboard!" I ran to the edge of the platform and was about to jump in after Sergei when someone yelled, "Don't jump in!" I looked over the edge of the platform and there he was floating, face-down, not moving. There was quite a bit of blood in the water, and a few people were in the water already pulling him to the side of the pool. Sergei was unconscious but still breathing.

At that point, I turned and walked to the back of the platform where the Canadian diver was standing. I could see he was pretty shaken, and I tried to calm him down by asking him about his next dive. I don't think I helped him much, but it gave me something to do.

When the diving resumed, we were all still shaken. I still had a job to do, but it was almost impossible to concentrate.

My next dive was a back three-and-a-half, which I did fine, but then my final dive of the prelims was the same reverse three-and-a-half Sergei had attempted. Before I did the dive, I asked my coach permission to jump it out, to push out farther from the platform so there would be more space between my head and the concrete as I passed the platform on the way down. I didn't want to take any chances, so I played it safe and jumped out. I got 4's and 5's, which wasn't great, but in the finals, I did the dive as I usually did and I got 8's.

When we left Canada, Sergei was in the hospital in a coma. The rest of us headed for the McDonald's International Invitational, which was being held at the Olympic swim stadium in Los Angeles. Toward the end of the L.A. meet, a reporter asked me if diving was getting too dangerous, given the example of the Soviet diver who had just died. I was stunned, and told the reporter that I hadn't heard the news yet. The reporter was very apologetic. I said I had no comment.

I was terribly upset and felt that Sergei's death was my fault. I know I didn't put a gun to Sergei's head and force him to do the dive. It was his own decision, his and his coach's. But I still felt responsible. What made me feel worse was that his coach was his mother. I'm sorry I inspired Sergei to try using that dive, and I hope his death made us more careful. It was a tragic reminder that diving could be a dangerous sport.

To make sense of what happened and make sure I never made the same mistake as Sergei, I decided to look at a tape of what had happened and figure out what he did wrong. I watched it alone, crying through the first few times, watching the dive through my tears.

I played the videotape over and over and over. By the sixth or seventh time, I saw what Sergei had done wrong: As he was initiating his takeoff, bending into the platform and then jumping off the platform, he had his weight on his heels, and his back was very straight. His shoulders were over his heels, which pushed him up over the platform instead of away from it. If his shoulders had been forward a little bit, his weight would have been over his toes, not his heels. Also, as he was pushing off the platform, he should have projected his hips farther forward to carry him up and away from the platform. I watched the tape several more times, to imprint on my mind exactly what *not* to do, so I would never make the same mistake.

And on that dive, at least, I never did.

10

AS AN ADULT looking back, I can see now that depression has been a major problem all my life. But as a child and adolescent, I just thought I was moody. Generally, my bouts of depression seemed to be triggered by a specific problem, like being called names or having a bad workout. Until fairly recently, I never thought of the depression itself as the problem.

Sometimes when I was young, the bad moods seemed like they would never end. One of those times was in the fall of 1977, when I was just going back for my senior year of high school. My strained back had kept me out of the pool on and off for nearly a year. Even when I dove, I was still in pain. I was beginning to think I'd never get the chance to redeem myself at the next Olympics.

I was also wrestling with my sexuality, mostly scared that I'd no longer be accepted if anybody found out. If I'd had somebody to talk to, I might not have felt so bad. I looked forward to my furtive meetings with the older man from the beach, but he wasn't someone I could really talk to. At that point I didn't even consider seeing a counselor or psychologist. I accepted my parents' view that psychologists were for people who were mentally ill. I was depressed, but I wasn't mentally ill.

I started to think that I should just leave, kill myself, commit suicide, but I didn't act on those feelings right away. But one day at school I decided there was no point going on. There was a report due in my English class and I didn't have it finished, so I made up an excuse that I'd been away diving. I did that a lot, especially in humanities classes. Most of the teachers would give me an extension, but a few of them would take off an entire grade for each day the paper was late, so I would get a C instead of a B. Even without the penalties, I was barely getting by.

My parents were unhappy about my schoolwork, but they figured I'd be going to college on an athletic scholarship, so my grades didn't matter. But the grades still mattered to me, and I felt like a failure that afternoon. So I went to my parents' medicine cabinet to find some pills.

As I looked through the various prescription bottles, I remember thinking to myself that I'd better be careful not to use too much of any one drug, because I didn't want to get in trouble for taking my mom's pills. So I tried not to take so many that my mother would notice they were gone, but I took what I thought would be enough to get the job done.

I wrote a suicide note explaining that I couldn't take it anymore, and I outlined all the reasons why I was doing it—except my sexuality. One of the lines in the note was about how I couldn't seem to do anything right. I told my parents not to blame themselves, because it wasn't their fault, and I explained that I was simply too sad to let them know what was going on in my life. I swallowed a handful of pills, got into bed, and prayed that I wouldn't wake up.

When I opened my eyes the next morning and realized I was still alive, I was angry with myself for being such a failure that I couldn't even kill myself. I grabbed the suicide note off my nightstand and ripped it up. I was feeling pretty groggy, so I told my mom that I was coming down with the flu. I stayed home from school and slept for most of the day.

The next day, my mother discovered that some of her Valium and codeine were missing. She confronted my sister and me, concerned that we'd stolen the medicine from her to sell it on the street. I told her I didn't know anything about it.

The next day, I went up to Belmont Plaza in Long Beach to train with Dr. Lee. I tried practicing on springboard, but my legs weren't under me at all, and I almost hit the side of the pool. I went to Dr. Lee and told him that I couldn't dive. I didn't tell him what I'd done, but I told him that I had to call home.

I called my mom and told her that I was the one who took the pills. She asked me why I took them and I started crying. I told her that I took them because I'd wanted to kill myself. I was more ashamed that I'd stolen medicine from my mother and that Mom felt it was her fault. Her biggest concern was that I was okay, that I hadn't hurt myself. It was easier for me to feel guilt and concern for my mom than it was to confront what my depression was really about. As soon as we got off the phone, I headed home.

My father spoke with Dr. Lee about the suicide attempt, and Dr. Lee suggested that I go to a friend of his who handled suicidal teenagers. My parents thought I would be better off talking with our family doctor, Dr. Easler. They thought, mistakenly, that since he was a friend of the family, I'd have an easier time talking to him.

Dr. Easler asked me a lot of questions, to which I gave my usual one-word answers. Before long, he gave up and I went home. I had learned this well-practiced tactic early on at school. If you just gave one-word answers, they gave up on you. I didn't know how badly I needed to talk to someone who could help me sort out the emotional mess I was in.

My parents didn't make me go back to Dr. Easler again. Instead, they grounded me for a few weeks for taking my mother's medication. Like most people of their generation and background, they didn't know a lot about mental-health problems or the psychiatric profession. They saw my suicide attempt as an isolated thing. I wonder how different things would have been if only I had dealt with my depression as a teenager. Maybe the rest of my life would have been changed for the better. That's why I urge parents to take their children's problems seriously.

≈

THE REPLACEMENT FOR therapy for me, as always, proved to be my diving. My back slowly got better, my diving improved, and so did my outlook. The turning point was when I started diving with Ron O'Brien, whose diving camp I'd attended a few summers before. In some ways Ron reminded me of John Anders. He was the kind of esteem-building coach who taught his divers the difference between competition and competitiveness—in other words, to be a good sportsmen rather than focusing on winning at all costs.

Dr. Lee recruited Ron to coach at the new diving center at Mission Viejo, about an hour north of where I lived. It was a great facility, with an Olympic-competition diving pool, 1-meter and 3-meter springboards, and 5-, 7.5-, and 10-meter platforms. So when Ron got there in May 1978, I started training with him on the days when Dr. Lee couldn't work with me.

I first met Ron in 1969, around Christmas, at the Swimming Hall of Fame in Fort Lauderdale. I was in a competition, and Ron was there to train his divers over the Christmas holidays. He came over to say hello to me and to meet my coach. I don't remember what Ron said to me, but I stood there with my arms crossed in front and my shoulders forward. When he talked to me, I kept my chin down and just peered up at him. Ron says that I came across as a "meek little guy," and I guess I was. I wasn't afraid to throw myself off a diving board, but I froze up when it came to meeting new people.

Years later, Ron told me that when he saw me dive in 1969, I had body lines, strength, grace, and control you never see in a kid that age. He said he knew I'd be a great diver if I stuck with it.

I didn't see Ron again until I was fourteen, in Decatur, Alabama, when I was competing in the senior nationals. I took twelfth place on platform and thirty-third on 3-meter springboard. Not exactly an impressive performance. But Ron still thought I had great talent, although it was clear that I needed some technical help, especially on springboard. He thought some of my problems came from trying to do dives that were harder than what I should have been doing at the time.

When I finally worked with Ron at his summer camp, I saw how well balanced his divers seemed. I learned that he believed it was important for his divers to get a good education and become happy and successful people. Although I agreed with Ron's philosophy that if you got too narrowly focused on diving, your whole happiness and self-worth would be dependent on it, somehow I still tied my self-worth almost entirely to diving. But I liked that Ron encouraged his divers to do more than dive.

Ron's coaching style, most of the time, was to remain calm and on an even keel. Ron wasn't the kind of coach who yelled at and belittled us the way Dr. Lee did. He was more nurturing, and he tried to instill a sense of calm in us by teaching us not to get riled up over one bad dive. As great a coach as Dr. Sammy Lee was, his pressurized coaching made me feel worse when I blew a dive. A competition involves many dives, so it doesn't help to feel bad just because you made one mistake. Ron's focus was always on doing your best on each dive. If you did a bad dive, you went on to the next and tried your best again.

Another thing I became more aware of after I'd been diving with Ron for a while was that when he critiqued a dive, he'd start with a positive comment, which always got me to listen, and then he'd go on to explain what needed to be improved and he'd offer some suggestions about how to do that. Then he'd finish with a positive statement about the overall dive or something specific about the dive that worked well, always ending on an up note, which helped me go into the next dive with a positive attitude.

A short time after I started training with Ron, I gave up training with Dr. Lee. I'd finished high school a semester early, so since January I'd been free of that obligation. Despite my low grades, I managed to accumulate enough extra credits from coaching and my outside part-time job to finish in three and a half years. With school over, I picked up another two part-time jobs to save money for college. Then I started diving with Ron, so I was working with two coaches, training double time. For example, on the weekends I worked with Ron's team on Saturday morning, but while they had the rest of the weekend off, I dove with Dr. Lee on Saturday afternoon and for a few hours on Sunday. I never got a chance to rest. Ron and Dr. Lee didn't communicate with each other very well, so I was getting conflicting messages about what I should be doing. I couldn't possibly keep both of them happy, and there was no way to keep my jobs and still spend so much time diving.

The decision to give up one coach was easy. Dr. Lee wasn't happy about it at first, but eventually he agreed that it was the best thing for me.

I surprised Ron by coming out of my shell when I joined his team. I was still a little shy, but I was a lot more open. I even became a bit of a joker, always trying to make people laugh. Somebody would be getting ready to do a difficult dive and I'd make a remark and break the tension. Or in the middle of my doing a handstand, I'd crack a joke. Ron didn't put up with a lot of messing around, but he encouraged us to have fun. He made us feel like a team.

But I could still be moody, and sometimes I would get very down. Ron noticed that one day I'd be fine and the next day I wouldn't talk to anybody. I still had no idea why I had such bad moods, but there didn't seem to be much I could do about it. Ron would sometimes ask me what was wrong, but my usual answer was a shrug. One time that summer, when I was in a really bad mood, Ron called me into his office and told me I wasn't leaving until I told him what was going on. He could tell I'd been upset, because he'd seen me at practice that morning standing in line waiting to dive with tears coming down my cheeks.

Often I got in bad moods for no particular reason, but this time there had been a reason. Eventually, I told Ron that I was exhausted from working the three part-time jobs and diving. My diving schedule didn't leave me enough time to work just one full-time job.

My average day started with opening the recreation center at 5:30 A.M., before my morning workout. Then I worked out for a couple of hours before going to my other job, at Chess King, a clothing store in Huntington Beach. Then I'd come back to the pool for my second workout. I'd have two hours off, and then I'd go to the Westminster Chess King to close that store. The pressure was weighing me down. Ron got me to talk about it and helped me adjust my work schedule so I could quit one of the jobs and not run around so much.

After that it was a little easier for me to talk to Ron about things that were going on in my life outside of diving. In Berlin a few months later, at the world championships, I suddenly clammed up again. I'd had a really negative attitude in practice and wasn't diving the way I should have been. I didn't really know what was bothering me, but I felt miserable and was letting my moodiness get to me.

In a competition, even if I was in a bad mood, I was able to kind of turn the switch when I got up on the board and still do a good job most of the time. Ron was pretty gentle with me when I was in a bad mood. This time he felt that I needed a jolt.

Between dives, I stood under the hot shower to warm up. The shower was located under the stand for the 3-meter springboard. I was there for a while, and Ron came to talk to me. While he was talking to me, I started to turn around to walk away, and he just kicked me in the butt—literally—and told me to get back up on the platform and dive. Well, he got my attention.

After the practice, Ron pulled me aside and told me we had to talk. He asked me what was going on, and at first I started bitching. Then I started crying. I couldn't explain why I was upset, but Ron kept me talking, and eventually what came out was my anxiety about going from the competition to the University of Miami for my first semester of college. I was already feeling homesick. Ron suggested that I call home, which I did, and I felt a lot better.

Ron convinced me that I could trust him, that I didn't have to keep all my problems to myself. I never liked burdening anybody with my problems, but Ron made me feel it was okay to tell him something that was bothering me. I knew he cared, because he kept pushing for answers; he really wanted to get to the bottom of what was bothering me, and he didn't let up until I opened up. And then he'd come up with some pretty insightful solutions.

Over the years I got better at going to Ron and asking him for help. And over the years I would need his help with things even more diffi-cult than a reverse three-and-a-half.

II

~~~~~~

THE

UNIVERSITY

OF

MIAMI

DESPITE MY MOODS, working with Ron was great. I made a lot of progress with my diving, especially on springboard, where I really needed the help. But we only got to work together full-time for a few months, because in September, I left for my first year at the University of Miami. I was scared, but I was also very excited, especially because I was the first one in my family to go to college. My mother and father didn't have the opportunity, and my sister had chosen not to go even though she did really well in high school. If it hadn't been for diving, I'm not sure I would have gone myself, because I certainly didn't have the grades.

When I left for the University of Miami, some people thought I was going there because Julie Capps was there. She was a sophomore and a nationally ranked diver. The real reason I went there was because they gave me an athletic scholarship and they had a great drama department, but I was happy to be near Julie. Even though I knew I was gay, I still thought it was wrong, and I thought I should make one more attempt to see if I could have a relationship with a woman. Julie seemed like the right woman.

From the time I arrived at school, the two of us palled around like boyfriend and girlfriend, although we weren't having a sexual relationship. In my mind we were dating, but then I heard around the pool that Julie was dating a swimmer, which made me realize I was only fooling myself. I was gay, and even though people thought it was wrong, even though I felt bad about it, nothing was going to change. I gave up on the idea of trying to have a girlfriend, and eventually I told Julie that I was gay. We continued our friendship without skipping too many beats.

I went to the University of Miami with the intention of spending only two years there. I planned to leave early at the end of my second year to go back to California and continue training with Ron O'Brien full-time in preparation for the 1980 Olympics. After that, I thought I might transfer to a school in Southern California or continue diving full-time. That decision would have to wait until after the Moscow Olympics.

My time at the University of Miami was a mixed bag of experiences, between diving, meeting other gay people, having my first relationships, and taking acting and dance classes.

Acting and dancing were great releases for me, because they were the only things outside of diving that I really enjoyed doing. I first got the idea to study acting after the 1976 Olympics. Several people told me that I could be an actor or that I could do commercials. Also, I was inspired by two Olympic athletes, Bruce Jenner and Mark Spitz. I wasn't sure I'd wind up acting or doing commercials, but if I did, I decided that I wanted to be prepared. I'd seen other Olympians try acting and commercial work. I didn't want people laughing at me, so I thought I should study acting before I went out there and tried it in public.

It wasn't difficult for me to get up in front of an audience—I'd been doing that for years—but it was a new challenge for me to get up in front of a crowd of people and speak. So, going into my first acting classes, I didn't have a lot of confidence in my ability to communicate feelings and ideas.

Frankly, I wasn't great. One of my teachers was even cruel enough to tell me that the only way I'd make it in acting was because of diving. I assumed he meant that without my celebrity from diving, I could forget about making it on my acting abilities alone. That was disheartening, but as bad as my self-esteem is, my stubbornness is stronger. I wasn't about to give up. Besides, I still had several years of diving left, which meant lots more time to study acting before I had to make a serious attempt at an acting career.

So whether or not I was going to be a great actor, I still had fun, and through the drama department I had the chance to meet and spend time with other gay people, which was great. I went to my first gay dance clubs and bars with other students from the drama department. Sometimes just two of us would go together, and sometimes we'd go in groups of boys and girls. Most of the girls weren't gay, but we all had a great time dancing together: boys with boys, boys with girls, girls with girls. I'd never seen two boys dance together before, and at first it was shocking. But once I got used to it, dancing with other guys seemed like the most natural thing in the world. I'd always been a good dancer, so I really had a great time. Suddenly there were all these other people like me out there. It was such a relief to know I wasn't the only one.

I was only vaguely aware of the gay rights movement and the gay student group on campus. I'd heard about Anita Bryant and the hateful things she said about gays. I knew that we were supposed to boycott orange juice because she was the Florida orange juice spokesperson, but that was the extent of it for me. I didn't pay much attention to those things. All of my time was taken up with trying to get my schoolwork done, getting to theater rehearsals, and keeping up with my diving.

My schedule at school didn't leave me much time to catch my breath. I had an hour and a half of diving practice in the morning before I went to class, followed by more diving before lunch, then back to class. Next was rehearsal for scene-study class, and then rehearsals for whatever production was being done at that time. I barely had time to eat.

Even though I was busy, I somehow managed to find the time to have my first real relationships. Given my usual turbulent emotions and my almost complete inability to communicate in any realm other than diving, the experiences didn't turn out all that well.

My first big crush at school was on Daniel (not his real name). We met in dance class, and I was crazy about him. I would have done anything for him. I thought about him constantly and always wanted to do nice things for him. He returned the affection and our relationship became sexual, but it didn't have the same meaning for him.

One major problem was that Daniel was still struggling to find himself. He was still coming to terms with his sexuality, which is a tough thing to do. I was also part of the problem. I was clinging to Daniel with such desperation that he couldn't breathe. After a few months, he told me he needed his space. I was crushed, and when I found out that he was seeing somebody else, I was devastated. All I knew was that the love of my life didn't want me, and at eighteen, that was the end of the world.

Unfortunately, the end of the relationship with Daniel came at the same time as one of my low periods. Things at school had been difficult: My roommate's girlfriend was practically living with us in our tiny dorm room, I was having a difficult time with Freshman English, finals were coming up, and I was terrified I wouldn't pass. All the negative feelings snowballed, and I decided once again that I'd be better off dead.

I don't remember exactly what I took this time, but it was probably a mix of Quaaludes and black beauties, the kind of recreational drugs I could get my hands on. I collected them over a period of a few weeks as I got more and more depressed, thinking that suicide might be an option. Once I found out that Daniel was seeing someone else, I took the whole mixture.

Again, I woke up the next day feeling like a total failure because I couldn't even manage to kill myself. I was pretty sick for a couple of days after that, and my friend Bob Strickland kept an eye on me, as did a couple of other friends. Bob brought me food and made sure I ate it.

A few of my friends suggested that I see a counselor, but I didn't listen. After having tried unsuccessfully to kill myself three times, I started thinking that there must be a reason why I was still alive, and maybe I should try to figure out what that reason was. But for the second time in my life, I passed up the opportunity. I wish now that I'd made the effort to seek serious professional help rather than waiting another sixteen years to do it.

It took me a few months to get over Daniel, and by the next fall, I was feeling ready to meet someone else. One day during diving practice, I noticed a guy hanging around the pool. He was handsome, with curly brown hair and a nice physique, and he was taller than I was. He came back the next day, and during a break we talked for a little while. He asked if I'd like to get together sometime, and I said yes.

It turned out that Jeff (not his real name) was a graduate student. I liked him a lot, although I didn't have the same intense feelings for him that I'd had for Daniel. A few weeks after we met, I moved in with him. This may sound a little crazy, but at the time it made perfect sense. It was coming up to the start of the next semester and it was time to pay for the dorm. I'd been complaining to Jeff about my roommate situation and he said he could help out, because he had a two-bedroom condo near the campus. I was over there all the time anyway, so moving into the second bedroom made sense.

I spoke to the coach's secretary about the logistics of moving out of the dorm. We made the necessary arrangements, and I moved in with Jeff. I didn't tell any of my diving teammates that I'd moved in with my boyfriend, but I'm sure at least some of them figured it out.

Moving in with Jeff was really nice, especially since we shared a lot of the same values. Unfortunately, we didn't share the same values about relationships, which should have been a warning to me. We both agreed that we wouldn't sleep with other men, but Jeff was still dating women. Sometimes he'd stay out all night, which made me furious. I didn't think he should be dating anybody else, women or men. He gave me the option of sleeping with women, but I wasn't interested. It was a strange and unfair double standard.

We had separate bedrooms, but Jeff and I usually slept in his bed unless he went out on a date with a girl. When that happened, I was in my own bed. If he brought girls home, I just shut it out.

Despite his dating women, I thought that Jeff and I were in a committed relationship—even though I was going back to California at the end of the semester. We both avoided talking about the future. Jeff was rooted in Miami, and I was determined to go back to California to train with Ron. Diving was more important to me than staying in Miami and having a relationship with Jeff. We talked about carrying on a long-distance relationship, but never very seriously.

Nevertheless, our breakup was dramatic and devastating. I was in the middle of finals, which I was trying to rush through because there was an international competition in Fort Lauderdale the first weekend in May. I was pulling all-nighters to get my studying done.

In the middle of all this there was a party that Jeff and I were invited to. We'd already been fighting before the party, over a grocery list. Things had been generally tense, because I was about to leave for California. At the party, I was determined to make him jealous—I admit it—and scoped out the cutest guy and started talking to him. I left the party early—alone—and went home to get some more studying done. I hadn't said goodbye to Jeff, and he figured I had gone home with the guy I was flirting with. So he decided to teach me a lesson.

I was in my room studying when Jeff came home. I had my books and notes spread across my bed, but I'd been having a hard time studying because all I could think about was how bad I felt about the fact we were fighting and that I was leaving soon. When I heard the front door open, I ran downstairs to greet Jeff with open arms, and there he was with another man.

Jeff introduced me to him. I was extremely embarrassed, and I made an excuse for myself: "Oh, I was just getting something to eat. Studying for finals. Good night." And I went into the kitchen and opened the refrigerator. I didn't take anything out, and after a few seconds of making some noise moving things around, I closed the door. I felt like a complete fool, rushing to greet him with open arms only to have the door slammed in my face.

After the introduction, Jeff and his friend went right upstairs, and I went back to my room and tried to study, but I couldn't handle the noises coming from next door. I grabbed my books and ran down the street to where Bob Strickland and his roommate, Jim Crum, lived. I was crying as I told them what happened.

I spent that night at Jim and Bob's, and the next day, when I knew Jeff was going to be at class, I packed my things and moved them over to Bob's. In a few days I went up to Fort Lauderdale for the international competitions. Jeff came by the pool one day to talk to me, and I told him to leave. I was in the middle of a competition and I needed to concentrate on my diving. I was very angry and didn't want to talk. We didn't talk again until several years later.

I look back now at my relationships with Daniel and Jeff and realize how young and inexperienced we were and how much I had to learn about relationships. I didn't exactly have a great model at home to start with, and I had no role models when it came to intimate and committed relationships between two men. I'm sure they existed, but I didn't know any adult gay couples. So I had plenty more mistakes to make, and lots of lessons to learn.

Unfortunately, I seemed determined to learn all of them the hard way.

12

~~~~~~

MOSCOW

1980

GOING INTO 1980, Ron and I talked about what we thought was possible for me at the upcoming Olympics in Moscow. Ron wasn't someone who talked about expectations, but based on how well I'd been doing at competitions, he thought it was possible for me to win both 3-meter springboard and 10-meter platform at the Olympic trials and at the Moscow Games. Ron didn't *expect* me to do it, but he thought it was possible, and we both thought it was something we could work toward. It was a goal to reach for.

One thing Ron didn't do, which I really appreciated, was talk to the press about the goals we set for ourselves. When he did speak to the press, he was always careful to keep things in a realistic perspective, especially after I started winning consistently. It got to the point where every time I got on the board or the platform, the press expected me to win.

Ron also helped *me* keep perspective by reminding me that on any given day someone could beat me. The danger, he said, was thinking I was unbeatable, because that was the day I'd get beat. Ron drove home the point that each competition was new, and I couldn't count on winning if I didn't make the effort every time.

It didn't matter how much effort I made in preparing for the Olympics, because history intervened and there was no 1980 Olympics for the U.S. Olympic team. The Soviet Union invaded Afghanistan in December 1979, and President Carter demonstrated the U.S. government's displeasure by deciding to boycott the Moscow Olympics.

The boycott was a terrible disappointment. All of us had been working toward the Games, and now suddenly it was gone. To make matters worse, we were all expected to fall in line and support the president. I never paid much attention to politics, so I really didn't care why we were boycotting. Whether the goal was to humiliate the Soviets for invading Afghanistan or to express dramatically our government's disapproval of the invasion, the bottom line was that we weren't going to compete. The athletes and the fans paid the price for the message.

In the long run, it wasn't too bad for me: I still had plenty of time left in my career. For some of my fellow divers, 1980 was their last best shot at making the team and competing in the Olympics. Megan was one of those people. She came in first at the 1980 Olympic trials in both springboard and platform, and she won the world championships two years later. She might have won medals for both 3-meter springboard and 10-meter platform had we gone to Moscow.

Despite the boycott, we still had the Olympic trials. At first it was like we were just going through the motions. The trials were held at the end of June, in Austin, Texas, at the Texas Swimming Center at the University of Texas. Fifty-three of the top men and women divers from around the country came to compete.

For the two weeks before the trials, Ron took our team, the Mission Viejo Nadadores, to a training camp in Cleveland, Ohio, to fine-tune our dives and help us get focused. Ron didn't give us much time to feel sorry for ourselves over the boycott, because he worked us really hard. His attitude was that this was a competition for the Olympic team, and if we wanted to be Olympians, then we had to prove it by doing our best.

The two weeks in Cleveland paid off, because six of the thirteen divers to make the Olympic team were from Mission Viejo. Some of the reporters asked us what we thought was the key to Ron's success. We said it was a raggedy doll we'd given him on Father's Day, but the key was Ron.

I don't think I surprised anyone when I came in first in both spring-board and platform. But success in diving is never guaranteed. All it takes is one mistake, and you can blow your entire lead. I had to concentrate from my first dive to my last.

In the springboard competition, I was happiest with my seventh dive of the final round, a reverse two-and-a-half pike, which is a difficult dive. I got six 10's and a 9.5, an almost-perfect score. My total score at the end of the final round was 940 points, 28 points ahead of the second-place finisher. Then on platform I finished 65 points ahead of the next diver. I scored several 10's in that round despite the fact that I cut my palm on a pipe at the bottom of the 18-foot pool on my first dive.

When you dive off the 10-meter platform, you're going at 32 miles per hour when you hit the water, and your hands hit the water first. So with a cut palm, it really hurt. But by that point in my career, I didn't let a minor injury get in the way of a good dive.

Ron once told me that I dove with more pain and suffering and sickness than any diver he had ever had. A lot of my injuries were just routine, sprains and stomach viruses, but sometimes I did klutzy things. One time I sat down on a glass when I was in a boat and cut my butt. That doesn't sound like anything big, but when you're in the middle of a dive and you're pulling your legs up to your chest, the stitches hurt like crazy.

A week later, I was diving on springboard and I slipped going up the ladder and gashed and bruised my leg right on the spot where I had to grab my leg and squeeze hard during the dive. Each time I dove I wanted to scream.

Another time, I had some warts on my hands and feet that I needed to have removed. I don't know why I decided to do it ten days before the nationals. That doesn't sound like such a big deal, but when I hit the water from the 10-meter platform, the pain brought tears to my eyes.

One time I almost didn't get through it. At the national championships in Indianapolis in 1986, I caught a stomach virus. I was very sick, but I did a few dives, went into the bathroom, threw up, and came back out and did a few more dives. I don't know how, but I won.

I may cry easily, but I never give up.

≈

THE ONE SOUR note for me regarding the 1980 Olympic trials came during the Olympic team's exhibition tour that followed. Some of my teammates didn't want to be my roommate because I was gay. This wasn't expressed to me directly—it rarely was—but I heard about it.

Most of the time, the fact that I was gay was ignored by the other divers, or I just never heard about it. Plenty of the divers knew I was gay, because I didn't exactly keep it a secret. Some divers clearly kept their distance. I don't know what they thought I'd do to them, but obviously they wanted to be sure never to be close enough to find out. Others were perfectly comfortable.

Over the years, a few of the younger male divers asked me questions about my sexuality, mostly out of curiosity. I had no problem answering their questions, and they seemed glad to have the answers. I explained that I was attracted to men over women. I made the point that I didn't hate women, that I could appreciate a beautiful woman, but that my primary physical and emotional attraction was toward men. One of the young divers who came to talk to me was clearly confused about his sexuality and was struggling to deal with it. He came from a family in which he felt that his being gay would never be accepted, so I knew he was going to have a rough time.

Generally if I was teased, it wasn't because I was gay; it was because

I was winning. It was frustrating for the other divers, who worked very hard, that as long as I was diving, the odds were I was going to win. After the Olympic trials, they started calling me GL, for God Louganis. I didn't like it, because it wasn't meant in a complimentary way. Usually if someone said GL, it was under his breath, like I was being booed. But for any athlete in a lead position, that kind of teasing just goes with the territory.

The one time the anti-gay stuff was the most blatant was in Baton Rouge, at a National Sports Festival competition in 1985. One of the divers, who whispered "fag" whenever I walked by and called me names behind my back, put up FAGBUSTER signs all over the dorm where we were staying. His inspiration came from the movie *Ghostbusters*. The signs had the word *fag* in the middle of a circle with a slash through it.

I never saw most of the signs, because Megan went around pulling them down. But the first time I saw one, I got a terrible feeling in the pit of my stomach. They were as much symbols of hatred as swastikas or burning crosses would be for someone who is Jewish or black.

Megan was afraid that someone would try to hurt me physically, which never even crossed my mind. I never heard most of the things people said about me, and Megan didn't tell me about them until recently. She remembers some of the divers saying that I wasn't human, that it was time to get rid of the fag, or they'd make jokes about specific sexual acts. Megan always defended me, and I'm grateful to her for that.

Megan wasn't the only one who would defend me, but there weren't many and most were women. These same women also sometimes said things to Megan like "Can't you convert him?" and "What a waste!" But the women didn't say these things in a threatening way. For whatever reasons, the men were threatened by me.

No one ever did anything as overt as the "fagbuster" campaign after the festival in Baton Rouge. The diver who put up the signs boasted about how he was going to beat the faggot, but he didn't. The faggot trounced him.

All I ever had to do was get on the diving board and let my record speak for itself. I stayed true to that belief for my entire career. Plenty of other lesbian and gay athletes had to put up with that kind of prejudice then, and they still do to this day.

I always wanted to tell the diver with the signs that his anti-gay attitude was not only bigoted, it also went against the principles of true sportsmanship. He wanted to be an Olympian, but he didn't know the first thing about Olympic ideals, which have nothing to do with hate. But I never got the chance to say anything—until I spoke about what had happened in Cobb County regarding the 1996 Olympics. And then I got to tell the whole world that there's no place for anti-gay bigotry in the Olympic movement. No young athlete should have to face the prejudice that I did.

13

~~~~~~

INTERNATIONAL

DOMINANCE

AFTER THE U.S. boycott of the 1980 Olympics, there was no question that I would train for the next Olympics. But 1984 was a long way off, so the challenge was to come up with goals that would keep me busy, focused, and in shape for four years, which was not an easy thing.

One major goal was finishing my college degree. In December 1980, after all the tours and competitions following the Olympic trials, I started school at the University of California in Irvine, where I had an athletic scholarship.

When I first started classes, there weren't a lot of diving competitions to get ready for, which meant I could concentrate on school. I needed all the time I could get. At the University of Miami we had had study groups for each of our classes. At U.C. Irvine I was left to fend for myself. It was a commuter school, so after classes were over, everyone headed home. There were no dorms where people got together for study groups. That wasn't only frustrating, it was a disaster for me. If you didn't maintain a certain grade point average, you couldn't participate in the sports program. I was doing so badly that I barely scraped by. I could have talked to the athletic director about my reading problem, but I still felt embarrassed about being dyslexic, so I never said anything. I just tried my best to keep from drowning.

The bright spot for me again was the drama department. Among other things, I got to be dance captain and one of the lead players in a production of *Pippin* and assistant choreographer for a production of *The Gondoliers*.

The two big diving events ahead of me were the world championships in 1982 and the Olympics in 1984. But competitions alone couldn't keep me motivated. On my own, I could never set goals. That wasn't how I thought of things. I could focus only on doing the best I could on the upcoming dive and not much beyond that. It was Ron who first mapped out my goals for me and worked with me to come up with some of my own.

Ron came up with a list of competitions for me to compete in each year. Over the next four years, I competed in about twenty meets a year. Of those, about six were major competitions. Then he came up with records for me to beat. He wanted to make sure that I'd leave behind a record that reflected my ability, one that would be remembered long after I retired from diving. So he'd say something like, "How about winning the most national championships for a male diver?" By the end of 1981, I'd won eighteen national titles, more than any other male diver. The next goal was to beat Cynthia Potter's twenty-eight national titles. I had to wait until after the '84 Olympics to break her record, but I did.

We also came up with a few personal goals, like scoring perfect 10's on a single dive and breaking 700 points in a 3-meter competition, all of which I did by 1984. As soon as I met a goal, Ron would come up with a new one. For example, he'd say, "Well, you have four gold medals from the Pan American games, but nobody's ever won more than five." I liked a good challenge, and Ron knew it was the best way to keep me going.

Another goal was scheduling enough training time to keep my dives polished and to learn new, more difficult dives. In 1982, the International Diving Federation approved a number of tough new dives for competition that had higher degrees of difficulty. That meant you could get higher overall scores, assuming you successfully executed the dive.

I learned the new dives, but not because I was a daredevil or anything. Given the competition, Ron and I felt I needed the more difficult dives for me to stay on top. We talked about the fact that the one way I could distance myself from the other divers, especially Bruce Kimball, was to do all these new dives.

Until Bruce Kimball came along, I didn't really have to worry all that much about competing with anyone but myself. It seems hard to believe now, but by 1980 I was accustomed to coming in first on both springboard and platform without a tremendous amount of effort. My diving had become more of a performance than a competition. With Bruce, suddenly I was getting beat on platform on a national level. We'd been friends since we met on our first trip to Europe back in 1973, so the competition was always fun. I often found myself rooting for him, even when that meant I was rooting against his main competitor—me. Friendship aside, I didn't like coming in second, and neither did Bruce.

I didn't think I could compete with Bruce dive for dive, because he had excellent mechanics and he was consistent. His entries were incredible. But he wasn't as strong as I was, so the only way I could beat him was by doing tougher dives and increasing my degree of difficulty. Because of the higher degree of difficulty, tougher dives receive higher scores than easier dives done equally well. Bruce had a more difficult time doing those dives than I did. I also hoped the new dives would give me a big cushion going into the Olympics.

But the new dives weren't easy to learn, and before I did each one, I had to be able to visualize it, which meant that I had to see somebody else do it before I'd give it a try. When I visualized the dive in my head, it would take about three seconds to go through the dive, but I would see it in slow motion. I don't know how I did that, but because I could see it in slow motion, I was able to take the dive apart and memorize it step by step. Fortunately, I had all of 1983 to see if the new dives worked for me. Then I added them to my standard routine.

One time, in 1983, at the Air Force Academy Natatorium in Colorado Springs at the National Sports Festival, they announced I was about to attempt a dive off the platform with a 3.3 degree of difficulty. The audience oohed and aahed. I was trying to get in position and concentrate, but I heard them and thought, If they think the dive's so difficult, why am I trying to do it? I started to laugh, and the audience started laughing, too. When everyone calmed down, I did the dive and landed on my head, just like I was supposed to, and won the festival, more than twenty points ahead of the second-place diver, Dave Burgering.

The Air Force Academy Natatorium was a memorable place for me. Three years earlier, during a workout for the National Sports Festival, I had come pretty close to hitting the ceiling on a dive from the 10-meter platform. After that, somebody dared me to touch the ceiling, so I jumped up from the platform and put my hand through the false ceiling up to my wrist. They raised a big square section of the ceiling over the platform by three feet, which was plenty of room for me to dive.

≈

BESIDES THE COMPETITIONS and training, there were also exhibitions at home and abroad, and there was testing, which I hated. But Ron has a Ph.D. in exercise physiology, and he was committed to having his team participate in various studies. Periodically, he sent us off to the U.S. Olympic Training Center in Colorado or the training center in Squaw Valley, where they would run us through a whole battery of tests to measure our flexibility and coordination, and see how high we could jump.

In one test, which we all despised, they put you in a tank of water to find out how much body fat you have. The test itself wasn't bad, but Ron rode us hard about ideal weight and percentage of body fat. When

I was in shape, it was easy for me to go down to around 6 percent body fat. But for a lot of the women, meeting their "ideal" weight and percentage of body fat was a terrible struggle. A number of them wound up with eating disorders. Even the men used laxatives and Ipecac to keep their weight down. If I thought I was going to be a pound or so over, I'd do laxatives the night before we had to go to the weigh stations.

At first Ron would let us know in advance what day we were going to be weighed. But after a while he'd just surprise us, because he knew we were trying to get around him. After 1984, Ron began to see that the focus on weight and fat ratios was doing more harm than good. It certainly didn't help our self-esteem or make us dive any better.

At the Squaw Valley testing center, they also put us on an isokinetic machine, which provides resistance to test arm, leg, and shoulder strength. All kinds of graphs then tell you the results and compare the left and right sides. The machine could tell when you were backing off because of pain from an injury, which was valuable information. If it turned out, for example, that your left leg was 20 percent stronger than your right, you would have an imbalance in your hurdles. The test helped you adjust your training to bring the two sides into balance.

The worst test, which also happened to be the most painful, was part of a study at U.C. Irvine to determine why certain divers were more explosive in their dives than others. That meant taking muscle samples from our legs to determine what percentage was "fast twitch" muscle.

It felt like you were having your quadricep muscles yanked out of your leg. They took a scalpel and put a little slit right at the top of the quadriceps on the side of the leg. Then they inserted a cylindrical instrument that had clippers on the end of it. Once it was inside, the clipper was used to snip a part of the muscle and then pull it into the cylinder and remove it. They gave us a local anesthetic, but when they cut the muscle fiber, I just about jumped through the ceiling.

My test came back showing that my quadricep muscles were 75 percent fast-twitch muscle, which meant I was extremely explosive. That had seemed pretty obvious *before* the test, but I guess it was interesting to see it confirmed. I came in at the top of the scale. By way of comparison, at the other end was one of the women divers, with 30 percent fast-twitch muscle.

≈

OF ALL THE competitions between the 1980 and the 1984 Olympics, the most important was the 1982 world championships in Ecuador. In some ways it was my 1980 Olympics, because I got to go up against some of the divers I didn't get to compete with in Moscow. It was also an event that set the stage for the '84 Olympics.

As with any major competition, I trained very intensely in the months and weeks leading up to the event. At my peak, I was training five to six hours a day, six days a week. On top of that, I took aerobics classes to build up my endurance. Divers are not endurance athletes, so aerobics training wasn't standard. I found it beneficial, although there were coaches who recommended against it. They believed that with aerobic exercise you'd lose some of your explosiveness. Apparently, it didn't seem to diminish mine.

The irony about divers is that, like dancers, we were never the healthiest lot. A lot of divers smoked and drank pretty heavily, me included. I remember that in 1978 I showed up at the nationals one morning still half drunk. The day before, I'd missed the world championship team on 3-meter springboard. I was feeling pretty sorry for myself and I went out and got smashed. The next day we had the 1-meter springboard competition and I wasn't in great shape. I'd only gotten a couple of hours' sleep and was still pretty drunk. I had no business being on the board, but it was only one meter, so I wasn't going to kill myself. As it turns out, I won, which wasn't necessarily a good thing, because it just made me think I could get drunk, stay out all night, and still win. You can't.

Going into the world championships, I stopped the late-night partying. As I did with every major competition, weeks before the event I started to withdraw from everyone. Early in my career, I did this without knowing it. After Megan pointed out to me what I was doing, I began to do it as a more conscious thing, to psych myself up.

Generally, I would pull back from everyone and isolate myself. I'd become less playful during practice. I'd go in, do my list of dives twice, and leave. Ordinarily, I would have stayed around and done some repetitions or just hung out, but not in the weeks leading up to something like the world championships.

In time, I even stopped hanging out with Megan. A week before we left for a competition, you could hardly get me to say a word, although I'd go to the movies if Megan dragged me. Most of the time I stayed by myself and listened to music with headphones on.

At the competitions themselves, I'd create a little space for myself in the waiting area and go there between dives and listen to my music. If I saw anyone besides my coach, it would be Megan, and then just for a good-luck kiss and a smile. Sometimes we'd just sit together and not talk, and sometimes we'd hold hands, like at the '88 Olympic trials, where I wasn't feeling that confident about my position. Most people didn't know what was going on inside my head, but Megan knew. She was great.

During a meet, I'd go out and do my dive, and then go back to my space. It didn't matter what country we were in, who the judges were, what the weather was, or who the competitors were. Most of the time none of that mattered. I just went out and tried to do my best because I wanted to be my best, not because I was focused the whole time on winning. If you focus on winning, you have to focus on other people. I would focus solely on doing my best.

At the world championships, I had to work hard to stay focused on each dive and not on the end result. I got to Ecuador with a cold, but that was nothing compared to that previous October, when I developed an impingement of the rotator cuff in my left shoulder, mostly from overuse. So I had to sit out until January. A week after I was back on the board, I dislocated the same shoulder diving in a dual meet for the University of California at Irvine. We were diving in a 12-foot pool in Northridge, and I didn't realize how shallow it was until I hit the bottom. I finished the competition, but after that, I couldn't raise my arm above my head for three months. I didn't start diving competitively again until May, which didn't give me all that much time to get ready for the worlds in September 1982.

My main competition at the world championships was Bruce Kimball on platform and Aleksandr Portnov on springboard. Aleksandr had won the gold on springboard in Moscow. In Ecuador, when they made the introductions for 3-meter springboard, they called Aleksandr an Olympic champion. Only gold medalists are called Olympic champions. I was introduced as the 1976 Olympic silver medalist. That made me angry, because I'd never had a chance to compete against Aleksandr for the gold. This was my chance to prove that if I'd been at the Olympics, I would have won the gold.

I wound up beating Aleksandr by 126 points. My nearest competitor was 116 points behind me, 10 points ahead of Aleksandr. The second- through fifth-place finishers were a total of only 12 points apart. If I'd skipped my final dive, I still would have won by 40 points. I also won on platform. Bruce got a bronze medal, which was incredible given that he was just back in competition after a near-fatal car accident.

I was very happy with my performance at the world championships, especially on two of my dives. For my final dive on springboard I did a front three-and-a-half pike. It had a 3.1 degree of difficulty, which at the time was the highest for any springboard dive. I really ripped it, and I got five 10's, a 9.5, and a 9. When you "rip" a dive, that means you enter the water with hardly a splash, and it sounds like someone's ripping a sheet. That final dive gave me a total of 92.07 points, which was the highest in the history of diving for a single dive on springboard.

The other dive I was proud of was on 10-meter platform. It was my fourth dive of the finals, and it was an inward one-and-a-half pike. I got a perfect score: seven straight 10's. That was my first perfect score, and it was the first since Mike Finneran got a perfect score on platform at the 1972 U.S. Olympic trials. It was something I'd always wanted to do.

Unfortunately, getting straight 10's can be distracting. I still had six dives to go, and I managed to hold it together until my tenth and final dive. It was a new dive that I'd only been using in the last year. Fortunately, it had a high degree of difficulty, 3.2, so I still earned enough points to win, but just barely. I beat Vladimir Alenik of the Soviet Union by less than 5 points.

That world championship marked the beginning of my dominance internationally. Several months later, I finished college, and for the first time in my life I could really focus on my diving. From that point on, I was ready to take on just about any diving challenge.

If only that confidence had spilled over into the rest of my life.

14

~~~~~~

KEVIN

IN THE LATE summer of 1980, a couple of months after I
first returned to California from the University of Miami to train with
Ron, I met Kevin. I didn't have anything to do one hot and sunny day,
and I went to Laguna Beach just to hang out. There are a lot of steps
down to the gay section of the beach, and because it was a weekday,
there weren't many people there. When I got down to the bottom of
the stairs, I saw Kevin.

Maybe I was just lonely or maybe I just thought Kevin was very
attractive, but I walked over and asked him if he'd mind if I sat beside
him. I didn't usually walk up to people, but Kevin looked like someone
who was friendly.

I found out he was a couple of years older than I was and that he
was an artist who also worked for the telephone company. We talked
for quite a while on the beach, and that was the start of our relation-

ship. Within a few months, we moved to a house in Costa Mesa, the first of three places we would live.

Very quickly, we settled into a comfortable routine. We never formally divided up the chores, but we each took care of different things, sharing the cooking. Most of the time we'd talk before one of us left for the day and I'd tell him that I'd pick up some chicken on the way home from my workout or he'd ask, "How does lasagna sound for tonight?" It was very domestic and very nice.

We always kept separate accounts and paid our equal share for things. For example, we took turns paying for the groceries. When it came to the day-to-day housework, I tended to have more time, so I did most of it. He was more handy with repairs and that sort of thing, so he did those jobs.

Kevin loved me more than anyone else I have ever been with, and I loved him with a passion that I couldn't control. He was lots of fun to be with and he was really uninhibited. We even held hands sometimes just walking through our neighborhood in Costa Mesa. For me to do that, especially in a suburban neighborhood in the early 1980s, was a very big deal.

Not everyone in our neighborhood was happy to see two guys holding hands. One time when we were out walking, a group of kids drove by and called us faggots and threw eggs at us. Kevin had noticed them driving by earlier, and then they came back. I was just relieved that they didn't hit Maile, my dog, which would have gotten me really angry.

Kevin had given me Maile for my twenty-first birthday. I'd told him that I wanted a Great Pyrenees, which looks like a big white polar bear. Kevin couldn't find one, but he found a beautiful Great Dane puppy. I came home and found her waiting for me. He left her a couple of toys to play with, but she found my books far more interesting. She ripped them up and scattered them all over the house.

It made me more sad than angry that those kids had felt the need to throw eggs at us. Here we were in our neighborhood, not hurting anybody. Kevin was somebody I loved and he loved me. Why shouldn't I hold his hand? It felt like the normal thing to do. We continued hold-ing hands after that and nothing ever happened again.

Kevin was very comfortable with being gay. I never had to worry about him wanting to date women because he thought he should be straight. He went to gay pride marches. I didn't feel that I could go, but I liked being with somebody who was comfortable enough to go. Also, Kevin's parents knew, so it was very comfortable not having to worry about who knew and who didn't. They always made me feel welcome.

As much as I wanted to be that open about being gay, I didn't see how I could do it. From around the time I first got involved with Kevin, I was getting more and more press because of my diving and it didn't seem possible to be open about my sexuality. That meant that most of the time Kevin didn't go with me to my competitions. When I brought him home with me, I never told my parents that he was my boyfriend.

My feelings for Kevin reminded me of what I had felt for Daniel. But from the very start, our relationship was passionate in the best and worst ways. At its best we were completely devoted to each other and very affectionate; we always slept in each other's arms. I hated being apart from him when I traveled to diving competitions.

Making love with Kevin was remarkable because it went so far beyond the physical experience. It was intense, deep love mixed to-gether with overwhelming physical passion. I'd never experienced any-thing like it before, nor have I since.

Unfortunately, we also brought out the worst in each other, and things could get pretty nasty between us. We fought about everything from what to buy at the grocery store to what to watch on television. He'd get high on pot with his friends, and I didn't like it and felt left out. I wasn't exactly a saint myself at that time, because I was using cocaine—which probably contributed to the explosions.

I don't know quite how we did it, but we successfully turned every-thing into an argument. We were both great at getting the other one angry, and we must have taken some kind of pleasure in it, because we did it a lot. Maybe it was that making up was so good.

Most of the time, when our arguments got physical, we would get into a wrestling match and it would end there. But on two or three occasions we threw punches at each other. The last time we got into that kind of fight, my ring caught him under his eye and I gave him a pretty good gash. I don't think he ever forgave me for that, because it left him with a permanent scar. I felt terrible and apologized, but that didn't help much. After that fight, Kevin disappeared for a few days, but he came back. A few times when he did things that got me really angry, I too disappeared for a few days.

I know this kind of relationship doesn't sound very appealing, but in some ways I felt more alive than I ever had. You never knew what was going to happen. All of which helped fuel the physical passion we experienced.

At the time, I didn't think the fights were anything out of the ordinary. From the start, we had trouble communicating verbally, and getting physical was a form of communication. We were just two guys working things out, and physically we were pretty well matched. It wasn't like one or the other had the upper hand. It may not have been the ideal way to communicate, but we both got our point across.

Looking back now, of course, I realize that throwing punches was no way to work out problems. Hitting someone you're in a relationship with is never okay unless it's in self-defense, and if your relationship has reached that point, you need to get professional help.

The worst and last fight we ever had started as a pretty standard yelling and screaming fight. Things had begun to change in our relationship, and not for the better. We'd talked about going to a counselor to try to work things out, but again I was resistant, so Kevin went on his own. I found his therapy very threatening, and the longer he went, the more tense things got between us. I couldn't handle it.

From that point on, when we got into disagreements, Kevin wanted to talk it out. I still had a lot of trouble being verbal. It was much easier for me to get angry and wrestle with him than it was to sit down and talk about what was going on. I didn't like the fact that he seemed to be communicating more with his friends now than with me. I realized that Kevin was getting emotionally healthy, but that just scared me. I was afraid of the mere idea of exploring my life in that kind of formal setting. I wasn't ready.

The longer this went on, the more defensive and nasty I got. By this point, in the spring of 1982, we were only communicating in shorthand with one- or two-word answers, expecting the other to understand what we meant. I felt like I was living out my parents' relationship, which of course was exactly the case. Neither of them was ever up front about saying what they were feeling, because they didn't want to rock the boat, my mother especially. She was always very cautious in what she said, because she was always walking on eggshells when it came to dealing with my dad. There was always the danger of an explosion.

With Kevin, the shorthand responses often led to even greater misunderstandings. For example, I would try to signal that I needed to be reassured, and when he didn't respond, I'd get resentful and angry that he wasn't able to figure out what I needed. I'd blame him for not reading my mind. The truth is, I was the one who was more responsible for the miscommunication, because he was really trying. I was being the stubborn child, standing my ground and refusing to bend.

So the tension built and built to the point where we got into an awful screaming match over his daily journal, which his therapist had suggested he keep. I thought if we were in a relationship that we should share everything, including the journal; otherwise, how could we be a couple? He considered my reading the diary an invasion of his privacy and refused to let me see it. So I went and read a part of it without his permission. I did this shortly before I left for the world championships in Ecuador in the fall of 1982.

To make it worse, I told Kevin what I'd done, and he accused me of not having any respect for him. He said that he didn't have to share every part of his life with me. I was being incredibly stubborn, and I thought, Okay, if I can't have you, nobody can have you. I was getting more and more out of control.

By this point, we were wrestling each other and Kevin was getting the upper hand. He was shorter than I, but he was strong and quick.

While I was struggling to keep from being overpowered by him, I had a flash of getting beat up after school, when the other guy always had the upper hand. That made me even angrier, and I broke free of Kevin and ran into the kitchen. I grabbed a knife and threatened him with it. I was just a few feet from where he was standing, holding the knife as if I were going to stab him in his torso. I don't think I'd ever been so angry before, and I don't think he'd ever been so scared. I had no intention of using the knife, but Kevin had no way of knowing that.

When I saw the look of fear on Kevin's face, I was shocked back into reality. I looked down at the knife and couldn't believe what I was doing. I felt like a crazy person. I had to get out of there, and I ran. I don't remember if I put the knife back in the kitchen or just dropped it, but I ran out of the house. I was afraid that if I stayed we'd wind up really hurting each other.

I showed up on Ron and Mary Jane's doorstep—in tears, as usual—and told them what had happened and that I needed their help to move my things out. They got me calmed down. I also called my mom and told her that Kevin and I had had a big fight and that I had to move out. She asked me if I needed her help, and I said that I did. She could hear the panic in my voice.

The next day, we all drove over to the house in the team van. My mom was sitting up front with Ron, and I was in the back with Mary Jane. We were talking about what had happened, and I said, "Mom, I've got to tell you something. Kevin and I are more than just roommates." Mom said, "That's okay, honey." She told me that she'd known for a long time and was glad I felt comfortable enough to share it with her. We talked a little while about it, and I asked her to tell Dad for me, which, it turns out, she never did. I was afraid he would throw a tantrum or lay on the guilt about nobody to carry on his name. But telling him was my responsibility, and I shouldn't have asked my mom to do it for me.

I'd never discussed being gay with Ron or Mary Jane before, so this was something of a first with them, too. I wasn't surprised when they said they'd already figured it out. It wasn't as if I'd ever hidden it. Ron knew about Kevin, although I'd never said he was my boyfriend. But I'd talked about our fights before, and it was pretty obvious that these were not fights between two people who were just friends.

When Ron and I talked about it later that week, he told me that his feeling was that you don't choose to be gay, just as you don't choose to be heterosexual. He told me that he didn't see it as a big issue other than how it affected me and how I felt about myself.

Before we got to the house, we joked a little about the possible scenarios and how we might be ambushed by Kevin, just like in the movies. But even without being ambushed it was still pretty dramatic. I'm really glad that Ron and Mary Jane and my mom were with me, because it was extremely tense with Kevin the whole time we were there.

Earlier that day I had called Kevin to apologize for pulling the knife. I told him that I was going to move out. He didn't argue with me. I suggested that he not be there when I came to collect my things, but he insisted that he wanted to be home, because he was concerned that I would take some of his things. He especially wanted to make sure I didn't leave with a painting he'd given to me for my birthday. It was a large-scale geometric painting of a sphere, a box, and a cone. The way he had painted it, the shapes popped out at you. Kevin was absolutely clear that I wasn't going to leave the house with it, and I didn't.

Once we were at the house, I didn't even bring up the painting. For one thing, we couldn't have fit it in the van. And also, I was so embarrassed about pulling the knife that I didn't have the courage to ask for it. There was no argument over who got Maile. We both took care of her, but she was my dog.

I think in some ways we were lucky to have survived the relationship without killing each other. We were a volatile mix, and we somehow brought out the best kind of passion and worst kind of rage in each other. That's what made it impossible for us to stay together.

I have a lot of regrets about my relationship with Kevin. We were very brutal to each other, and there's nothing I can do to change that. Unfortunately, we never talked about what had happened. We spoke briefly in 1985, and then, in 1987, Kevin wrote to tell me that he had HIV. From the tone of his letter, I got the sense he was blaming me. In the letter, he stressed that I should get tested. I did, in 1988, and I was HIV-positive. Kevin had blamed me for infecting him, but it just as easily could have been the other way around.

We talked one more time in 1989, one year before he passed away, and I told him that I wanted to come see him. He was still angry with me, and I was afraid to push. Now he's gone, and it's too late to tell him anything.

Too late to say I'm sorry, and too late to say thank you for the love we shared.

15

LOS

ANGELES

1984

A FULL YEAR before the '84 Olympics in Los Angeles, the sports pages began heating up with predictions about my sweeping the gold in the springboard and platform competitions. They called me "the Baryshnikov of diving," "the Superman of his sport," and "the finest diver in the world today." Just about every sportswriter crowned me the favorite to win.

I tried not to pay attention to the hype, but Ron and I both knew that if I dove as well as I normally did, I could win two gold medals. If I did, I would be only the third man in the history of the sport to do it. Peter Desjardins of the United States won both in 1928, and Albert White, also an American, did it in 1924.

Before I could even get to the Olympics, I had to make the Olympic team. The first big step came in July with the Olympic trials in Indianapolis. It's a one-shot event—if you're sick or you're injured or if your legs just buckle and you fall in the water, you are out of the running. You never know, so you can't count on winning. Fortunately, I nailed most of my dives at the trials, and I came in first on both springboard and platform.

I was disappointed by my springboard performance, because I trailed after the first four dives. With my fifth dive I took the lead and kept it through the eleventh dive, winning by about 30 points.

On platform, Bruce Kimball continued to be pretty stiff competition. He had beaten me in six of the last eleven national competitions. If it hadn't been for my new tougher dives with the high degrees of difficulty, he might have won, especially because I missed my ninth dive and got only a 5.5 and 6's. That cut my lead to less than 10 points. But on my last dive, which had a degree of difficulty of 3.4, I got 9's and 10's. Bruce's last dive had a difficulty of 2.9 and he got 7's and 8's.

So I made the team, and a few weeks later, I was off to the Olympics, which were being held just up the road from where I lived. I tried to stay calm, but I was too excited. I'd been waiting since 1976 to compete in the Olympics again, and after training and competing for eight years, I couldn't be more ready. But walking into the Olympic swim stadium for the first time, all I thought was, Could I finally win a gold? Would I win two?

The one down-note for me was the boycott by the Soviet Union in response to the U.S. boycott in 1980. I wanted to see my Russian friends again, but in diving, my main competition came from other American divers and the Chinese.

Springboard was my first event, and from the start I was steady and focused, until the middle of the final round. Even though I tried to concentrate on nailing each individual dive, I got caught up in wanting to win the gold. After all those years this was my chance, and I had trouble not thinking about the final outcome.

Up until that point, everything was working so well that after each dive, I couldn't wait to get to the surface of the pool to hear the reaction of the crowd. Every time I mounted the board to do my next dive, the twelve thousand people in the stadium cheered, "Greg! Greg! Greg!" as they waved little American flags. It was incredible.

Garvey, my teddy bear, helped calm me down. Between dives I would go for walks with him and listen to "Fame" and "Chariots of Fire" on my headphones.

Mary Jane had given me Garvey before the start of the springboard preliminaries. I got so attached to him that just before the springboard finals, when I realized I'd left Gar in my dorm room at the Olympic Village, Ron ran back to get him for me. All the reporters wanted to know how I came up with his name. It was easy. His name was tattooed on his butt.

Garvey wasn't my first Olympic teddy bear. Back in 1976, just before the Olympics, Dr. Lee's wife had given me a little Paddington Bear dressed in overalls. There was a note in his pocket that said "Take me to the Olympics," which I did.

Garvey was my constant companion at the '84 Olympics. He actually did give me strength, because he was the one safe person I could talk to. I never had to worry about him judging me or talking back. It's amazing that a stuffed animal can give you strength, but it did. Many athletes use a small object to focus their concentration. Thanks to Mrs. Lee, my object of choice was a teddy bear, which for some reason the press and the public felt matched my personality.

With Garvey's help, I got myself focused, and a few dives later, I won my first gold and broke 700 points—the first time anyone had done that on men's springboard at the Olympics. When I got out of the water, Ron gave me a big hug and told me, "If anyone deserves to have a gold medal around his neck, it's you." My total score was 754.41, more than 92 points ahead of the second-place finisher. I'd really done it. After all that waiting and diving, I was an Olympic champion, a gold medalist.

It was an incredibly happy moment, but I was more relieved than anything. Now the pressure was off, and I didn't have to worry about winning a gold in the upcoming platform competition, because I already had a gold medal. I still intended to win the second medal, but it was a different kind of pressure than before, because I'd already proven myself.

I knew the platform event was going to be more competitive, because the Chinese were always close on my tail. There was no way I was going to win by the same kind of margin as I did on springboard.

One of my goals at the Olympics was to break 700 on platform, which Ron had warned me would be very difficult to do. I would have to nail every dive and get at least 9's. I wasn't sure I could do that, because one of my dives, an inward three-and-a-half, wasn't as strong as it needed to be. If I got 7's, I might win the gold but not break the record.

The morning of the finals, Ron and I went to the pool around nine to warm up. We always went through the same ritual. I'd do one of each of my dives and then I was done. When I got to the inward three-and-a-half, I ripped it—no splash at all. I usually had good entries, but not like that.

When I got to the side of the pool, Ron asked, "Where did that come from?" I shrugged my shoulders, because I really had no idea. Ron didn't think I could do that again, especially in competition. But later that day, during the final round, I ripped it again, and I got all 9's. That's when I started getting really scared, because with that kind of score, breaking 700 was within my reach. Now I had to hit all my other dives.

I had three more dives after that. I knew I could do those well enough to win the gold, so now I became terrified about the world record. I started second-guessing myself: What if I come close to 700 and don't make it? What if I get real close and I never get that close ever again? And then, What if I *do* break 700? What would I have to look forward to? It was fear of success, fear of failure, and fear of just getting through it all mixed together.

Throughout the final round, Ron's primary goal was to keep me relaxed and on an even keel. After each dive, I went back to one of the tents in the training area and Ron came back and talked to me. Sometimes I asked him if I was doing as well as I should, but most of the time we just joked around. Then Ron would leave me to myself, and I'd sit down with Gar and listen to music on my headphones until it was close to the time for my next dive.

My final dive of the Olympics was a reverse three-and-a-half—the same dive that had killed Sergei Shalibashvili. I was scared, but not so much because of the danger. I was afraid I would blow my final dive. As I stood on the platform getting ready, I quickly glanced down at my mom in the stands and reminded myself that she would love me no matter how I did. Then I started playing "If You Believe" in my head, and I executed the dive.

Despite my last-minute jitters, I earned 92.82 on the dive, which gave me a total of more than 710 points. Bruce Kimball did an incredible job, and he came in second, 67.41 points behind me.

I was genuinely thrilled about winning that second gold medal. Today, when I watch the videotapes of my two awards ceremonies at the '84 Olympics, I can easily tell which is which. I look relieved in the first one but not really excited, because I still had the platform competition to get through. But you can see that I really enjoyed the second awards ceremony, the one for platform. It was a dream come true. I won platform exactly the way every athlete dreams it: You want your best performance ever to be the one in the Olympic Games for which you win the gold medal. In Los Angeles, I don't think I could have done much better.

Ron told me recently that it gave him chills to watch the old videotapes of my performance on platform. Years ago, Ron was more restrained than he is now. Back then all he told me was that I'd done well.

≈

WITH THE OLYMPICS behind me, there was only one more diving event to compete in before I could take a break and hang up my Speedos, possibly for good. There was still Cynthia Potter's record of twenty-eight national titles to be broken. I already had twenty-six, so I needed only three more wins to do it. Two weeks after the Olympics, I competed in the U.S. Nationals in Santa Clara and won my twenty-ninth title.

For the first time, I thought seriously about retiring from diving. I'd been diving for a long time and I'd had a number of injuries. I'd met my goals of winning the two golds, and it was time for me to think about doing something else with my life other than diving.

At the time, the other good reason to consider retiring was money. The existing rules made it impossible to retain my amateur status and take advantage of some of the opportunities from endorsements and commercials that were likely to come my way after the Olympics. I didn't care about getting rich, but I wanted to make a decent living, especially after struggling for so many years. Shortly after the '84 Olympics, in part because of my efforts, U.S. Diving revised the rules to allow divers the opportunity to earn money through commercials and endorsements and still maintain their amateur status.

There were good reasons to keep going after '84. If I wanted to be remembered as one of the best divers of all time, there was a major record out there to be broken: No male diver had ever won *four* Olympic gold medals. And there were always more national and international competitions to be won. So if I chose not to retire, I could continue building my record. Besides, I didn't have any clear direction, and setting my sights on '88 would at least give me something to work toward.

Whether or not I retired, what I needed after the nationals was a break from diving and a vacation. I got the break from diving, but it was no vacation after the Olympics. It was an absolute whirlwind. I did appearances, exhibitions, and speaking engagements, one after the other.

I also did all kinds of other things, from appearing in an anti-drug commercial to visiting the Children's Hospital of Orange County, where I gave away the two dozen teddy bears that I'd received from fans during the Games. I even gave away Garvey. There was a seven-year-old boy named Rex Ryan, who was recovering from a burst appendix. His mom told me that whenever he got up on the diving board, he'd say, "Look, Mom, I'm Greg Louganis!" He was this cute blond-haired kid with blue eyes. The way I looked at it, Garvey gave me strength during the Games, and maybe he could give Rex strength, too. I was sorry to say goodbye to Garvey, but from the way Rex held him, he needed Garvey more than I did.

I would need more than teddy bears in the next four years.

16

~~~~~~

TOM

I THINK I gave Garvey away too soon.

After the 1984 Olympics, I moved in with Tom, whom I'd been seeing for about two years. By then, Tom was also my manager, and we would be together for the next four years.

Before I say another word about Tom (that's not his real name), I have to explain how difficult it is for me to write about this part of my life. For one thing, many of the memories I have about Tom are painful to recall. I'm embarrassed by what I allowed Tom to do to me and by the fact that I stayed in a relationship with him for as long as I did. I've decided to write about this experience because I think it's important for people to know what happens in an abusive relationship. Maybe I'll save someone from what I've been through. Perhaps my story will give someone in an abusive relationship—straight or gay—the courage to find help and get out. If you're in one now, get help now.

The first time I remember seeing Tom was in late 1982 at a bar in

Orange County, just a few months after I broke up with Kevin. I was there with my friend Kris from the University of Miami, who was also my roommate. He'd moved to California to look for work, and we shared a house in Costa Mesa. At some point, I glanced across the room, saw Tom, and our eyes met.

Tom wouldn't be on a magazine cover, but I found him attractive. He was bigger than I, which was something that had always appealed to me. He was about six feet tall, and he had broad shoulders and a good-size upper body. He told me he was a rower, which made sense given how he was built. He had brown hair and hazel eyes and he was about five years older than I was. I was twenty-two at the time.

Before Kris and I left the bar, he passed Tom my telephone number. I'd told Kris that I was interested in Tom and that I was too shy to go over and introduce myself, so he decided to help. The next day, Tom called and asked me if I'd like to come to his condo for dinner. I was delighted and said yes.

During the phone conversation, Tom reminded me that we'd met a year or two earlier at a mutual friend's birthday party. I had been talking to some guy and smoking a cigarette. I was trying to blow the smoke away from the guy I was talking to and didn't realize that I was blowing it right into Tom's face. Tom tapped me on the shoulder and said, "Get that fucking cigarette out of my face." He was nasty, and I didn't feel like dealing with someone like that, so I left the party. Until Tom reminded me on the phone, I didn't realize he was the one who'd cursed at me. I should have hung up right then, but I didn't.

Tom prepared the whole dinner by himself—or so I thought—which impressed me. Although he wouldn't let me help in the kitchen, he let me help clean up. It was then that I saw empty frozen-dinner boxes in the trash. Despite the boxes, I appreciated the effort and I was charmed.

Tom lived in a small one-bedroom condo in Laguna Beach, about a half hour south of where I lived. It was modest, but it was furnished with a number of antiques. Tom owned the place, so I was impressed, especially since I was still renting. He told me that he had gotten started by buying a fixer-upper, going in and tearing everything out, rebuilding, and then selling it. After he fixed up and sold the first one, he was able to buy the condo and his next fixer-upper.

In explaining his work and the finances of the whole thing, Tom was very logical and methodical, much like my dad. He was very articulate, and it sounded to me like he knew what he was talking about. I appreciated that he took the time to explain everything in a way that I could understand. That required a lot of patience, because I had trouble following what he was talking about. Finances were a mystery to me, and I wasn't all that interested.

After our first date, we started seeing each other three or four times a week. Very quickly, he made himself indispensable to me. I'd talk about how the yard needed cleaning, and he'd do it. I needed to paint the kitchen. Done. The wood next to the house needed stacking. Done. When I moved to El Toro, a half hour east of where I'd been living in Laguna Niguel, Tom had the gas turned on and put in my name. He had the phone connected while I was at a workout. I didn't intend for him to do so much, but every time I mentioned something, like, "Oh, I'll get to that on my day off," it was done before my day off. I thought he was wonderful. I could concentrate on my diving and not worry about anything else.

Tom also helped Megan and me with diving. Tom seemed to care what happened to us, and he encouraged us to stand up for ourselves. Sometimes he served as our advocate, especially in anything that had to do with business. He was a big help to Megan when she won the world championships and had a number of different offers to consider. Megan and I were young and naive. Neither of us was very verbal. To us Tom seemed smart, charming, and self-assured.

As Tom spent more and more time doing things for me, I began to wonder how he could take so much time from his own work. When I asked him, he told me that he had money saved up from his last real estate deal to carry him until the next one. He told me not to worry about it, that he was happy to do it. I just assumed that he did all of these things for me because he loved me and wanted to take care of me. That was my fantasy: to be loved and taken care of. And I loved Tom all the more because he showered me with so much attention.

Tom had a lot of personality. He was a quick wit. Whenever we were at dinner parties, he could be witty and articulate and I didn't have to say much. It took some of the pressure off me to carry on a conversation or entertain people. He created a comfort zone for me—once we got through all the standard dinner conversation about my training and my diet, he would pick up the ball no matter what direction the conversation took. He was great at challenging people on their ideas and their views. I didn't know very much outside of diving, so with Tom there to carry the conversation, it saved me from having to pretend that I knew what people were talking about. It also saved me from having to pay attention to anything beyond my work. That turned out to be not such a good thing.

During the first several months of the relationship, Tom made things so easy and was so agreeable that we didn't fight a whole lot. Everything changed one day, in the fall of 1983, over the fact that Tom wasn't the only man I'd been sexually involved with during that time. We had been seeing each other for about a year and we hadn't made any sort of commitment yet. I'd been enjoying my freedom after having been involved in a demanding relationship with Kevin. Tom and I never set any sort of ground rules, so I just assumed that it was okay to date other men, which I assumed he was doing as well.

I can't remember exactly how Tom found out, but I think he asked me about someone whose name I'd mentioned, and I told him that it was someone I'd gone out with a month or two before. He was absolutely calm and then casually asked if there had been anyone else, and I said yes. I didn't think to hide the fact I'd been seeing other men, because we'd never talked about making a commitment. I thought we were about to have that conversation now.

Tom got very angry. He called me a slut, and then went off on a tirade, calling me all sorts of names. My instinct, as it always had been, was to feel guilty, as if I'd done something terrible to make Tom so angry with me. But I was confused—I'd had no idea Tom thought we had an exclusive relationship. I felt dumb again, as if I had missed something important.

Tom demanded that I tell him who the other men were. He made me write down their names and telephone numbers. I wrote down the names of the five men. I really thought I was losing my mind. I didn't recall ever talking with Tom about being in a monogamous relationship, but I wasn't going to question him, because he'd done so much for me and been so good to me. How could I have disappointed him? How could I have cheated on him? And how could I have cheated on him when we didn't have an exclusive relationship? Now I wonder what made me instantly assume that it was all my fault, but I guess I've always reacted like that. I blamed myself for everything, even for my confusion. I was so afraid of losing him that I would have given in to almost anything he asked me to do.

Tom made me call each one of the five men and tell them that I was sorry, that I'd been in a relationship, that I hadn't been honest with them, and that I couldn't see them again. It was humiliating. I'm shy to begin with, so to have to make those calls was terrible for me. But I felt like I had no choice. Tom stood there right next to me watching me dial and making sure I said everything he had told me to say. He was right there, his head next to mine, listening to each conversation.

After I made the phone calls, Tom grew even more enraged. He kept calling me "slut," and "lying whore." I was paralyzed with fear. All I could do was stand there and take it. Then he said, "I'll show you!" and he went into the kitchen and grabbed a knife. I was terrified.

Tom grabbed me from behind, held the knife to my neck, and forced me facedown onto the bed. With the knife at my throat, he tore off my clothes. To keep control, he grabbed one of my arms and held it behind my back. Then he raped me.

All I can remember saying to him while it was happening, was "Please don't." I was crying and begging him to stop, but he told me I deserved it and didn't stop until he was finished. Part of what made it so terrifying was that I didn't know if Tom would go a step further and kill me.

The whole time, my mind was racing from How do I get out of this? to I deserve this and I better keep my mouth shut. I didn't see any way out, and I just lay there crying quietly. It wasn't the physical pain that made me cry—it was the shock that he wanted to hurt me.

When Tom was done, he got off me and stood there, still holding the knife, not saying anything. I was crying and telling him that I was sorry, sorry for what I'd put him through, sorry that I'd pushed him over the edge and made him so angry, sorry that I'd forced him to punish me like that.

Tom didn't say anything, and left the room. For a few minutes I couldn't move. I was numb, totally drained and exhausted. I just lay on the bed crying, thinking that what he had said was right, that I deserved it, but also not believing that anybody could do what he had just done to me. How could one person hurt another like that, especially someone he loves?

Once I collected my thoughts and realized he was gone from the room, I grabbed my clothes, put them on, and left. I didn't shower. I just had to get out of there and get home. I was afraid of him and had to get away. I no longer thought he was going to kill me, but I had to get out of there.

Driving home, it never occurred to me to go to the police or stop at a hospital or tell anyone what had happened. In fact, I didn't tell anyone for five years.

When I got home, the first thing I did was bring my dog, Maile, in from outside. Then I got out of my clothes and into the shower. After I dried off, I brought Maile into my bedroom, closed and locked the door, and brought her onto my bed and held her.

As I lay on my bed holding Maile, I thought about what Tom had just done to me. I was so confused, because I thought he loved me. I had chosen to be with him because I thought he would protect me, look after me. Yet he hurt me more than anyone had ever hurt me before. With so many thoughts running through my head, I couldn't sleep, so I tried a relaxation exercise I usually did when I was having a lot of anxiety. I went to a special place in my mind and imagined I was running through a field. This time, I took Maile with me to that field, so it wouldn't happen again. No one would rape me or hurt me if she was there to protect me. We went to a place we used to go in Costa Mesa, a wetland area called Back Bay. We'd go there and get all muddy and play. That's where I went that night as I drifted off to sleep.

The next day I had my regular practice session to go to. Before I went, I called Tom. I told him again that I was sorry. I wasn't being rational. I believed what he had said to me, that I was a slut and that I'd cheated on him. I also thought that nobody else would have me after what he had done to me, so I needed him to love me or I would be alone. I couldn't risk waiting for him to call me. Rape victims often think they are spoiled forever. I certainly did.

We saw each other that day, and he didn't say anything about the rape: no apology, nothing. It was as if it had never happened. I didn't expect him to apologize, because I thought I was the one who was in the wrong. I felt grateful that he wanted to see me again, grateful that he didn't tell me again that I had deserved it.

I was still scared of him and afraid of what he could do to me. The only way I could justify what he had done was to tell myself that this was an isolated incident, that I had driven him to this. I took full responsibility for what had happened and told myself that as long as I was good, it would never happen again.

I've since learned that my behavior is very much like that of battered spouses, primarily women in heterosexual relationships. But abuse occurs as well in lesbian and gay relationships. I wish it didn't, but it does.

Tom was violent toward me only one other time during our years together. In general, I did everything I could to keep the peace for most of our years together. It was a lot like how my mom was with my father, except that Dad never physically harmed her.

The only other time that Tom hurt me, we were in bed one night and I leaned across to his side to kiss him good night. He reached across the bed and slammed his elbow into my mouth. He said that I had startled him, but I find that difficult to believe, given how hard he hit me and that he aimed for my head. I knew it wasn't an accident. It was, however, an accident that he chipped one of my front teeth. He harassed me about going to the dentist and didn't stop bothering me about it until I got it capped two weeks later. My chipped tooth concerned him more than anything. Tom didn't want me being photographed until I got it fixed. He didn't want me to have to answer any questions about how it had happened.

≈

THE CHRISTMAS FOLLOWING the rape, still convinced it had been my fault, I tried to make it up to Tom. For months, he'd brought up my "cheating" over and over again, making me feel guilty for betraying him. Also, over the months he'd gone on at great length as to how he'd never had a real Christmas growing up in Mesa, Arizona, because his mother was crazy with so many kids. He had six brothers and sisters. He told me that he'd been reared by his sister and that he was physically and sexually abused by his father. At the time I believed everything, but now I don't know what was true and what wasn't. I do know that abuse is a vicious circle, so it's very possible he had been abused as a child.

So I showered Tom with Christmas gifts. I wanted him to love me, and I thought this would show him how much I loved him. I thought it was a way to keep him. One of the things I got Tom was a gold ring that matched my grandfather's ring, with a ruby added. I also gave him five teddy bears, as a peace offering. Tom had demanded that he be allowed to sleep with five other men because that's what I'd done. When I gave him the five teddy bears, I told him that it was okay for him to sleep with five other men. It wasn't okay, but I felt the need to tell him it was.

Tom always claimed that he was true to me, and I believed him. But Tom held those five men over me long after that incident, bringing it up whenever he wanted to remind me how I had betrayed him. It never occurred to me to remind him that he had raped me.

I don't know what I expected from that Christmas, but it was more scary than anything, because Tom hadn't yet decided whether he was going to stay with me. I hoped the gifts would help him make up his mind to stay with me.

Looking back, it makes me sad that I thought so little of myself that

I didn't just walk away from Tom. Like most battered spouses, I just wanted love and approval, and I thought Tom was the only one who could give it to me. I kept thinking, if I'm better, if I try harder, then maybe he'll love me.

I should have thought, Run for your life!

17

SIGN

HERE

TOM AND I moved in together right after the 1984 Olympics. I'd been renting an apartment in El Toro with two other divers, Kevin Machemer and Michele Mitchell, and our lease was up. They were going off to find another place to rent, and I was either going to find a place to rent on my own or move in with Tom. To me, it was logical for Tom and me to move in together. My plan after the '84 Olympics had been to buy a house, something bigger and more suitable for two, but I hadn't saved up enough money yet to do that. So Tom gave me "permission" to move into his condo in Laguna Beach. He acted as though he was doing me a tremendous favor, and I acted suitably grateful.

Shortly after I moved in, we started looking for a house. Actually, it was Tom who started looking, because I was out of town so much doing appearances. Tom told me he looked at hundreds of houses all up and down the coast from Santa Barbara to San Diego. I really don't know how many he looked at, but I was with him when we looked at the house we wound up buying. It was a spacious four-bedroom at the northern end of Malibu in the hills overlooking the Pacific. I liked the fact that you couldn't see it from the road, and it had the most incredible views of the ocean from every room. It was perfect for the two of us. There was space for an office for Tom and a workout room for me.

The house was a little beyond what I could afford. But after asking my agent from the William Morris Agency to come see it, I decided to do whatever I could to get the place. I had to borrow money from both my mother and Dr. Lee to swing it. My mom had divorced my father a year before, so she had money from the sale of the house. I wasn't comfortable borrowing money from either of them, but I really wanted the house.

Tom told me that his contribution toward buying the house was putting up the collateral to qualify for the mortgage. The way he explained it to me, it seemed like a fair deal. To this day, I really don't know exactly what the financial arrangements were with the bank. All I know is that we bought the house jointly, using my down payment. Tom was selling his Laguna condo, but somehow he didn't put up any of his own money toward the new house.

Wally Wolfe, my attorney and manager, went over the details of the arrangements with me. He asked if I understood what I was doing, and I told him I did, even though I didn't. I didn't understand finances, especially mortgages. I'd always paid cash for everything, and I'd never owned a house before. I didn't want to tell Wally that I didn't understand, because I was embarrassed. Tom was at that meeting, too, and I didn't want them to think I was stupid. Of course, I had no idea just how stupid I was until it was much too late.

Tom and I moved to the house in Malibu in May 1985. That August, Ron announced that he was moving to Florida and would continue coaching in Boca Raton at a new diving facility. I'd already decided not to retire from diving, and I wanted to continue working with Ron, so my plan was to go with him to train that winter.

Until I left for Florida, Tom kept me very busy with as many personal appearances and speaking engagements as he could put together for me. By this time, he was working full-time as both my business and personal manager. I always thought he was setting up more engagements than I needed to do, but he told me I had to make enough money to pay the mortgage during the six months I was away. I would only be able to do an occasional appearance while I was training, so we needed to build up our savings.

Before Tom started working for me, he didn't seem to have any kind of steady job, and I wasn't supporting him. He told me that he had put away some money from his real estate investing, but I wondered why he'd want to live off his savings for so long. During those two years, he'd occasionally go away, explaining that he had work to do. He led me to believe that he had to do paperwork associated with his real estate investments.

I learned a lot in life too late, and it hurts to learn too late. What I learned about Tom, years later, from people who knew, was that his "work" was hustling on Santa Monica Boulevard. Tom was a prostitute. If someone had told me in 1984 that Tom was a hustler, I wouldn't have believed it. Tom always gave me the impression that he was true to me, that I was the one who had strayed, and I couldn't imagine him lying to me, let alone hustling.

Not that I didn't have reason to be suspicious. One time before we moved in together, I went over to Tom's house to surprise him one morning. He hadn't stayed with me that night and I just assumed he was home. I knocked on the door, but no one answered. I looked in the window and saw two naked men. I thought one of them was Tom, but I wasn't sure. I pounded on the door. No one answered, so I drove to a phone booth and called. Still, no one picked up. I drove home and called again. This time Tom answered. He said that I'd scared the hell out of a friend of his who had borrowed his condo, and that he hadn't been there when I came by. He told me he had stayed with some friends that night. I believed him.

Of course, one of the naked men was Tom. But I wanted to believe what he told me. I was so desperate to have Tom's love and approval that I was willing to believe he was faithful to me even when I could see that he wasn't. If I was unwilling to believe he was cheating on me, how could I have ever believed he was hustling?

It was shortly after we started living together that Tom began managing my business affairs—not the contracts, but he took care of the checkbooks and all my financial matters. I was happy to have him take responsibility, because I had never had much confidence in my own ability to handle it all.

Tom thought we should put our arrangement on paper, so I had Wally draw up the contract. Dr. Lee had introduced me to Wally, and I'd hired him to handle arrangements for my personal appearances. The contract he drew up for me gave Tom the legal right to handle my business affairs, allowing him to sign checks and other business documents for me. It also stated that Tom was to be paid a set amount of money for the work he did. Again, Wally asked me if I understood, and I said I did.

Tom took a lot of interest in my work, and he started coming along to meetings with Wally. He was very observant, and when he believed that Wally wasn't being aggressive enough, he'd push to make sure I was getting what he thought was a fair deal. This went on for quite a few months before Tom started saying, "I can do what Wally does. Save yourself some money and just pay me. Then we can keep it in the family."

I wasn't in any rush to fire Wally, because I was generally happy with what he was doing. After a while, Wally made a series of decisions that Tom pointed out weren't in my best interest, and then Tom started giving me examples of what he called Wally's incompetence. Soon after, Tom convinced me to get rid of Wally. With Wally out of the way, Tom was in a position to manage virtually everything, and I was happy to have him do it. I was convinced that Tom had my best interests at heart.

I had a new contract drawn up with Tom, giving him 20 percent of everything I earned. But to me it didn't really matter what percentage he got, because we were keeping it all under one roof. In my mind, we were a team. I also figured that if anything went wrong, there was a contract.

After that, if there were contracts to negotiate or events to arrange, Tom did it. I would sign whatever papers I had to sign and show up. I was profoundly naive and trusting when it came to money and property. I would never do anything to harm anyone or to take advantage of anyone, and I just assumed the same of Tom. I should have been more cautious, because I'd already been taken advantage of by an overeager and greedy manager I signed with when I was twenty-one. From that experience I should have learned to ask questions and protect myself. But I saw my arrangement with Tom as different, because I loved Tom. Tom was family.

≈

TOM KEPT ME very busy after the '84 Olympics with appearances and speaking engagements, but the big product endorsements, which Tom had been counting on even more than I had, never materialized. I figured it was because I wasn't blond and blue-eyed or because I was shy or because people thought I was gay. That's business, I thought. These companies are selling products, and it's their choice. Just because I won gold medals, they weren't obligated to give me advertising contracts.

Whenever a rejection came in, Tom would tell me that the main reason I wasn't getting the big endorsements was because I wasn't masculine enough. He'd always say it as a put-down: "Just think of the endorsements we could have had if . . ." He made me feel guilty, as if I wasn't doing my best to earn a living for us.

Tom's attitude about my bookings was that he was making do with whatever he could get me. Since the commercials weren't coming in, he got whatever he could for me, from speaking to business groups to opening new shopping malls. These may not have been big product endorsements, but in a very short time I earned what I thought was a lot of money—enough to pay off my loans to my mom and Dr. Lee, and more than enough to make payments on our house and cover our other expenses.

Even though Tom was disappointed with me, I still got a few advertising contracts and did some product endorsements. I did some print ads for Banana Boat suntan and skin-care products and for California Pools and Spas. I appeared in a national television commercial for

Carefree sugarless gum with four other Olympic gold medalists. A number of companies that manufactured or distributed alcoholic beverages expressed interest in having me represent their products, but I'd stopped drinking by then, so I didn't pursue it.

The one big advertising contract I got after the '84 Olympics was with American Express. That was a lot of fun, because I got to work with photographer Annie Leibovitz. We were on location in Florida, and her vision was to do a photograph à la Tarzan. She thought my physique would work well with that idea. So they put me in a loincloth, which was fine with me, because it wasn't nearly as revealing as a bathing suit.

Speedo also approached me after the '84 Olympics, and a year later, I signed with them as their representative. I've been with Speedo ever since, and that contract has meant more to me than just a business arrangement. When people come to my appearances, they bring all kinds of things with them, from teddy bears to notes telling me what I've meant to them. I especially love the kids. There was one little boy who came to an event just after the '88 Olympics who said, "Oh God, I can't believe you hit your head—I hit my head taking diving lessons, and I'm still taking lessons, because I figured if you could hit your head and win a gold medal, then I could hit my head and still keep taking lessons." That's the greatest reward of all.

Tom often came with me to my Speedo appearances, and when he was along, it wasn't much fun. I always tried to make sure that I got to everyone who was waiting on line, even if that meant staying beyond the scheduled two hours. But when Tom was there, he wanted me finished in two hours flat, no matter how many people went home without seeing me.

One time when there was a really long line of people waiting for me to sign autographs, Tom suggested that he sit next to me and sign my name. I heard this later from the Speedo rep, and I couldn't believe it. It was classic Tom.

It was always tense at appearances when Tom was there. Often, people brought magazine articles about me or pictures of me that they wanted me to autograph personally to them. I was willing to take the time, but Tom insisted that I sign only my name and nothing else. He'd actually say, "Time is money," and push the people along. That really irritated me, because I felt that these people had made an effort to see me and the least I could do was sign what they asked me to sign.

On many occasions, if somebody was telling me a personal story about what they'd been through and what I meant to them, Tom would say, "C'mon, hurry up, move along. We've got a long line." That really embarrassed me. No one ever said anything, except for one woman. She was trying to talk to me, and as Tom was telling her to move along, she put her hand on mine and quietly said, "He's an asshole." I laughed, because she was right. But I have to wonder: If I really thought it was true, how could I have stayed with him?

There was one time I was particularly glad that Tom didn't come with me. In the major cities, many of the people who came to see me were gay men. Even though I wasn't publicly out, I had plenty of gay fans, which I always appreciated. Tom was uncomfortable whenever I had anything to do with other gay men—I pretty much stopped spending time with any of my gay men friends after Tom and I moved in together. So I know Tom would have been really upset when a gay man brought a poster of me from *Playgirl* for me to sign. That was one of those things Tom had arranged for me to do, but we'd specifically said that I didn't want to be the centerfold. We thought that would be too much attention, but they did what they wanted anyway and used me for a poster-sized centerfold. It's a picture of me with a small towel draped across my body, with a parachute flowing behind me. This guy was trying to be very discreet and opened just a corner of the folded poster, enough for me to see what it was and sign it. But the Speedo rep saw it and said, "What's that?" and took it before I could do anything and unfolded the whole thing, with everyone standing there in line. This guy was dying of embarrassment. I signed it and thanked him for coming by.

At another appearance, in the Bible Belt, a woman in line was showing everyone the *Playgirl* poster. She was so proud that she had it and asked me to sign it. This time, the Speedo reps teased me, saying, "Where's the Speedo?"

Speedo has always been good to me. Several months before this book was scheduled to come out, I sat down with Linda Wachner, Speedo's dynamic CEO, and told her that I would be revealing my HIV status in the book. My contract was coming up for renewal at the end of 1994, and I wanted her to know the whole story before we talked about a new contract. Linda was most concerned about my getting proper medical care, and she assured me that I could always count on her support. She also told me that she wanted to continue our business relationship and renewed my contract for another two years. You can imagine what that kind of unconditional support has meant to me.

With all the appearances I did, I always imagined that someone would show up claiming to be my natural mother or father. It happened at a Speedo appearance at a big shopping mall in Honolulu. Tom came over to me while I was signing autographs and said, "Your father is here." I knew my dad wasn't in Hawaii, so I immediately knew what Tom meant, that someone there was claiming to be my natural father. I told Tom that I'd talk to him after I was finished signing autographs.

I don't know if I had any mental picture of what my natural father would look like, although I figured he would look something like me. He was shorter than I am, with rounder features, and had a heavier stature. He had dark eyes and wavy, dark hair, gray at the temples. And there was no mistaking his heritage: He looked like a Pacific Islander.

Our conversation was very emotional for him. His voice was shaky as he explained that he needed to tell me that he hadn't wanted to put me up for adoption and that he did care for me. Then he started crying and said that he was glad I'd been adopted by a nice family that could offer me the kinds of opportunities that he couldn't have.

I was pretty wary, especially because certain facts didn't jibe: I had been told that he and my mother were fifteen at the time I was born, but given what this man told me his age was, he would have been around nineteen when I was born. Later, I realized that he might have lied on the original records, because if my mother was fifteen, he could have been accused of statutory rape.

I was pretty reserved through the whole thing, and after we finished talking, he asked if he could introduce me to some of his family, whom he'd brought with him. He introduced me to his son and two daughters. I had to get to the airport, and told him that I had to go. He asked if I minded if they came to see us off, and I said that was fine.

At the airport, he loaded us up with macadamia nuts and pineapples to take home. He gave me his phone number, and I gave him an address where he could reach me, but not the house address, because I was still suspicious. We said goodbye, and Tom and I got on the plane.

All the way home on the plane, I thought about whether this man was my natural father. I couldn't help but wonder if he wanted something, if maybe he was just bragging to his friends that he was my father. But then I thought about how genuinely emotional he had been. I decided to call the adoption agency.

It took me a while to get around to calling the agency, because I really didn't know what I wanted to do. On the one hand I didn't care, because Pete and Frances Louganis were my parents. They had been there for me. There when I skinned my knee. There to pick me up and dust me off. But in the back of my head I knew that I wanted to know once and for all.

Eventually, I called and the people at the agency explained to me that they'd had a fire several years back and that my records might have been destroyed. They said they had some of the records on microfilm, but they weren't sure, and it would cost $75 to check. They emphasized the possibility that my records were gone, so I didn't bother. I could have tracked down the hospital records, and I'm sure there are other ways of finding out, but it wasn't that important to me. I had my family and I knew that my natural parents had wanted the best for me. That was enough.

Since 1985, I've been back to Hawaii more than once and the man who says that he's my father has come to my appearances to see me. He also sends me a Christmas card each year. But over the years, I've never called him. And I've never asked him about my natural mother.

18

~~~~~~

SHOW

BIZ

AFTER THE '84 Olympics I was very excited about my acting career. The William Morris Agency in Los Angeles signed me up just days after the Games ended, to "represent me in all areas of the entertainment industry," so I thought they'd help open some doors for me, especially in television and film. But except for a few good experiences, my career in show business turned out to be one disaster after another.

William Morris sent me to some general meetings and a handful of auditions. I don't know how it happened, but whenever they sent me out, I would show up in jeans and a T-shirt when everybody else was in suits. Or I would be in a suit when everybody else was in jeans and a T-shirt. And since they sent me out on so few auditions—two or three the first year—each one was incredibly important. I was never sure that I'd ever get to go on another one.

Fortunately, I had plenty of other things to keep me busy. Between taking acting and scene-study classes in California and making appearances and doing exhibitions around the country and training in Florida, it wasn't as if I was sitting by the pool waiting for the phone to ring.

The one movie I did during that time was called *Dirty Laundry*. I hated the script and told Tom that I didn't want to do it. But Tom and my agents talked me into it because they wanted it for my reel, which didn't have much on it. Sonny Bono, Frankie Valli, and Carl Lewis were in the cast. I played the womanizing beach bum roommate to Lee McClosky. It went, as they say in the film industry, straight to video.

Over the next few years, I did things like *Hollywood Squares* and *Family Feud*, *Night of 100 Stars*, and *Circus of the Stars* as a sports celebrity. I met all kinds of people, including Anita Morris and Grover Dale, Louie Anderson, Roseanne, Richard Simmons, Milton Berle, Wil Shriner, Dionne Warwick, Estelle Getty, Brooke Shields, Michael Feinstein, Katharine Hepburn, Jimmy Stewart, Dick Clark, and Raquel Welch.

I also did a lot of benefits, where I met other celebrities. At one benefit, an AIDS fund-raiser in Dallas, I met Angela Lansbury, who is my absolute hero. I've always admired the range of her work, from the Broadway stage to television. I'd seen her in just about everything she's done and knew that in person she would be completely accessible. I wasn't at all disappointed, but I was incredibly nervous.

For the benefit, we were supposed to waltz across the stage for my introduction. But in rehearsals I kept stepping on Miss Lansbury's feet, so we gave up on that idea. In the end she wound up introducing me from one side of the stage, and I walked out from the other. She was very gracious, but I was embarrassed. After all, I had lots of dance experience, so doing a waltz should have been second nature for me.

While I had lots of fun, none of the television game shows or celebrity specials involved acting. In fact, it wasn't until a year after the 1988 Olympics that I was cast as Prince Charming in *Cinderella* at the Long Beach Civic Light Opera. The prince had plenty to do but, thankfully, it wasn't a lead role. I didn't feel at all prepared to carry a show. I did get to sing a few songs, and the reviews weren't bad.

I'm never one to shy away from a challenge, but I hadn't taken voice lessons in eight years, so I knew that I needed a vocal coach. I went down to San Diego to see Cathy Rigby, the Olympic gymnast, in *Peter Pan*, and I asked her advice about studying voice. She suggested a coach in Los Angeles, and I began weekly lessons.

To mentally prepare for a diving event, I'd always look around the stands at all the empty seats and then visualize them full. That way, I was comfortable when the seats were filled with spectators. So when I walked out onstage for the first rehearsal, in my mind I filled in all the empty seats with people. That terrified me, because I was going to be singing solo in front of all those people, which is something I'd never done in front of such a big audience before.

By the time the show opened, I felt secure with the acting and dancing, but vocally I wasn't completely sure of myself. There's always a feeling of being exposed when you're onstage, but when I sang, I felt totally naked, especially with my family there watching. Despite all my anxiety over my voice, it was great fun during the three weeks of rehearsal and three weeks of performances. I especially enjoyed working with the wonderful cast. And the audiences were great—close to three thousand people for each performance.

I learned from that experience that I wanted to do more dramatic work. It was easier for me to get musical theater because I can act and dance. But after *Cinderella*, nothing much happened for a while, not even auditions. I kept telling myself to be patient and continued with my classes, hoping something would happen. When nothing happened, I began to think that I should probably start thinking about doing something else.

Finally, I got another offer, which I really should have turned down, for the lead in *The Boy Friend* at the Sacramento Music Circus. I wasn't getting a lot of other offers and I thought I'd better not be too picky. I wish I had been.

From the start, I wanted to play Bobby, which is a supporting role. I still didn't want the pressure of the lead role, and I thought that the lead character, Tony, was a cardboard figure. The producer was adamant that I had to play Tony. The draw was going to be "Greg Lou-ganis, starring in *The Boy Friend*."

I would have been even more comfortable in the chorus, but no one wanted me in the chorus, because I was too famous to blend in. The cast knew that I had been given the lead role because of my name, and some of them resented that. So from the first day, I was out there on my own.

My performance was okay. I had three songs, and my voice was about the same as it had been for *Cinderella*. We didn't have much re-hearsal time, so I didn't even feel fully prepared with my acting. The only thing I felt good about was my dancing.

The reviews were so awful that I didn't want to go back, but I still had about a dozen performances to go. At least I got some positive comments from people in the audience, and nobody threw things.

That experience made it clear to me that I wasn't cut out vocally for musical theater. I wasn't sure I'd do any acting again at all.

Not long after that, I was asked to go onstage and perform with the Cincinnati Pops Orchestra. It was a variety show in which a number of baseball players and other athletes had been asked to recite a poem about baseball. I had to read part of the poem and dance, which helped make it easier for me to get back onstage, since dancing was one of my strengths. Pamela Myers, who had also been in *Cinderella*, and I sang some music from the show. I also sang and danced "I Can Do That" from *A Chorus Line*, which was in many ways the story of my child-hood. The emphasis was on the dancing, and I had an entire orchestra behind me. Pam helped me through it, and I was glad I did it, because I really love performing.

After that, I did a small job for the Playboy Channel that required a lot of body makeup. It was just a short sketch about Max the fish, whose owner is in an awful relationship, in kind of a *Love, American Style* television show with eight- or nine-minute stories. In mine, the fish turns into a "man-fish" (man's body, fish's head) and rescues the owner from her terrible life and takes her back to the fish tank with him. They used my voice for Max the fish and my body for the man-fish. It was called, unfortunately, *Wet Dreams*. I must have been dreaming when I said yes to that one.

Maybe I should have called it quits then, but not me. Along came a film offer, for *Object of Desire*. I was cast as the love interest for the leading lady. I loved working in front of the camera, because when they're ready to shoot, you've got to be there instantly, which is like diving, although with diving at least you know you have another dive coming up. With film, there's usually not much rehearsal time and an awful lot of waiting around.

We had two weeks of work in the can when one of the producers was thrown in jail for writing bad checks. Fortunately, I had a round-trip plane ticket, otherwise I would have been stranded in Belize. I was disappointed, because it would have been a good break for me. When the production collapsed, we all went into the editing room and watched the dailies. It was beautifully shot, and I was proud of my work.

There were other offers that came in occasionally for parts where I would get to play a diver or play myself in a cameo, but I didn't want to do that, because it wasn't acting. At one point I was cast as the Finnish runner in what was supposed to be a movie adaptation of *The Front Runner*, but it never got made. So after the debacle in Belize, I pretty much gave up, and by 1992 I got so frustrated that I even quit my acting classes and voice lessons. I was spending money every month to study and my efforts were going nowhere.

≈

I'D LIKE TO set the record straight about something. For years, people have spread rumors linking me to various Hollywood moguls.

In 1989 my agent set up a meeting for me with a casting director for a part in a police drama. I finished my reading and she asked me whom I was studying with, and I told her. She told me that I had some promise and that I should really talk to Barry about my career. I asked, "Barry who?" She looked at me skeptically and said, "Barry Diller." I told her that I'd met "Barry Dillard"—which is what I thought his name was—only twice and probably wouldn't even recognize him. She said, "You mean you're not . . ." and then she caught herself and said she was sorry.

That wasn't the first time I'd heard that rumor, and I've long suspected that Tom was the source. He probably thought it would be good for me to have my name linked to one of Hollywood's biggest producers, and I guess he didn't care how it was linked. It bothered me to think that I wasn't getting work because people thought I had some kind of connection to him. It bothered me even more to think that people assumed he bought my house in Malibu for me. I paid for that house myself, with a lot of hard work. I started thinking that I should just call Barry Diller up and say, "As long as you're not keeping me, the least you can do is get me work!"

For the record, I've never been kept by anyone, although it sounds like a nice life. But people believe what they want to believe.

I kept going to the occasional audition but pretty much put my performing career on the back burner and concentrated instead on training and breeding my dogs. And for the record, I keep *them*, and it *is* a nice life.

19

TOM'S

RULES

AFTER TOM AND I moved to Malibu in 1985, we had a pretty easy time sorting out who did what. I cleaned the house, Tom took care of the grounds, and he did most of the grocery shopping, but we often did it together. Tom was supposed to take care of the cars, but he wasn't terribly responsible.

I had a Corvette that had been leased to me for a year at no cost, in exchange for my doing advertisements for a local car dealership. After the lease was up, Tom returned the car with the oil run down to a dangerous level and the engine ruined. My name was on the lease, and no one else was supposed to use the car. I was away in Florida, and I didn't know there was a problem until years later, after Tom and I had split up. One of my contacts at the dealership told me that they couldn't do anything with the car and then explained the condition it was in when Tom brought it back.

When it came to preparing meals, I did all the cooking. I liked to cook, so I didn't mind. Sometimes Tom and I would eat together in the kitchen and sometimes I just delivered his meals to the office. If I ever called downstairs and said, "Tom, dinner's ready," he'd get angry. I would have to walk down to the office and ask, "Would you like your dinner down here, or would you like to have dinner upstairs?" I fell into such a servile role so easily, I can hardly believe it now.

If Tom was on the phone, I'd write him a note that dinner was ready and set it down in front of him. I once made the mistake of trying to hand him a note when he was on the phone, and he got pretty irate. He put the phone on hold and yelled, "What the hell do you expect me to do, you idiot? Just put the fucking note down on my desk."

Looking back, it seems pathetic and sick that I was so deferential to Tom. But I never wanted him to get upset with me, because he really knew how to hurt me. He could have me feeling stupid in a matter of seconds, and I'd retreat with my tail between my legs. So I tried to keep the peace and not rock the boat.

Tom and I didn't entertain much. In the beginning, sometimes my diving friends would come over and we'd all play Scrabble or Uno. Tom liked playing board games, but you had to play by "Tom's rules," which meant that Tom always had to win.

Tom also liked to correct me in front of other people. During conversations with people, if I used a word improperly, Tom would interrupt and say that clearly I hadn't meant what I said. Then he'd translate what he believed I'd meant to say. When I told him that I felt bad when he corrected me in front of other people, he said, "Give me an example. When did I do that?" If I didn't remember the exact circumstance, he would say, "Until you can get your facts straight, I don't know what you're talking about, so don't bring it up to me." At the time, I didn't think of any of this as abuse, because Tom wasn't hitting me, but it still made me feel awful.

Once we moved up to Malibu, Tom started handling our social life entirely. He told me, "You don't know your schedule. I know your schedule, so you talk to me before you make any plans." Sometimes I suggested that we have people over for Easter or Thanksgiving or just

for a dinner party. Tom would take it from there and make the arrangements and do all the inviting. He needed to control my every move,
and I allowed him to do it.

I began to realize that I didn't enjoy being home with Tom. In general, his attitude toward me was that I never did anything. He was always saying, "Somebody's got to work in this house." My diving was
nothing. My appearances were nothing. *He* was doing the real work,
because he was on the phone, talking to people and making deals.

All I really wanted from Tom was for him to love me and to show
me affection, but he was never the kind of man you would describe as
loving or affectionate. In the beginning, we would cuddle at night, and
sometimes if he was watching 60 *Minutes* on TV—he never missed 60
Minutes—I'd have my head on his lap and he'd stroke my hair, which I
loved. Unfortunately, that stopped happening after the first few
months of the relationship.

When it came to our physical life, after the first few months, I was
the one who always had to take the initiative. When we did have sex,
Tom could be anywhere from extremely tender to indifferent to brutal,
which I didn't like.

By the time we moved in together, I always felt like I was begging
for his attention, including begging for sex. When we did have sex, it
felt like he was doing me a favor. That was a horrible feeling. Over the
years it got worse, and after a while I just assumed that he didn't love
me anymore.

Part of the problem was that I spent several months at a time in
Florida training, but even when Tom came to visit, he would avoid
making love. For example, if I made an advance, he'd suddenly get busy
on the phone or tell me he had to take care of business. Often he would
leave me at a hotel and go out until the early hours of the morning. A
lot of times he'd say, "I didn't want that house—*you* did. Now we've
got to figure out how to pay for it. I've got to go take care of business,
because somebody has to." So he'd put me to bed at eleven or twelve
o'clock and give me a kiss and say, "Good night, my little dummy," and
leave. I didn't see him until four in the morning. And I *was* a dummy,

because I believed him when he said that he was going out to do business. It never occurred to me he was out hustling or picking up men just for fun.

Once, when we were in Indianapolis, I asked Tom what he did during those late-night/early-morning hours. He said that I had no right to question what he was doing because he was taking care of my business. He turned the situation around by bringing up my so-called unfaithfulness to him: "*You're* the one who can't be trusted. How dare you! I'm taking care of everything, and all you have to do is show up!" Where, I wonder now, was my self-respect?

Megan tried to tell me that Tom wasn't exactly out signing contracts at three in the morning, but I didn't want to believe her. If I had, that would have meant he was lying to me. If he was lying to me, then I'd have to think about what other lies he was telling me. I would have to think about ending the relationship, and I couldn't imagine life without Tom. He had convinced me that I couldn't survive on my own.

I try now to remember a time with Tom that was truly happy. There were a couple of times that stand out: driving home from Los Angeles after the '84 Olympics, having just won two gold medals. He was proud of me, and I was proud of myself. Then there was a time walking down the beach in Laguna and going to get a frozen yogurt. But the Tom of my happy memories is a different person from the Tom he was the rest of the time.

I can't remember if he ever said he loved me. He wrote me notes sometimes and said in the notes that he loved me. The note would usually be about how when I was home he couldn't wait for me to leave and now that I was gone he missed me.

One of the most confusing letters I got from Tom was one he sent to me from Puerto Rico, where he'd gone for a vacation while I was in Florida training. First he talked about how romantic the setting was, but how there was something missing. I thought he was going to say that if I was with him, the romantic setting would be complete. But instead, he went on to say that he didn't think my being there would help, and that life never lives up to the fantasy. Then he switched gears again, talking about all his regrets for not treating me better and how he'd always love me even if we broke up.

As if I wasn't confused enough, Tom would follow a letter like the one from Puerto Rico with a totally positive and supportive note that usually said something like, "Hi Honey! I miss you! Please do well at the competition. Don't forget to believe in yourself! And most importantly, I love you and only you!"

If Tom's goal was to keep me off balance, he did a good job. Just when I was thinking he didn't love me, he'd toss me a bone and I'd think I was wrong, that he really did love me. Then he'd come for a visit to Florida, and it would be pretty awful, but after he left I'd get a loving letter, and I was sure I was losing my mind.

Tom was good at manipulating me, and I was a willing victim. I wanted to believe he loved me, and I convinced myself he did because he worked so hard to keep me busy. And he did some genuinely positive things, like getting me to quit smoking and drinking.

Tom's constant criticisms had me look at a lot of things in my life to see how I could improve myself. By this time I'd already stopped using cocaine, because it hurt my diving, but smoking and drinking didn't seem to have any noticeable effect, so I didn't seriously consider quitting those until Tom raised the issue.

Before I met Tom, it was typical for me to have a six-pack of beer a day. I'd been drinking since junior high, and a few times over the years my coaches told me I should cut back, but compared to my father's drinking, a six-pack didn't seem like that much.

Tom had me write out the reasons why I drank. I came up with two reasons: to escape and to cope with my depression. We talked about it for a while, and before the end of the discussion, Tom had me convinced that I was an alcoholic and that I had to quit.

Not drinking turned out to be pretty easy in the short term, but in the long term it was tough. Invariably, at parties I'd be offered a drink before dinner and then wine with dinner. For a few years, I stayed away from alcohol entirely. These days, I'll have a drink occasionally.

My smoking came up because of something that happened before

Tom and I had our self-improvement talk. I was a closet smoker. I never smoked at diving events or in public places where there were a lot of people. I was at Mission Viejo one day judging an event, and between rounds, I went out to the parking lot to have a cigarette. I hadn't lit up yet when I ran into one of the kids on the team. He was smoking a cigarette, and I asked, "What the hell are you doing?" He said, "When I grow up I want to be just like you, and *you* smoke." I was stunned, but I couldn't deny it.

I wrote down the reasons I smoked: My parents had smoked. It gave me something to do. It filled my time. It was also a rebellious act, something I wasn't supposed to do. I had the reputation of being a goody-two-shoes athlete, and I didn't want to be.

Tom and I reviewed the list together and decided I would quit smoking. I was allowed to have three more cigarettes, and that would be it. I smoked one cigarette the next morning, one that evening, and then the next morning I smoked half a cigarette. That second evening I smoked the other half and it was disgusting. Smoking a re-lighted cigarette is awful—and a wonderful way to quit. I didn't even finish it.

I felt good about quitting. I knew it was the right thing to do in terms of my health and in terms of being an Olympic athlete whom kids looked up to. I had a responsibility not to smoke.

In an odd way, quitting both drinking and smoking at the same time made me feel even more dependent on Tom. I needed him to be there for me on my bad days because I'd used both the drinking and smoking as a way of coping with my bad feelings about myself. Now all I had was Tom. On his good days he was a strong support. He would tell me how proud he was of me, that I was doing the right thing.

Another thing Tom did that I was grateful for was that he got me to pay more attention to what was going on in the world. He encouraged me to read the paper and watch CNN. He also got me to read books. The first Christmas after we met, he loaded me down with a bunch of books to take with me when I went home for the holiday. They were mostly self-help books, like *The Art of Loving* and *The Intimate Enemy*. I wonder if Tom read them first.

But it wouldn't have mattered what books Tom read, because the problems we had facing us couldn't be solved by reading books.

20

DIAGNOSED

YOU WOULD THINK that because Tom and I were a gay couple, the subject of AIDS would have been something we talked about early on in the epidemic. But we didn't. In fact, AIDS didn't really register with me in a big way until 1986, when I heard about Ryan White, a hemophiliac teenager in Kokomo, Indiana, who wasn't allowed to go to school because he had AIDS. Ryan got AIDS through tainted batches of the clotting factor he had to inject himself with every day.

Before Ryan, I had been vaguely aware of what was called gay cancer. In 1985 I heard, along with the rest of the world, that Rock Hudson had died from AIDS. But it didn't seem like AIDS was something I needed to worry about. The way I understood it, you got it from having sex in bathhouses or public restrooms, and you had to have a thousand sex partners. I was in a monogamous relationship, and while I'd had relationships before Tom and dated several men along the way, I never had that many partners.

It's quite possible that Tom knew a lot more about AIDS from the beginning. Unlike me, he had contact with the gay community. He had gay friends, and when I was away, he spent time in Los Angeles. But Tom never said anything to me during those early years of the epidemic, and I was so focused on my diving that unless Tom told me what was going on in the world or it was major national news, I didn't pay attention. I depended on him to be my eyes and ears to the world.

The Ryan White story was impossible to miss, and it really caught my interest. I first saw Ryan on CNN. I was very impressed by this kid who had gone to court to go to school, especially because I had always hated school and would have been happy if someone had said I couldn't go. Ryan was sick, but instead of people having compassion for him, they were terrified that he'd spread AIDS by going to school. I thought if I showed I wasn't afraid of Ryan, then maybe others would follow my example.

As oblivious as I was in those days, I knew of course that most of the people who suffered from HIV and AIDS discrimination were gay men. There was no other way I felt I could get involved in the issue of AIDS without risking some reporter asking questions about my life. Helping Ryan was a way of lending my name and stature to the AIDS cause without having anyone get suspicious. And then I met Ryan, and my life changed.

I invited Ryan to come to our national championships in Indianapolis in April 1986. It wasn't a big public event, and all I wanted was to earn Ryan's trust. I also wanted to get to know his mother, Jeanne White, and make sure that Ryan wasn't just being pushed by her. I'd known plenty of stage moms in my day.

After the competition was over, I gave Ryan my gold medal, and I took him and his friend from school on a tour of the diving facility. I brought them up to the top of the 10-meter platform, to show them what it was like from my point of view. Ryan thought I was crazy. He said he'd never jump off anything that high, even if someone paid him.

Ryan was a kid, but it was clear from talking with him and Jeanne that he was the one calling the shots. I remember one time when I was over at his house visiting, Jeanne and I were talking about the different magazines that were trying to buy his story. She didn't know which one to go with, and Ryan yelled out from the living room, where he was playing video games, "Hold out for the money, Mom. You're going to need it when I'm gone."

Despite his maturity, Ryan was still a teenager. Later, when we did press interviews together, he'd keep me in stitches by making faces at me from behind the reporter's back. But he never failed to impress me with his intelligence and his perseverance. Ryan was determined to go to school, and once he'd accomplished that, his goal was to live a normal life for as long as he could and take every opportunity to educate people about AIDS. I was amazed at how he handled himself, whether it was one-on-one or on national television. He was—and is—an inspiration.

Because of Ryan I got involved with AmFAR, the American Foundation for AIDS Research. I was asked to be an honorary board member and I agreed to be part of a calendar they put together. Over the years, whenever I've been asked to donate autographed bathing suits and photographs to be auctioned off for AIDS hospices all over the country, I've gladly helped. I would like to have taken a more active, high-profile role in AIDS education and fund-raising, but I was afraid that people would start asking questions. I was especially afraid after I found out about my own HIV status. I intend to do everything I can now for the rest of my life, but I wish I could thank Ryan for the inspiration he gave me. Jeanne always reminds me that he knows.

Getting to know Ryan and being involved with raising AIDS awareness, there was no way I could ignore the fact that Tom and I were at risk. It wasn't just gay men with a thousand sexual partners who were getting sick. Tom and I could easily have been infected before we met each other, before anyone knew how to prevent AIDS. It didn't matter that we were in a relationship. We were still at risk.

I started getting more scared when some of Tom's friends got sick and died and then when Kevin wrote to tell me that he was HIV-positive. He urged me to get tested, but somehow I managed to stay in denial. When Tom came down with shingles in the summer of 1987, I convinced myself that it had nothing to do with AIDS, despite the fact that shingles is often the first sign that someone is HIV-positive.

We had just come back from a European tour when Tom got shingles. He met me in Italy for part of the trip and then headed back to California. I returned to Florida to continue with my training. When we parted, Tom was fine, but shortly after he got home, he started complaining about itching and burning. He was in excruciating pain before he went to the doctor who diagnosed it. Plenty of people who get shingles don't have AIDS, and I took comfort from the fact that a straight guy about Tom's age who worked in my attorney's office had shingles. I figured that if he could get it from stress, so could Tom.

It was too frightening in 1987 for me to think that Tom could have AIDS. First of all, despite all my problems with him, I still loved him very much, and the thought of losing him was terrifying. If Tom was sick, then I might be sick—we'd been having unsafe sex for years. He could have infected me or I could have infected him, even though I apparently wasn't showing any symptoms and didn't yet know I was positive. It was the twin terror of facing the death of the person you love most and the possibility of your own death at the same time. The whole thing was so overwhelming that I couldn't let myself think about it. Tom's shingles was stress. That *had* to be it.

≈

TOM GOT OVER the shingles and we went back to life as usual, or at least usual for us. We talked about getting tested for HIV, but we didn't do it. I don't think either of us wanted to deal with the real possibility that one or both of us was positive, so we pretended nothing was wrong. All around us gay men were getting sick, getting tested, getting educated, but we remained in denial. We were also in denial about safer sex: When we did have sex, we continued not to take any precautions. Despite the fact that one or both of us could have been infected from before we met each other, I convinced myself that everything was okay because we'd been in what I thought was a monogamous relationship. That dumb assumption was more denial, because it was clear to everyone but me that Tom hadn't been monogamous. Too many gay men—too many people—blinded by love make the same dangerous assumption. If you really love each other, be safe—every time.

In early 1988 we went on another trip, and while we were away, Tom started to have trouble breathing. He seemed always to be out of breath lately whenever we walked anywhere. Again, I chalked it up to overwork. Tom went back to California and I went back to Florida. By now this was late February, and I was in training for the national championships, just a few weeks away. The Olympics were only five months away, so this was the beginning of a very intense period of training. Little did I know how intense.

After Tom got home, he got worse and worse. He was having high fevers and night sweats and he could barely get up and down the stairs. During our phone calls, Tom didn't let on how sick he was, but on March 8, he called me to tell me he had to go to the hospital. I don't know how he got there, but he did. I waited in my apartment for him to call me back. A few hours later he called from his hospital room. He was very out of breath. He told me he had pneumonia, that they were asking a lot of questions about his sexual history, and that they were running blood tests, including an HIV test.

Tom told me he was scared and that he thought he had AIDS. My stomach sank and I could feel my eyes filling with tears. There were times during the conversation when he talked about wanting to end it. I knew he was in a lot of pain, and I knew he couldn't bear the thought of dying the way some of his friends had.

There was no denying it now. Tom probably had AIDS, and it would only be a matter of time before we got the results. After I put the phone down, I sat in my room with my head in my hands and cried.

Oddly, I'd had blood drawn for an HIV test that very day. I'd gone to my doctor, John Christakis, to have my ear checked for an infection. While I was there, I talked to him about how he would handle doing an HIV test. Just in case I decided to have the test at some point, I wanted to know how it would be done. I guess my denial was weakening.

John is my cousin by marriage, so I felt comfortable asking him. I didn't know him well, but I knew I could trust him. He explained to me that he would draw my blood and put it under an assumed name. I looked at him, not saying anything. I couldn't actually say that I wanted the test, because saying it meant acknowledging that I had more than a casual interest in being tested. John picked up on my anxiety and said, "Let me see some other patients. You think about it, and if you want to get tested, we can draw blood today and have it sent out. The results will be back in a few days."

As I sat in the examining room, I thought about the reasons why I should get tested: I should do it for my peace of mind, and I should do it because this was an Olympic year. I thought through the worst-case scenario and decided that if the test came back positive, I would pack up and go home. First of all, I needed to be with Tom. Then, what if I made the team and couldn't compete? I would be depriving someone else of the chance to go to the Olympics. Since I expected to qualify in both 3-meter springboard and 10-meter platform, that would mean depriving *two* other divers of the opportunity to compete.

Olympians are not made overnight. I had worked out with the other divers for years and years. I knew what we'd all been through, how hard we'd worked to be good enough to compete in the Olympics. So for me, the thought that I might make the team and prevent two other divers from going to the Olympics and then not be able to compete myself was terrifying.

Then there was Ron. He would be wasting his time training somebody who might not be well enough to go to the Olympics when he could have been working with someone who could win a medal.

Testing positive meant not being able to compete. It hadn't yet occurred to me that I might test positive and still go to the Olympics.

If I was negative, I'd go home for a while to take care of Tom, and then once he was better, I'd go back to Florida and continue with my training. The test would be out of the way, and I could go on without that worry in the back of my mind. But in my gut I knew I was positive. This was before Tom went into the hospital, but deep down I knew from the shingles and breathing difficulty that Tom had it. And if he was infected, I probably was. I already knew my ex-lover was infected, so that increased the odds.

When John came back into the examining room, I told him to do the test. I knew I had to take it, and I felt comfortable and confident that I could trust him to do it.

Before John drew my blood, he explained that he could draw just enough to do the test, but that if I came back positive, I would have to have more blood drawn to determine my T-cell count. The number of T cells you have is an indicator of how far the disease has progressed. Or, he said, he could draw enough blood to do both tests. I told him to draw enough for as many tests as there needed to be. He drew my blood and shipped it off.

So when Tom called me from the hospital to tell me that they were testing him for HIV, I said, "Funny you should mention that, because I just had my HIV test today as well."

We hadn't planned it that way, but it turned out that Tom and I were tested on the same day. Tom got his results back first. He wasn't just positive. He had PCP—pneumocystis carinii pneumonia—which is a very serious kind of pneumonia that people with AIDS get. We cried on the phone. I wanted to be with him. This was not the kind of conversation you want to have on the phone. My first reaction was to feel guilty for not being there. In my mind I was blaming myself: What if I'd given this to him? What if I had made him sick? I didn't know he'd been hustling. All I knew was that my ex-lover Kevin was HIV-positive and now my current lover had it. And for all I knew, the test would come back saying I had it too.

I asked Tom if he wanted me to come home for a while. He said, "No. Stay in Florida. I don't want you changing your plans. I want you to stay focused on your diving." He was very upset and crying and said, "Please don't quit. My biggest fear is that you'll leave your diving, and then I'll feel like a burden." He told me I had to be strong, that we had worked so hard to get to the '88 Olympics, that I hadn't yet reached my full potential, and that we couldn't give up now. He said, "I don't want to bring you down. I worked so damn hard for everything, for our future, and . . ." but he was crying too hard to go on.

Once Tom stopped crying, he made me promise that I would stay in Florida and continue to train. I told him that he had to be strong and get better, that there was time to decide what I would do. I told him that it all depended on my test results.

Then Tom brought up Ryan White. He said, "Well, Ryan's still fighting this, so I can fight it, too."

My doctor didn't want me diving because of the ear infection, so I had a few days with a lot of time on my hands to contemplate what I was going to do. I ran through all kinds of scenarios. If I was just positive and my T cells were close to normal or okay, then maybe I'd continue training while I remained asymptomatic. But then what about my obligation to Tom? We had always said that we'd be there for each other, and with him in the hospital, I wasn't meeting my commitment. But Tom wanted me to stay in Florida and train.

If I was positive and my T cells were low, the question was: How long did I have to live?

One thing I didn't have any doubt about was keeping the whole thing secret. This was no one's business. Tom's attitude had always been that certain things were kept between just the two of us. In this case, our doctors had to know, but that was it. I wouldn't tell my family or my coach. Of course, the press couldn't know. Whatever I did, it was my business and I didn't have to offer anyone any explanations. I couldn't even begin to contemplate my conflicting responsibilities to the members of my team, the other athletes, the public, the Olympic Committee. The issues were so complicated that I still don't know how to think of what I did. I imagine some people will think I was irresponsible and others may think I was heroic. All I know is, at times of crisis like that, you just do what you think is best.

During the days between when I was tested and when I got the results, I spent some of my time working out, lifting weights and taking aerobics classes. So far, it was just an ear infection, so the only thing I couldn't do was get in the pool. One of those days I didn't get out of bed. I pulled the covers over my head, not wanting to deal with anything, like I used to do when I was depressed.

John called me up at home and said, "I've got your test results. How about if I come by your place after I make rounds?" I said, "Fine." There was nothing in his voice that led me to think this was good or bad news. Nevertheless, I knew.

When John came to the door, I invited him inside. At the time, I was living in a two-bedroom town house that was provided to me while I was training. I had MTV on the television and turned down the volume as we sat down.

We started with some informal chit-chat, but I didn't let too much time pass, because I wanted to know. I said, "Well, what are the results?" He said, "It's positive." And that was it. I nodded my head. I felt strangely calm. He had just confirmed what I already knew. In a way, it was a relief. But what came next was a shock: My T cells were 256. I didn't know what normal was, so I asked. He said that people typically have about 1,000 T cells, although the normal range is from 600 to 1,200. According to the latest Centers for Disease Control definition of AIDS, when your T-cell count falls to under 200, you're considered to have full-blown AIDS. John told me that he wanted to draw more blood to run some tests to see how much of the virus I had in my system. He told me that he wanted to "treat this very aggressively."

All I could do was nod my head, because by this time I could hardly hear anything except the pounding of my heart.

21

THE LOW T-CELL count was pretty crushing news, because I figured it meant giving up the Olympics. As soon as I could manage to get the words out, I asked John what he thought I should do. He surprised me and said there wasn't any reason why I couldn't continue training for the Olympics. He thought that staying in shape would be good for me and that I posed no threat to the other divers. I just had to be careful, and I had to take care of myself. He also wanted me to talk to a nutritionist about my diet, to help keep my immune system strong during training.

Before he left, John and I talked about some of the treatment options, like AZT, and also a drug called Bactrim, which is used to prevent the development of the pneumonia Tom had. He told me that once I was on the various medications, he wanted me to think of my treatment as part of my training program. It didn't have to overwhelm my life. I just had to take my medication and take care of myself.

On his way out, John was very considerate and said the appropriate things, that he was sorry and that this was a tough challenge. He gave me a hug and left. I called Tom to tell him the news, but I didn't tell him about my T cells because I thought, as always, that he was the one who needed *my* support. He was the one who was sick, and I had to encourage him to take care of himself and get well. I could have used some moral support, too, but I never asked him for it and he didn't offer it.

The only other person I called was my attorney in California, Debbie Shon. Debbie was more than my attorney. She was also a friend and something of a big sister. She's also Dr. Lee's niece, which is how I met her. I'd spoken to Debbie briefly after I'd had my blood drawn for the test. I told her all about Tom, and she said that if I were positive, she'd talk to the people she knew at the National Institutes of Health to find out what drug-trial programs I'd be eligible for. One of my concerns was handling the cost of the various medications. I knew that AZT was pretty standard treatment, and it was incredibly expensive. I had health insurance but, like other people who are afraid of having their HIV status revealed, I couldn't use it because of the danger that someone would leak the news that I was on AZT. So whatever my doctor put me on was going to be an out-of-pocket expense. In fact, I've paid for most of my medical expenses related to HIV since then, such as tests, X rays, and medications. I wonder how many people have been through the same thing because they're afraid of being found out. I've been very lucky, however, because both John and my doctor in California, Kathy Shon (Debbie's sister), have never charged me for their professional services. I'm grateful to them for their generosity.

Shortly after I was diagnosed, Debbie flew in from California to meet with John and me. She was incredibly supportive and was quick to remind me how many people cared about and loved me. I told her how scared I was, and she held me. As soon as I put my head on her shoulder, I started sobbing.

When I finally stopped, Debbie made me promise her that I would call her whenever I needed to talk to someone. She warned me that I'd feel like I was on an island all by myself, with no one around for miles. She said, "Call me at any time of day or night from anywhere."

Debbie made me feel like we were a team working together to get me to the Olympics. John was responsible for taking care of the medical side. Debbie was making sure that Tom was well taken care of, and Ron took care of the coaching. I had to take care of myself and focus on my diving.

Debbie was great, because in no time she helped me apply to the appropriate drug-trial programs, and fortunately, I was accepted.

I hadn't yet told Ron that I was HIV-positive. John had wanted me to tell Ron right away, but I was afraid that if he knew my health status, he would take it easy on me. This was a time when I really needed him to push me. The Olympics were only a few months away. I didn't want him making allowances because of my health.

I also thought that telling Ron I was HIV-positive would be a burden. This may sound dumb, but anyone I told had to keep this an absolute secret. I was sure that if it ever got out to the press, it would be a major scandal. I wasn't sure I'd be allowed to go to the Olympics. I wasn't even certain I'd be allowed into Korea, where the Olympics were being held. The U.S. Olympic Committee and the International Olympic Committee hadn't yet addressed the issue, and they still haven't.

At the time, no major athlete had ever come out about being HIV-positive, so there was no way to know how it would be handled by the Olympic officials or what the reaction of the other athletes would be. People were still pretty ignorant about AIDS in 1988. People are still pretty ignorant now, in 1995.

It turned out to be impossible to hide everything from Ron, because I had trouble holding it together all on my own. I lost it at a workout one particularly cold and windy morning. The girls on the team were bitching and moaning about how they couldn't believe they had to dive on such an awful morning. I wanted to scream at my teammates. With as much anger as I think I ever expressed in my life, I told them to be thankful for their health and to stop bitching and moaning, because they had nothing to bitch and moan about.

Here they were moaning and groaning about the weather, and

Tom was in the hospital. He might die. I've just found out that I'm HIV-positive and I'm wondering how soon before I'm going to get sick.

I was furious, but it wasn't just at my teammates. I was furious with myself for not going home to take care of Tom. I was furious at the world for my being HIV-positive. It's not my nature to wonder "Why me?" but after all the challenges I'd faced and tried to overcome in my life, I felt overwhelmed and beaten down. There was just so much one person could take.

Ron could tell something was up, because when I'm angry I usually take it out on myself. It's very rare for me to lash out at someone else that way. Ron pulled me into his office and asked what was up. I couldn't pretend that everything was okay, so I told him that Tom was in the hospital with pneumonia, that Tom had AIDS.

Ron wasn't really shocked. He'd known about Tom's shingles and his lung problems, so he already suspected that Tom had AIDS. Then he asked me how I was doing. I tried to speak but started to cry instead. Ron came around his desk to where I was sitting and he held me, like he always did.

I calmed down and told Ron that I was okay. I could tell he was relieved. I wasn't ready to tell him the truth about my HIV status for another month. I told him that with so much to worry about, it had gotten to be too much being around the other divers complaining about the weather.

Ron was genuinely sympathetic about Tom. I know he didn't care much for Tom, but Ron knew how important Tom was to me, and he could see that I was devastated.

Over the next few weeks, I continued with my training routine as if nothing were wrong, but something wasn't right. I was constantly tired and had no energy. Back in '84 I was always up for going out after practice, but now after a workout, all I wanted was to take a nap.

John had warned me I might have side effects from the AZT, including fatigue, but I couldn't tell if I was tired because of the AZT or because I had to get up every four hours during the night to take the pills. My training regimen might also have had something to do with it. I was training extra hard to prove to myself that I could do it, to prove that there was nothing wrong with me. One week I took six aerobics classes in addition to my regular training. By the end of the week, I was so sore that in the morning I had to sink into the hottest tub I could stand just to get my joints moving.

It wasn't only the exhaustion that was getting in the way of my regular training. It also turned out to be impossible to look at my HIV treatment as just another part of my training regimen. AZT is no vitamin pill—it is strong stuff, designed to keep the HIV from completely destroying what is left of the immune system. I tried to put that frightening thought in the back of my mind, but I carried around a little alarm clock to remind me to take the AZT every four hours, a six-times-a-day reminder that I had a deadly disease.

I also had to carry around a pillbox with lots of different compartments, for the AZT, the Bactrim, and all the vitamin supplements I was taking. Fortunately, because it's common for divers to be taking lots of aspirin for injuries, no one ever questioned me about the pills.

With all of this going on, you can imagine my emotional state. It was a constant roller coaster. Sometimes I was okay. At other times I would cry for no apparent reason. I'm sure a lot of people thought I was in a perpetually bad mood.

After I told Ron about Tom, I lasted through a month of ups and downs before I finally told him that I was HIV-positive. He had noticed that my moods were pretty bad and that I was having a difficult time staying motivated in my workouts. But it was typical for me to be anxious and unfocused several months in advance of any major competition. If I was any worse than normal, Ron figured it was because Tom was sick, although by now, Tom had come home from the hospital and was doing pretty well.

I decided to tell Ron when we were in Washington, D.C., for a U.S. Olympic Committee event. It was just the two of us on the trip, and it seemed like a good time to tell him. We got to Washington at midday, and that afternoon, around three o'clock, I called Ron and told him that I wanted to come by his room. I was sure that he would be supportive and that he'd love me no matter what.

Ron opened the door and we went over to sit at a small round table by the corner window. Ron knew something was up, because normally if I wanted to talk to him, I'd do it informally during practice or I'd drop by his office.

I told Ron that I needed to talk about something and then I told him I was HIV-positive. I explained that the reason I didn't tell him initially was because I was afraid he would go easy on me with my training. I told him that I knew there was no way to make it through the Olympics unless he treated me the way he always did. I had to go through the program as if nothing were going on, because I needed the confidence I got from my training to compete at the Olympics. I also told Ron my fear of qualifying for the team and then not being able to compete if I got sick.

This conversation wasn't nearly as emotional as the one in which I had told Ron about Tom. The whole time I talked, Ron sat and listened calmly. Ron and I are similar in that we can be terrified, but we don't necessarily show it.

The first thing Ron said was, "We'll get through this together," amazing words to hear from anyone. Then he asked me what I wanted to do. I told him that I wanted to continue. I explained my T-cell count and that I was on AZT. I told him what my medical care was at that point and said that he was free to discuss any of this with my doctor, John.

Ron said I shouldn't worry about him holding back in my training because he wasn't going to let me off that easy. We both chuckled. He also told me not to worry about being unable to compete after qualifying in the Olympic trials, that we'd cross that bridge when we came to it. He said, "We can't think about that now. We've got to get ready for nationals first."

Before I left Ron's room, we agreed that we each had a job to do. Ron said he wasn't going to neglect his part and that we all had to work together. Then he added, "It just makes this year that much more important." Ron gave me a big hug and we parted.

Ron and I didn't discuss it much after that first day. On occasion he'd ask me how I was doing, but he didn't push. As long as I was getting to my workouts and training, I was okay. He kept in regular contact with my doctor to keep current on my course of treatment.

Ron talked with John as soon as we got back to Florida, and their biggest concern was fatigue. Ron had promised not to let up on my training, but he worried about working me into the ground. Both he and John had a lot of concern about maintaining my training at its normal level and what the stress might do to my immune system. John's feeling was that as long as I did what I was supposed to do and took good care of myself, I'd probably be okay, but there was no guarantee I'd perform as well as I had in the past.

After he met with John, Ron told me that he would train me the way he thought I needed to be trained, but that I needed to tell him if it was too much. One thing Ron didn't tell me was that he worried about my having some kind of accident, one where I cut myself. The danger, of course, would be the potential for infecting others if they were exposed to my blood. Ironically, Ron worried about this during my training, but it never occurred to him that I might hurt myself at the Olympics.

One of the things that I know was hard on Ron was the fact that he couldn't talk to anybody about my being HIV-positive, not even Mary Jane. I told him that I didn't want anyone else to know at that point. He and Mary Jane always talked about everything, but I was terrified that this news would get out, and I didn't want anyone, not even Mary Jane, to know. Looking back, I realize this wasn't fair to Ron or to Mary Jane. Ron really needed someone he could talk to, and I know Mary Jane would have kept the secret.

I also needed someone to talk to, because even after I told Ron, I continued to struggle with my emotions. From week to week, my moods got progressively worse. On top of all my fears about what would happen to Tom and whether or not I'd stay healthy enough to get through the Olympics, I started being haunted by the feeling that somehow I deserved AIDS. I was a faggot and this was the faggot's punishment. Intellectually, I knew it was ridiculous, but emotionally, I couldn't shake the feeling that I deserved to be HIV-positive.

Growing up, I learned that being gay was a bad thing. I'd rejected those lessons long ago, but the negative feelings about being gay stayed with me. Now I was infected with what many people misguidedly called a "gay disease." So it just followed that God was punishing me for acting on my feelings. Rationally, I knew those thoughts made no sense. If AIDS was God's way of punishing gay people, how can you explain that babies and children get AIDS and that lesbians have the lowest incidence of the disease?

Now that I've talked with other gay men who are infected with HIV, I've discovered that I'm not the only one to have those feelings. But at the time, I was alone with my thoughts. The way I handled the emotional turmoil, as always, was to withdraw. If I had a workout, I'd get there just before it started, do my stretching exercises, dive for an hour and a half or two hours, and then break for lunch. I kept to myself during lunch, and then it was back to the pool for another couple of hours of diving. After that I would do weights or have an aerobics class. Then I'd go home.

If I didn't have a workout, I stayed in my apartment all day. Usu-ally, I didn't get out of bed, but sometimes I moved to the couch and turned on MTV or watched cartoons. Occasionally, I played tennis with John or went out with a couple of the divers after weight training for a bite to eat, but only if I was invited. I didn't go out of my way to spend time with other divers, mostly because I was afraid that I'd slip and say something. I was afraid they'd hear my AZT timer go off and ask about what vitamins I was taking and why I needed an alarm clock to remind me. It was easier just to be on my own and pretend that nothing was going on.

At one point, shortly before the Olympic trials, when the depres-sion was really bad, I talked to John about it. He asked me if I'd thought about harming myself. I told him that I'd thought about it plenty. He asked me how I would do it. I didn't have access to any kind of sleeping pills or painkillers at that time, but I did have syringes that John had given to me so I could give myself injections of vitamin B_{12}. I told him that injecting myself with air was a realistic option.

John immediately asked me to hand over the syringes, which I did.

He knew that this was something out of his realm, so he suggested that I go to church and talk to a priest. John belonged to a strict Greek Orthodox church, and I was brought up Greek Orthodox. He thought that talking to a priest would help me deal with what was going on in my life.

For me, talking to a priest was totally out of the question. I don't agree with a lot of what the Greek Orthodox Church teaches, particularly when it comes to homosexuality. I had every reason to think that if I went to talk to a priest, he'd want to talk to me about "my sin" and tell me that it was never too late to "repent." I had nothing to repent for.

I told John I'd think about the priest—knowing full well that I had no intention of going. He also recommended that I go on an antidepressant, and gave me a prescription. I only took the pills for a few days, because they seemed to throw my equilibrium off. I wasn't stumbling into walls, but the side effects were more than enough to mean the difference between winning and losing. Again, I definitely should have been talking to a psychologist, but no one was pushing it, and besides, I wasn't ready.

What really saved me from my depression and thoughts of suicide was the approaching competition. I was training more and more and had less free time to be preoccupied with the HIV. I had something to look forward to. That gave me purpose. As long as I had a workout, I was there on time or even early. I had a goal, and there were people counting on me to reach it.

Deep down, there was something else going on. I had something to prove to myself. Besides proving that I was good enough to win two more gold medals, I wanted to prove that even though I was HIV-positive, I could still win. Like always, I wouldn't have to say anything. I'd let my diving speak for itself. Unfortunately, if I won, no one but me, Ron, John, Debbie, Tom, and a handful of other people would know the true meaning of my victory.

22

OLYMPIC

TRIALS

AFTER HE GOT out of the hospital, Tom bounced back pretty quickly, and when he was well enough to travel, he came to visit me in Florida. I hoped we'd get to spend time together. I needed his support. Unfortunately, Tom was back to his routine of taking care of business, which meant that most nights he was out until long after I'd gone to sleep. I tried to accept that he had things to do, but when I complained, he just got angry.

Once he got better, Tom was even more hurtful and controlling than before. He would tease me about my T cells, which were lower than his, making childish comparisons like "My T cells are better than yours." He was desperate to prove that he was healthier than I was. He did it in a sort of sick, joking way, which I didn't think was very funny. The fact was that even though I had fewer T cells than he did, I had a stronger constitution and was in much better health. I had no problem throwing off a cold or the flu.

Tom started pointing the finger at me again, saying that I'd infected him. When he first got sick, he was briefly concerned that he had infected me. As soon as he was feeling better, he quoted an article to me from *Newsweek* that explained the disease could lay dormant for years and that you could still infect other people and not be sick.

I'd made the assumption that since he got sick first, he was the one who infected *me*, but now it turned out that I could have infected him even though I was still healthy. To me it didn't matter who infected whom—maybe we were both infected when we met. My attitude was, however it had happened, we both had it and pointing fingers wasn't going to make either of us better. I just wanted us to be there for each other.

When it came to exercising more control, there wasn't a lot Tom could do, since I was in Florida training full-time. So what he started doing was taking more control of my financial assets. Tom also tried even harder to control the media's access to me, but I didn't pay much attention to that. The only way Tom's tightened reins really affected me was in a battle over whether my parents were coming to the Olympics. That was an ideal opportunity for him to show who was in charge.

One of the major Olympic sponsors had a program that helped get the families of competing athletes to the Olympics. I don't know exactly what the program was, but Tom decided that he was going to be the one to benefit from the program and not my parents. He tried to pass himself off as my brother, which didn't work. It was pretty easy to figure out that he wasn't my brother. So in the end he had to pay his way, which meant, of course, that *I* paid his way. My parents still could have come to the Olympics on that program, but Tom said that if my parents came, he was staying home.

My parents didn't like Tom, and he didn't like them. My father had made it very clear that he didn't trust Tom, that he thought he was an opportunist. My mother felt that Tom was ruining my career, and she accused him of trying to cut off her relationship with me. She even said all of this to GQ in a 1988 profile of me. She told the reporter that Tom didn't let me answer my own phone and that he didn't pass along messages from her, which was true. When the reporter asked her how long she thought the relationship between Tom and me would last, she said, "I hope until tomorrow." That really upset Tom.

Tom's goal was to drive a wedge between me and my parents. He claimed that my mother got off on my stardom and told me that she was a "whiny bitch" and a "star fucker." He said that my father was a "control freak" who just wanted to tell me what to do with my finances. Tom would always put a negative spin on whatever they did, which made me think that maybe he was right. That made me feel awful, because I'd always counted on my mother, at least, to be in my corner. Deep down I knew she still loved me, but Tom's remarks made me wonder.

It seems incredible to me now that I ever believed what Tom said, but he was still the person I trusted most, and I foolishly chose to see the world through his eyes—at least for a while longer. At the time this happened, I was still very dependent on Tom. I was attached to him, and I needed and wanted his approval. So I felt like I was being torn in half. I couldn't imagine him not being at the Olympics, but I wanted my parents there, too.

The only way I felt I could survive the dispute was to step aside. The Olympic trials were fast approaching, and I just couldn't deal with it. I told my mother, "Mom, I love you, but you and Dad are on your own. Argue it out with Tom." I washed my hands of the whole thing. It was the cowardly thing to do, but I was afraid to challenge Tom. So Tom went to the Olympics with me, and my parents watched it on television.

I got to the Olympic trials in Indianapolis about six days before the start of competition, which was four more days than we usually gave ourselves when we were going to a national meet. The trials were obviously very important and we wanted to be totally prepared. I wanted plenty of time to get familiar with the diving board and the pool.

I had a good workout the first day, but I woke up the next morning feeling pretty lousy. I went through my morning workout, and then Ron and I decided I should take the afternoon off and rest. The next day was horrible. I was achy and feverish, the whole nine yards. I was scared. I thought this was it, this was the HIV kicking in, it would all be over soon.

I stayed in bed all day and thought about what was going to happen. Would I recover and then be able to get through the trials? What if I got through the trials and got sick at the Olympics? Should I talk to my friends at U.S. Diving and let them know my situation so we could have an alternate there just in case? What if they decided I shouldn't go to the Olympics because of the HIV? I couldn't risk saying anything. I prayed it was only the flu.

During the night the fever broke, and the next morning I felt a lot better. I realized by then that a lot of other people at the trials had caught the same virus. Fortunately, with my surprisingly strong constitution I fought off the virus faster than some of the other athletes did. But it was scary, because with every sniffle or upset stomach, I couldn't help but think it was the beginning of the end.

The next morning, with only one day to go before the trials were set to begin, I got back in the pool. I was so thankful to be diving again, and after getting through my list a couple of times, I felt confident that I'd do well in competition.

Everyone expected that I'd get two spots on the team, one for 3-meter springboard and one for 10-meter platform, but I had some anxiety about how I'd do on springboard. If I was having a bad day, there was always the chance I'd wind up not making the team.

Despite my last-minute doubts, I did really well on springboard and platform, winning both with a comfortable lead. It was a huge relief to be past that hurdle, because if you make the team, you know that at least you have a shot at the gold. If you don't get through the trials, it's over.

Ron was also relieved. It wasn't just that I'd won; he was also afraid that my fever had to do with the HIV. As if that wasn't enough to worry about, while we were in Indianapolis, Ron's son-in-law, Andy, committed suicide. He'd been suffering from depression for many years, but his suicide still came as a terrible shock to them. Ron and Mary Jane decided not to say anything to any of the divers, because they were afraid it would affect our diving. We all knew the whole family, including Andy, and it would have upset us. But it must have been a terrible burden for Ron to be there with us, not being able to say anything and having to be away from his daughter at a time of real crisis. Ron's good at shutting out the world and focusing on what has to be done. That's what he taught me, but it's tough when something like that happens.

The six weeks between the Olympic trials and the trip to Seoul were pretty much a whirlwind. From the trials, we went right to New York to do one of the morning TV shows. From there we went back to Indianapolis to go through processing for the Games. We had photo shoots and paperwork to deal with.

From Indianapolis, we headed back to Florida and took a few days off. Then we started training again, six days a week. The goal with those final weeks of training was to build up to the Olympics and peak at the event. This was no standard six weeks of training. After the first three weeks at Mission Bay, we did an exhibition in Boca Raton. For the first time in my diving career, I almost missed an event because I was late.

John wanted me to have a gamma globulin infusion before I left Florida. After the exhibition, we were heading out for two more weeks of exhibitions across the country, then flying to Hawaii for a week of training. From there, we were flying to Seoul. John was concerned that I was going to a foreign country, where I'd be exposed to all kinds of bacteria and viruses, and he wanted to build up my immune system as much as he could before I left.

The only time I had a long enough break to get the infusion was between my morning workout and the exhibition. Gamma globulin isn't just an injection. It's a full infusion, and it takes time. I was angry with John for making me come in, because it was just one more reminder that things were different now. But I knew he was right, so I drove to his office after morning practice.

There should have been more than enough time to get to John's office, do the infusion, and get back in time to dive. But they had trouble with the machine, and it took a lot longer than the two hours it should have taken. I was watching the clock the whole time, getting more and more panicked. I was never late, and I didn't know how I'd explain where I was. What was I going to say—that I was getting a gamma globulin infusion because I was HIV-positive and had a low T-cell count?

As soon as the needle was out of my arm, I ran for the car and drove like crazy. I ran into the pool area, and everybody was relieved to see me, because they were afraid I'd been in a car accident. I wanted to say, "I wish that's all it was."

I'd been in such a rush that I'd forgotten to stop at home and get my suit and chamois. Luckily, someone had an extra suit for me to borrow, but I didn't have my chamois. That might not sound like a big deal, but it's unheard of for a diver to forget his chamois. It's basic equipment. Ron took me aside and said, "Don't worry, we're holding. People are still coming in. Just calm down." He was the only person who knew where I'd been.

I got through the exhibition just fine, but mentally, I didn't know where I was.

≈

EVEN WITHOUT THE added burden of HIV, Ron and I knew that getting through the 1988 Olympics—and coming home with two gold medals—was a much bigger challenge than it had been in 1984. I still had a good chance of winning, but a lot had changed in four years. To start with, I was four years older, and most of the divers I was competing against were a lot younger. My strongest competition on platform, Xiong Ni of China, was half my age. Some of the divers were calling me Grandpa.

It wasn't just that my competition was younger. They were also better than they were in '84, especially the Chinese. They'd been studying my techniques, and now they were doing the same difficult dives that I'd counted on in Los Angeles to give me a substantial edge. In other words, the competition had caught up.

On top of that, I wasn't in the same peak shape I'd been in four years earlier. My body had changed. It wasn't that I'd gotten heavy, but I'd gotten bulky as my body matured. That's my Samoan heritage. In

1976 I was skinny. In 1984, I was just about right. And by 1988, I was a little bulky.

These factors were out of my control, but what I *could* control was my training, and it wasn't nearly as focused or consistent as it had been in the years leading up to the '84 Olympics. Back then, I'd spent nearly a whole year training. I was very single-minded. After '84, my world really opened up and diving was only part of what was going on in my life. I was busy with lots of things other than diving, from public speaking to Speedo appearances. I always seemed to be running to my next appearance, and I never had enough time to train for competitions. I was still winning, but the difference was that now I always felt unprepared. I'd get three months of concentrated training during the winter, and then, in the off season, I'd get two or three days here and there, depending on my appearance schedule.

Tom and Ron wound up struggling over how much time I got to train. Tom wanted me out there as much as possible making money. Ron wanted to make sure I was prepared for competitions, and sometimes he'd have to rein Tom in. Finally, they came to an agreement that I could have at least six weeks to get ready for a competition. But then something would come along that was too good to pass up and Tom would insist that I do it. That happened a few times where it really hurt my performance. One time I hit my hand on the board during a dive, and then in April 1987, I came in second—not first—in all three events at the U.S. indoor diving championships in Baton Rouge. That was it. Ron put his foot down and insisted that there were no exceptions: I had to have the six weeks of training before every major competition.

Despite the fact that I had a lot more than six weeks of training for the '88 Olympics, I just wasn't as well prepared as I had been in '84. I'd already won two golds at the Olympics and I knew what it was like to compete at that level. But whatever I gained from the '84 experience didn't make up for the fact that I wasn't as focused going into '88.

Then, as much as I wanted to deny it, there was the HIV. After I got over the virus at the Olympic trials, I managed to push my HIV worries to the back of my mind, but I couldn't forget about it completely. I still had my AZT clock to remind me to take my pills every four hours, and there was John pumping me full of gamma globulin. I tried to act as if there were nothing to worry about, and Ron did the same thing. We didn't want to alarm each other.

Still, there was plenty to worry about as the departure date for Seoul approached. To start with, I was scared about the drug testing they do at the Olympics. Would the medications show up in my urinalysis? Among other things, they checked for high levels of caffeine and steroids. Were any of the medications I was taking banned substances? I talked to John about this before the Olympics, and he made some calls. Fortunately, none of what I was taking was on the list.

What scared me more than anything was that someone would find out about my HIV before we left and stop me from going. I was also scared that they'd decide to implement HIV testing at the last minute. And then there was customs in Seoul. How would I hide all my medications?

Before I left home, I put my AZT in a medicine bottle that didn't identify what the pills were. I left the rest of the medications in their containers. Unless you were a doctor, you couldn't tell that they were prescribed for someone who was HIV-positive. When I got to customs in Seoul, the agent asked me what the pills were for. I was so scared that I could hardly breathe as I told him the pills were vitamins and antihistamines. He just nodded and continued going through my bags.

I was relieved to get through customs, but that wasn't the end of it. I was also afraid of being found out during the Olympics. I had a room to myself, so at least I had some privacy. Normally, you're two to a room, but because I had qualified for two different events, I got my own room. Still, when my alarm went off during the night, I shut it off as fast as I could. I didn't want to wake anybody up.

The rest of the day was more of a problem. I was swallowing pills from morning till night. I was afraid all the pill popping would raise some eyebrows, but only one of the divers asked about it. I said it was aspirin for my shoulder. Funny thing is, when he asked, the pill I was taking happened to be aspirin.

23

~~~~~~

SEOUL

1988

I'VE OFTEN SAID that diving was my refuge. If ever I
needed a refuge from what was going on in my life, it was during the
1988 Olympics. In the past, it had always been a struggle to keep the
turmoil of my daily life and the ups and downs of my own emotions
from getting in the way of what I did on the diving board. In Seoul, it
was almost impossible.

This time, there was just too much going on to push it all aside.
Starting with that first night in Seoul, there was no way I could clear
my head and fall asleep. I'd toss and turn for hours, and once I finally
drifted off to sleep, my alarm would go off for my next dose of AZT.

Ron was under a lot of pressure beyond diving. Mary Jane still calls
the weeks leading up to the Olympics the "five weeks from hell." On
August first Bruce Kimball, my friend and rival on the 10-meter platform, had a terrible car accident in which the car he was driving killed
two people. He'd apparently been drinking. All of us were upset by the

accident and the controversy that followed. A lot of people didn't think Bruce should be allowed to compete in the Olympics because of what happened, but he wound up not making it through the Olympic trials anyway. The whole thing hit Ron's family especially hard because Bruce and Ron's son were good friends.

Then two weeks later, Ron and Mary Jane's son-in-law killed himself. Right after that they had to put their dog, Amity, to sleep. Amity had been Ron's constant companion for fourteen years. I don't mean to put a suicide and the death of a dog in the same league, but losing an animal's love is still a blow. Then Ron's mom became seriously ill and went into the hospital. Ron wanted to be with her, and I was honored and grateful that he chose to stay with me in Seoul. I could never have made it through the Olympics without him.

Just hours before the springboard preliminaries got under way, Ron got the call that his mother had died. He didn't think it would do any of us any good to know about it, so he didn't say anything. He didn't want to burden me. I've never in my life had someone show as much concern for me.

I had no idea what Ron was going through, and I was feeling pretty good the day of the preliminaries. Through each round my confidence grew. By the end of my eighth dive, I had a comfortable lead, and my next dive was the reverse two-and-a-half pike, which was usually one of my best. As I was getting ready to climb the ladder, Ron was debating whether to warn me that earlier I'd been a little too close to the board on another of my reverse dives. But he decided not to say anything, because I was never close doing a reverse two-and-a-half pike. My distance on that dive had always been just right, so Ron decided that he didn't want to give me another thing to think about.

In one of the articles published during the Olympics about my diving, the reporter estimated that I'd done 180,000 springboard dives in my eighteen-year career. During that time, I'd had some close calls, like hitting my hands and hitting my feet on the board, but I'd never hit my head, at least not on springboard. I guess the lesson there is that you always have to watch out for dive number 180,001.

News of my accident on the diving board was reported around the world. I can only imagine the number of times the videotape of me hitting my head was played over and over again on the news. Every major newspaper published a picture of my head making contact with the diving board. It was a shocking moment, not only for me. I was the top diver in the world, and almost no one imagined I'd hit my head on the diving board at the Olympics.

I'd been upset that my parents weren't in Seoul to see me compete, but now I was glad that my mom, in particular, wasn't there to see me hit my head. It would have been terribly upsetting for her. Given the time difference between the U.S. and Korea and the tape-delayed TV coverage, she saw the videotape only after she had been told what happened, so she knew that I was okay. It turned out that she wasn't surprised. After I had left for Korea, she told some of her friends that she had a feeling I was going to hurt myself at the Olympics. She told them that I was under too much stress, not knowing, of course, that I was also dealing with HIV. They told her that she was being silly, that nothing was going to happen.

Because I was back on the board so quickly and apparently in good humor, people didn't realize how badly shaken I was. In fact, it wasn't until after I'd completed the preliminary round and made the finals that I allowed myself to really think about what had happened. If I hadn't blocked it out, I would never have made it through the last two dives.

That night, between my sore head, trying to sort out what I'd done wrong, and worrying about whether or not I'd put anyone in danger, I couldn't fall asleep. I eventually drifted off, only to be awakened by the AZT alarm clock. After that, I gave up and just stayed in bed until six o'clock, when I got up to get ready for practice, having had less than three hours of sleep.

Normally, finals are in the evening, so you have twenty-four hours between prelims and the final round. But because of the live television broadcast schedule for the finals, they were being held at eleven in the morning, and I had to be at practice at eight. I didn't really like having finals in the morning, but I was glad they weren't in the evening this time. With so much going on in my head, I couldn't have held it together until the end of the day.

At eight o'clock, I met Ron at the bus to go over to the pool to work out. I barely said hello, and when we got on the bus, I took a seat by myself. I just wanted to be alone and listen to music on my headphones. Ron sat in a seat nearby. He could tell just by looking at me that my confidence was badly shaken.

He realized that his plan to take it easy on me that morning would only make the situation worse, so he decided to be tough on me, to help me regain my confidence. Before a major competition, Ron usually had me do two of each of my dives and that was it. The whole idea was to get the feel of the board and get warmed up, to do just enough to feel relaxed. That had been our routine for the past eight years.

Before we even started the workout, Ron warned me, "Don't have high expectations. Just get through the workout. Get through your dives. That's your goal this morning." Ron knew that I had to get through my dives safely to start building up my confidence. I had to be sure of myself in that final round. When you're competing on a world-class level, there's not much room for error. I had to be on.

If you saw the start of my workout that morning, you would have thought that there was no way this guy could do it. The first thing Ron made me do was the dive I'd missed the day before, the reverse two-and-a-half, to prove to me that I could do the dive, that what happened the day before had been a fluke. I did the dive, and when I came to the surface, Ron said very sternly, "C'mon, don't be a wimp! You were too far out there. Do another!" He was right, I was way out in the middle of the pool, but I was terrified of being too close to the board. So I did another, and he said, "C'mon, stand up a little bit. Do another!"

Ron was being a real taskmaster, really kicking butt. Usually, he's very positive and sort of gentle. This time his whole attitude was different; even his voice was different. He was very aggressive, almost like Dr. Lee had been. At that point, I needed him to tell me what to do, to help push me over the hurdle of my own fear.

Whatever Ron told me to do, I did. I trusted him and I surrendered myself to him. I had to, because I didn't trust myself anymore. I didn't have my own confidence, so I was drawing on Ron's confidence and strength. It's ironic that this kind of selfless faith in someone else was key to my success as a diver while it was devastating in my personal life.

Whatever it was, it worked. After the first four dives I felt stronger, and my last two were pretty good. My legs were starting to feel solid under me again. Ron would have made me do a dozen of those dives if he had to, but after a half dozen, satisfied that I'd gotten past it, that I'd be able to do it in the finals, we moved on to my other dives, and I did two or three of each of them. The rest of the practice was pretty routine, and by the time we finished, Ron and I even managed to joke a little with each other.

To get through the final round of the springboard competition, I had to stay focused on the diving or I'd never do well enough to win the gold. Practice had helped a lot, but it was still a struggle to put everything else in the background. Fortunately, putting everything else in the background was what I'd been trained to do. I'd been through adversity before. I'd had rough conditions before. I'd hurt myself before. I'd learned to dive even when I didn't want to, when I didn't feel well, when the weather was bad, when I was injured, when I was depressed. Still, this time was harder. I'd never faced a challenge quite like this before, and I was scared that I just couldn't do it this time. The worst part was, I still hadn't figured out what I'd done wrong the day before. I was having a block; I just couldn't process it. So I had to put that out of my head, too. I had to trust my body to do the right thing, even though my mind couldn't understand what had happened.

An odd advantage to my having hit my head was that all of a sudden I became the underdog. It's a position I'm comfortable with, so it alleviated some of the pressure of being first in prelims. There wasn't that automatic assumption that I was going to win.

It was the first time in a long time that I had to come from behind. Several years before, at the nationals, my legs had given out on a dive, and I landed with my hands and feet together. I got all zeroes and dropped to twelfth place in the preliminary round. They took the top twelve, so I went on to the finals, and in the end won. But this was the Olympics, and hitting my head was worse than having my legs buckle.

I was still feeling shaky by the time the competition got under way. I tried to concentrate on taking the dives one at a time. That's the way I normally did it. Ron was there the whole time for me to lean on. I let him know that I needed a little extra support by giving him my chamois before each dive. Although we never discussed it, Ron knew if I gave him my chamois that I needed a little more attention, an extra push. It was my way of signaling that I had some doubts.

I felt timid in the first few rounds, not diving as aggressively as I normally did. I still did my dives well, and with each one I felt stronger and more confident. Through five rounds, I built up a 9-point lead on Tan Liangde, a Chinese diver who'd beaten me twice earlier that year at international meets. In the seventh round, when Tan had trouble with the reverse two-and-a-half, which, of course, had been my ninth dive, I opened up a 20-point lead.

≈

IN FINALS YOU do the same exact dives you did in pre-lims. The momentum was building with each dive, and I grew more and more confident, through the eighth dive. But the thought of doing the ninth dive scared me. I was afraid of hitting my head again, of embarrassing myself, of not winning the gold—or any medal. Ron said only one thing to me before I headed up the ladder: "Just do it like you always do it."

Standing on the board, I could feel the tension. I knew everyone in the stands was waiting for me to do the ninth dive, to see how I would handle it. Some people wonder how I could concentrate with all those people watching. When I was in shape, I knew that my timing would be automatic, so I could afford to experience what the crowd was feeling—the excitement, the tension, the support, the enthusiasm—and I'd used that energy in my dive. That's what I did at the '84 Olympics. When I could experience the audience, that gave me a more emotional and fulfilling performance. It was a lot more fun to dive in those circumstances. It's like being onstage performing in a play, because you're getting the audience involved.

Now I couldn't afford to experience the audience at all and just screened them out. I took a couple of deep breaths and an extra moment to concentrate. I jumped it out a little bit, but not too much, because I couldn't afford to lose any points. When I came to the surface, I was laughing, just from the sense of relief. The scores were good, ranging from 8 to 9.

My next dive was fine. And for the final dive, I did a reverse three-and-a-half tuck. I didn't rip it, but it was certainly good enough for me to win. My total score was 730.80. Now I just had to wait to see how the final two divers did. Because I'd finished third in the preliminaries, I was the third-to-last diver. At the time, we dove in reverse order of finish. It was nice for a change not to be the final diver. Usually, there's a lot of pressure on you if you're the final diver, especially if it's close.

With my job done, the pressure was off me. I went over to Ron at the side of the pool and he gave me a hug. He told me that I'd done a great job, that I was tough, and added, "It's a good thing you have a hard head." We didn't talk about winning. We never talked about it before the fact.

I went back to the waiting area, where the divers hung out between dives, to gather my things and see what was going to happen. I was just thankful that I'd gotten through the finals in a respectable way. I still hoped I'd win the gold, but the ball was in Tan's court. I had no control over what he did. I tried not to watch, but I couldn't help but peek.

As soon as Tan did his dive—which was a little back and a little short—I knew I'd won. It was a big relief, much like I'd experienced in 1984, when I won my first gold. Ron came looking for me to tell me that I'd won. By the time he found me, I'd already gotten the news and was changing to get ready for the awards ceremony. Ron was thrilled, and thought we'd done a pretty good job of showing everyone how tough I was. But I didn't feel very tough. As Ron hugged me, my legs felt wobbly and I was on the verge of passing out.

The awards ceremony was a complete blur. I can't remember if I was crying, and when I asked Ron if he remembered if I was crying, he said that he couldn't see, because *he* was crying. You can't go through something like that and not be emotional.

Before they gave us the awards, I congratulated Tan. He nodded and turned away. I couldn't blame him for being upset. I had kept him from winning the gold at the Olympics for the second time—he had also come in second in '84. After I hit my head, I imagine the Chinese thought that this was finally their chance.

When the official put that award around my neck, I thought of Ron. We won the gold medal together, because I could never have done it without him. He still jokes that *he* couldn't have done it without *me*.

After the awards ceremony, there was a press conference, at which I was asked all the predictable questions: How was I able to get up and do that dive again? What was going through my mind when I did the ninth dive in the finals? Was I afraid that I'd hit my head again? One of my answers was "It would have been really embarrassing if I hit my head on the board twice." Not to mention painful.

Following the press conference, I had doping. They take a urine sample right after your event to make sure you weren't taking any drugs to enhance your performance. Despite John's reassurance that the AZT and the Bactrim wouldn't show up, I was still nervous. Before I went back to the Village, Ron and I talked briefly about what came next.

There really wasn't the chance to enjoy our win, because we both knew that the next day we had to start again. Ron suggested that I take a day or two off and let my head rest. He knew I could take a couple of days off and still have enough time to get ready for the platform competition. But I told Ron that I wanted to do my dives the next day as planned. We'd had a schedule going into the Olympics, and planned to train for three days prior to the platform event. I didn't want to change it. The fact that I had stitches in my head and a bruised skull made me even more determined not to change anything. I was still battling to keep myself together. I had to build up my confidence, and taking any time off would have been giving in. Sticking to our original schedule would help me prove to myself that I could do it no matter what. After the Games were over, I could take off as much time as I wanted—but not yet. I still had a job to do.

Ron and I said good night. He and Mary Jane went to dinner, and I went back to the Village. I was completely exhausted, but I had to have something to eat and have the stitches in my head checked and the dressing changed. Then I went back to my room and I went to sleep. I don't think I even looked at my medal. I just got undressed, got into bed, and pulled the blankets over my head. And for a change, I fell into a deep, deep sleep.

At practice the next day, Ron suggested that we start with some of the less difficult work, like practicing lineup and takeoff routines, and save the platform for the second day. You get sore from diving off the platform and you can't do it day after day, but I wanted to do all my dives that day. It had been five days since I'd done any training on platform, which meant that I hadn't done any training on platform since I'd hit my head. I wanted to get through all my dives right away just to be sure I could still do them, to remind my body what it had to do.

I also wanted to be sure I'd be able to endure the pain. My head still hurt quite a bit, and I thought it would hurt like hell when I hit the water. It did, especially when I missed my hands. When you do it right, you clasp your hands together just before you hit the water, and your hands break the surface, rather than your head. If your hands are apart, your head absorbs a lot of the impact. From the few times I missed, my ears were ringing from the pain.

Ron went back to his normal style of coaching, and actually gave me more room than he usually did. He left it up to me to decide how hard I wanted to push myself.

During those three days before the platform preliminaries began, Ron and I never talked about what was going to happen or not happen. In a sense, we were in denial and just focused on the job at hand in the way we always did. When you're under stress like that, you have to stay with your normal routine or the stress takes over and you start getting uptight. Whenever that happened, one of us would make a joke.

I've tried to remember if I even saw Tom during this time. I must have, because he was there. But oddly enough, I don't remember. I only remember seeing Ron. He was the most important person to me, the only one I knew I could count on.

By the time the platform preliminaries began, I was feeling pretty good about my diving, but I was awfully sore. I still had stitches in my scalp, and my head ached. For my bad shoulder, I needed two ice and E.G.S. (electro-galvanizing stimulation) treatments every day, to kill the pain and maintain mobility. My bad wrist had to be taped to keep a bone chip from aggravating a ganglion cyst. I had sinusitis, and after that one good night's sleep, I was back to being up most of the night. I was really beginning to feel like Grandpa.

The preliminaries were totally routine—no surprises. I got through it basically on autopilot, and then I won. To me, it was particularly important to win these prelims, especially after what had happened in springboard. I wanted to show the judges that I was still one of the top players. I wasn't used to being beaten in a major world-class competition, and I didn't want that to happen again.

Most of the time I looked at my diving as a performance. Part of me was a competitor, but mostly I felt like I was a performer. By the time I got to the finals in the platform diving, I was 90 percent competitor and 10 percent performer. I *had* to be a competitor, because it was going to be very close.

Normally, in a major competition, I would rise quickly to the top of the scoreboard and stay there. But this time, I moved between first and third throughout the whole ten rounds. The real struggle began in the seventh round, when fourteen-year old Xiong Ni, from China, moved from fourth place to second, and I moved from third to first, leading by only 8 points. In the eighth round, Ni took the lead by 2 points, and increased it to 3 points with his ninth dive.

I knew all along that it was close, just from the tone of Ron's instructions to me before each of my dives: "Just do a good dive"; "Just do your normal dive"; "Reach back and go for something special"; or, "Greg, you've got to bump it up a notch. Hang in there and keep going." He never told me that I was in trouble. He never told me I had to win the gold. That was Ron's philosophy. Just stay focused on letting your ability go, relaxing and doing your best, and the rest would take care of itself. He just kept encouraging me to fight, to keep going for it.

This wasn't the first time I'd competed against Ni. In the past, I'd always been able to count on his missing at least one of his dives and scoring 4's and 5's. So far he hadn't missed a single one.

It came down to our final dives. Ni was diving second to last and I was diving last. I knew that I was trailing by 3 points, because I'd peeked at the scoreboard, which is something I never did. I always tried to do my best and not pay any attention to the scores, but this time I looked when they flashed up all the scores for the last round.

At the '84 Olympics, before leaving the waiting area to go do a dive, I always rubbed Garvey's head. Garvey was long gone, but after I hit my head, I received a lot of teddy bears. One of them was a teddy bear with a bandage on its head, and so before I walked over to the platform to prepare for my final dive, I rubbed his bandaged head.

When Ni was on the platform getting ready to do his last dive, I climbed up the stairs to the platform and started giving myself the usual verbal reinforcement: "Relax in your shoulders. You can do it. Believe in yourself." Then I went through the dive in my mind's eye to the beat of, as always, "If You Believe": arms through, strong jump, draw your legs up to your chest into a tight tuck, spot, spot, spot, kick, stretch for the water. "Believe you can go home. Believe you can float on air. Click your heels three times if you believe."

Ni's dive was an inward three-and-a-half. I figured he was bound to miss it, but as soon as I heard his entry, I knew that he'd ripped it—no splash at all. He got 8.5's and 9's from the judges, giving him 82.56 points and a total of 637.47. He hadn't missed a single dive.

My final dive was the reverse three-and-a-half that killed Sergei Shalibashvili in 1983. It had a 3.4 degree of difficulty and was considered the most difficult dive in the sport. Lee Kongzheng from China was the only other diver at the Olympics doing the reverse three-and-a-half in competition—he won the bronze on platform at the '84 Olympics. Ni's dive only had a 3.2 degree of difficulty, which meant I had a slight edge. But I was trailing by 3 points, so I had to do a perfect or near-perfect dive to beat him. I had to get at least the same scores he did. I'd never been that close in a major competition before.

I knew from the expression on Ron's face that I couldn't hold anything back. Not that I ever held back—I always went all-out—but I really had to give this dive everything and more.

As I climbed the platform, the crowd was going nuts. They were still screaming and hooting and hollering and applauding for Ni. I used to have to remind myself that they were applauding *for* my competitor and not *against* me.

This time I had to narrow my focus and shut everything out. I had to go into my own world: just the pool, the board, and me and Ron. I had to be intensely aware of my body and my timing to make sure that everything was in sync. I couldn't afford to be distracted by the audience. And I couldn't let myself think that this was the last dive of my career.

With a reverse three-and-a-half, you go forward and then you spin backward toward the platform. There's always the danger of hitting the platform, but that wasn't on my mind. I wasn't at all afraid of hitting my head. I was afraid of not doing the dive well enough to win.

From the top of the platform, I glanced down at Ron and he gave me a hand signal telling me that we were even, that it was a 1-point contest. What he was really thinking was, Oh my God, we're behind! but he didn't want to add to the pressure. He didn't realize that I'd already taken a look at the scoreboard, that I knew I was trailing.

As I was getting ready, Ron was looking up at me, visualizing me coming off the platform, doing my dive, and going straight into the water with no splash. He was trying as hard as he could to push that image into my brain. I didn't know he was doing that, but I could feel how intensely he was watching.

I walked out to the end of the platform and removed the hand towel that Ni had placed on the edge. Some people were having problems with the surface, which was a little slippery, and Ni had been using a towel to give himself surer footing.

I took my chamois and squeezed some water onto my hands and then tossed it down to the deck below. Then I rubbed my hands together to get them equally damp, and rubbed them on my thighs to get off any of the extra moisture. I needed my hands to be damp, because with the reverse three-and-a-half you have to make sure your hands don't slip off your knees when you grab them. If you slip, which can happen because of the centrifugal force, you're in deep trouble. You can get pulled right out of your dive.

I got myself set about five steps away from the end, and they announced my dive. I knew at this point that there was a better chance I'd come in second than first. I wasn't resigned to that possibility, but I considered it briefly. I thought to myself, What's the worst that can happen? I do a dive that's not so great and win a silver. I thought about some of the people I'd dived with in the past who would have loved to have won a silver medal.

In the twelve years since I'd won the silver in Montreal, my appreciation of that accomplishment had grown. I was proud of having won the silver, especially at such a young age. That helped make the prospect of winning the silver this time around okay. It would still be a hell of an accomplishment, and it was all right. I prepared myself in case I didn't win the gold.

As I prepared for the dive, there was one other thing that I took comfort in. Whenever I was in a real tough situation—and this was the toughest situation in my diving career that I'd ever been in—the one thing I always told myself was that no matter what happened, my mother was still going to love me. In that moment, I had an image of my mother sitting at home, watching me on TV. Even if I did a bomb of a dive, she would still say, "Oh, wasn't that a pretty splash?" That image made me smile and helped me to relax.

I took some comfort in knowing that I wasn't facing the possibility of coming in second because I'd been diving badly. Ni had done all ten of his dives without missing one, which is incredible to do at the Olympics. Even if I came in second, there would be nothing to be embarrassed about.

And then it was time to dive. I rubbed my face with my hands, and then clasped my hands in front of me and closed my eyes, as if in prayer. A lot of people thought I was praying, but I was actually trying to get focused. Maybe that's what prayer is. I took a deep breath, and as I exhaled I said to myself, "Breathe, relax, get your arms through."

I walked out to the end of the platform. Facing the water, I got my feet set, with my big toes barely over the edge. With my arms out in front of me at a 45-degree angle to the platform, I checked my body alignment, looking down my arms to the water. As I drew my arms back into my body, I pulled my head up and focused on the edge of the pool, across from where I was standing. I lifted my head just a fraction, to focus about a foot higher than I normally did. By making that adjustment with my head, my weight was pulled back just a little bit more, so when I jumped I'd be closer to the platform. If you jump closer to the platform, you have greater height and more time to execute a good dive. It's also more dangerous, especially when you make that kind of adjustment in a competition where the pressure is great. I took the chance because I had to do the best dive I possibly could.

I focused across the pool and then raised my arms, forming a T with my arms and body. I counted myself off: one, two, three, go. With each count, I moved my arms slightly to build momentum, and then I began my arm swing. As I did that, I had to remind myself to stay relaxed in my shoulders, because I couldn't afford to tense up. If I tensed up, then my shoulders might rock back or forward and that would throw my alignment during the dive.

I relaxed my shoulders, letting my arms swing freely. As I reached through and left the platform, I kept looking at my spot across the pool. I circled around through the air, grabbing my knees, and then picked up my spot on the surface of the water. Another rotation, spot the water, another rotation, spot the water.

When I spotted the water for the third time, I gauged how far off the water I was. Based on that and the feeling of the spin, you adjust your kick to make your entry as close to vertical as you can. I knew that I was closer than I'd wanted to be, so I kicked for the sky and stretched for the water. With the reverse three-and-a-half, when you come out of the dive, the water's right there. You're right on top of it, so it feels like you're assuming the crash position as your hands hit the water.

I broke the surface with my hands, and as I entered the water, I had

A moment of concentration just before my final dive at the 1988 Olympics in Seoul. I was in second place and there was no room for error, but I knew that no matter what happened, my mother would still love me.

(AP/*Wide World Photos*)

Ouch! The ninth dive in the springboard preliminaries at the 1988 Olympics. (*AP/Wide World Photos*)

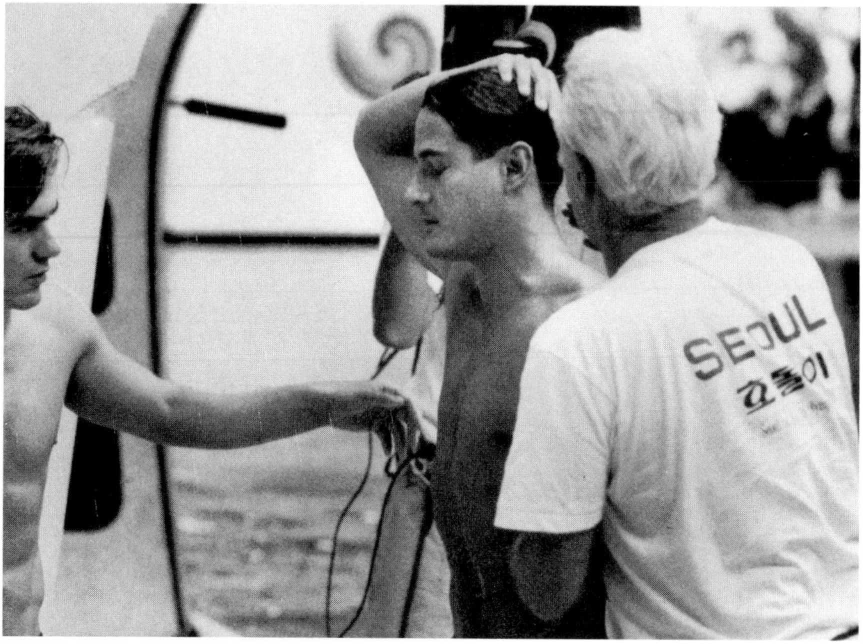

Just after I hit my head. Everyone wanted to help, but they didn't know what they were dealing with. (*AP/Wide World Photos*)

The day after, during practice the morning of the springboard finals, with stitches and waterproof patch. (*AP/Wide World Photos*)

The 1988 Olympics.
(*AP/Wide World Photos*)

The awards ceremony for 10-meter platform at the 1984 Olympics in Los Angeles.
A moment of pure joy. (*Collection of the author*)

I'd finally accomplished my goal: winning two gold medals. Now what?
(*Courtesy Dan Helms/Duomo*)

My final gold medal at the 1988 Olympics; it was a very bittersweet moment.
Xiong Ni of China is at left; Jesus Mena from Mexico is at right.
(*Courtesy Mary Jane O'Brien*)

At the team dinner following the end of the diving competition at the 1988 Olympics. I told everyone that no one would know what Ron and I had been through, and then I started crying. That's Ron I'm hugging in the final picture.
(*Courtesy Mary Jane O'Brien*)

"Star of the Day" in 1989 at Universal Studios in Orlando, Florida.
(*Collection of the author*)

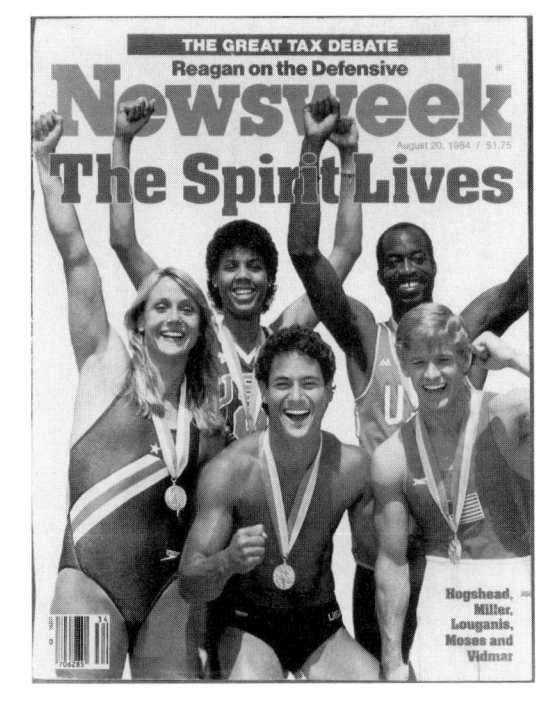

The cover of *Newsweek!*
August 20, 1984, following the
Los Angeles Olympics.
(© *1984 Newsweek, Inc.*
All rights reserved. Reprinted
by permission.)

With Elizabeth Becker Pinkston, 1924 U.S. Olympic gold medalist in 3-meter springboard and 1928 gold medalist in 10-meter platform, and Pete Desjardins, 1928 U.S. Olympic gold medalist in 3-meter springboard and 10-meter platform—at the International Swimming Hall of Fame, Fort Lauderdale, Florida. (*Photo by Bob Taylor,* THE DIVER *magazine*)

Getting the Orange County Sports Celebrities of the Year award with fellow Olympic champion Edwin Moses. (*Collection of the author*)

It was a thrill to meet the presidents, but I wish they had been the leaders we needed in the fight against AIDS. (*Collection of the author*)

With Brooke Shields at *Night of 100 Stars*, Radio City Music Hall, New York City. Of course, we were just friends. (*Collection of the author*)

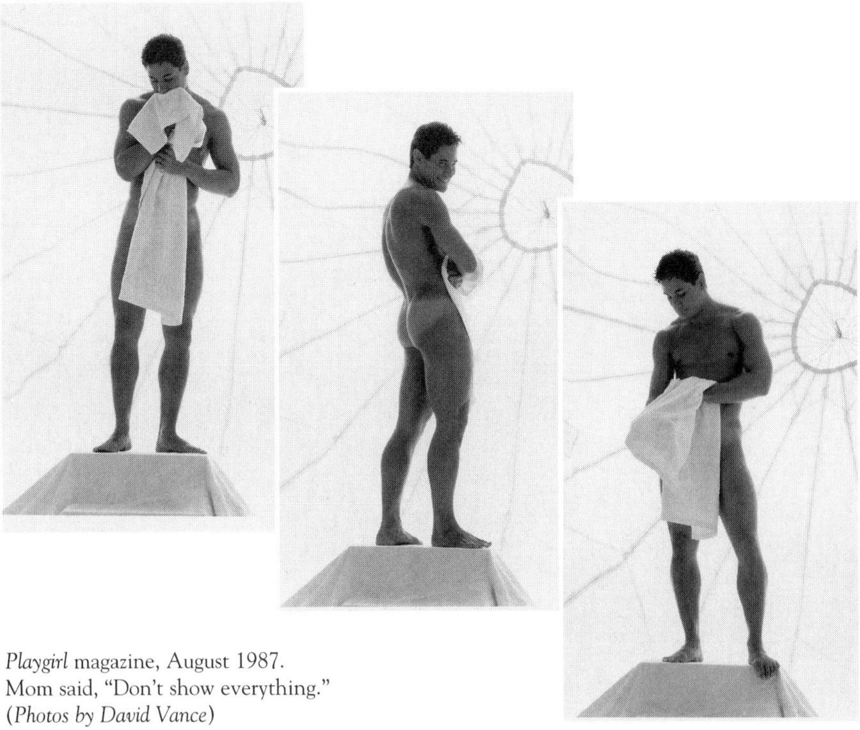

Playgirl magazine, August 1987.
Mom said, "Don't show everything."
(*Photos by David Vance*)

At the Kentucky Derby with Megan (seated, second from the right) and an all-star cast. Standing, that's Hal Holbrook, Dick Van Patten, Dick Sargent, David Birney, Patrick Duffy, me, and Lloyd Bridges. In front, Dixie Carter is holding Hal Holbrook's hand. Megan guessed the winner of the race; no wonder she looks so happy. (*Collection of the author*)

With Pam Dawber and Marvin Hamlisch at a New York City awards event. (*Collection of the author*)

At an awards dinner in Los Angeles with Dawnn Lewis,
my old college friend and confidante.
(*Collection of the author*)

Mom and my friend Michael Feinstein at Thanksgiving in Malibu.
(*Collection of the author*)

Showing Donna in "the classes" at the Burbank Kennel Club, 1993. No medal that day, although I still love her. (*Collection of the author*)

With Donna (foreground) and Brutus. They may look intimidating, but they're very sweet. (*Photo by Greg Gorman, courtesy of* OUT *magazine and Viking Stuido Books*)

"It's great to be out and proud!"
Gay Games IV, June 1994, New York City. (*AP/Wide World Photos*)

to reach back pretty hard to try to pull my body in line, because I was going short of vertical.

I heard my hands breaking the surface of the water and then felt the water rushing against my body. From that point on, I couldn't hear anything except the hum of the water pump. It's a deafening silence that only divers know. Even though I was in a building with thousands of people, I was all by myself for those few moments before I surfaced.

≈

FROM THE SOUND of the entry, I knew it wasn't a complete rip. It wasn't a perfect dive, but it was a pretty good dive. I was a little close to the platform on the takeoff and a little short on the entry. I realized all this while still underwater.

It was the final dive of my career, and that brief time underwater seemed a welcome relief from the events of the past few months. For much of my career, that time underwater had been a peaceful respite, a kind of friend. And now I was saying goodbye to my friend. I didn't linger, though, because I wanted to get to the surface to find out if I'd won.

As I came to the surface, the crowd was cheering, but I could tell they were holding back to see the score. There was a dialogue going on in my head. I was reassuring myself that I had nothing to be ashamed of, that I'd competed well and done the best I could under less than ideal circumstances.

I swam to the side of the pool and climbed onto the deck. The cameras were right in front of me, and I tried to make my way to Ron, who was over at the side of the pool. I grabbed my chamois and put it over my face. I didn't know if I should be embarrassed or happy, so I was just trying to be playful, although I wasn't feeling all that playful.

I turned the corner to head toward Ron, and I could see he was fixated on the scoreboard. I didn't want to look. So I just looked at Ron. Then all of a sudden he turned and he was jumping up and down hugging his son. Then the crowd started cheering, and I knew we'd won. After all we'd been through, none of it was in vain. Ron and I embraced and I just sobbed. I wasn't just crying, I sobbed.

As he held me, Ron said, "Nobody will ever know what we've been through." I said, "I know, I know." Ron reminded me that in 1976 I was the young upstart and Klaus Dibiasi had to fight for his life. Now the tables had been turned, and I had done the same as Dibiasi. I didn't say anything. I was completely overwhelmed.

People thought I was crying because I'd won. They didn't know that it was the emotional culmination of an incredibly difficult few months and my last competitive dive. It was all over, and we had done it. There was no need to hold anything back now, and I didn't. I couldn't. I just cried and cried.

I'd like to think that despite the crush of people I managed to congratulate Ni as Klaus had congratulated me, but I'm not sure that I did. It was one of those moments when I was pretty self-absorbed. But it was my moment, and for the first time I didn't feel at all guilty about enjoying it.

My final score was 638.61, only 1.14 ahead of Xiong Ni. It was my closest win ever in a major international competition. I became the first male diver to win a pair of gold medals in consecutive Olympics. I also equaled Klaus Dibiasi's record for total diving medals.

At some point after all the hugging and crying, Ron and I separated. I had to get ready for the awards ceremony, and Ron stayed on the deck and tried to get Mary Jane to come down from the stands.

Once I left Ron, it was pretty much a blur. I made my way back to the athletes' waiting area to change into my sweats. In those situations, with so many people converging on the same place, you just wrap a towel around yourself and get changed. I don't remember changing, but somehow I made it onto the podium with my sweats on.

When the ceremony began, Ron was on the deck with Mary Jane, near the podium. I could tell they were both crying. And, of course, I was crying too. I wish I could say they were only tears of joy, but they weren't. The whole thing was very bittersweet.

On the one hand, my sense of joy for having accomplished what I did was great. I had an incredible sense of pride that I'd managed to come through for the whole team of people who were supporting me.

On the other hand, this was it. My diving career was over, and I was HIV-positive. Tom already had AIDS. Standing on the podium, I wondered, How soon before I get sick? How soon before I die?

It made me sad that I couldn't share the truth about my accomplishment beyond our small group. What would the people cheering for me think if they knew I was gay and HIV-positive? Would they still cheer? And lurking in the back of my mind was the fear that I might have infected someone with HIV following my accident.

As soon as the awards ceremony was over, I had interviews with the press, and afterward they took me off for doping. Then I went back to the Village to rest for a while and get changed for the team banquet that evening.

The banquet was very emotional. Each athlete got up to give his or her thanks. When it was my turn, I went up to the podium, thanked all the appropriate people. Then I turned to Ron and said, "Ron, I couldn't have gotten through this without you. It took all ten years of our experience together, and a lot of love and trust, to get through a very difficult week. Nobody will ever know what we went through, nobody." I started crying, and that was the end of my speech. I simply couldn't say any more. I left the podium and went to Ron's table and we hugged and cried. We didn't talk. We just cried.

24

~~~~~~

SEPARATE

WAYS

I DIDN'T GET much time to reflect on what I'd just been through, or even catch up on sleep, because Tom had me on a plane back to California even before the closing ceremonies. He'd booked me to guest-host *Improv Tonite*, a cable stand-up comedy show, which was taped at The Improv, a comedy club in Los Angeles.

After the 1976 Olympics, I decided that I never wanted to go on television unprepared in the way some other Olympians do. You'd see them embarrassing themselves. But here I was, totally exhausted from the '88 Olympics, on my way to host a comedy show. I've never been a comedian.

I got to Los Angeles, and they handed me a script that made fun of my hitting my head and how I brought back this wonderful jewelry from Korea—two gold medals. They got their mileage out of the Olympics at my expense. The script was horrible. I was horrible. The whole experience was horrible. It was exactly what I'd said I'd never do.

I could have said no to the whole thing, but I was still taking the path of least resistance with Tom and that meant doing whatever he told me to do. He booked it—I had to do it. What I should have done was force them to rework the script, but there is never time with television. So I came off looking like a dumb jock. Even worse, I thought the whole thing was a disaster as far as positioning me to pursue acting after the Olympics, which was what I'd hoped to do.

Right after the *Improv Tonite* taping, Tom and I were on a plane back to Seoul. Just before I'd left for Los Angeles, the U.S. Olympic Committee announced that I was the winner of the Maxwell House Olympic Spirit Award, which honors the American Olympian who best embodies Olympic ideals. So after another thirteen-hour flight across the Pacific, I went to accept the award. It was an incredible honor, but I didn't know where I was.

I decided to use my acceptance speech as the time to announce my retirement from diving. I said, "This is a great way to end my diving career. I have decided that this was my last competition." The next morning, I flew back to L.A. and watched the closing ceremonies from home. I was so wiped out that I couldn't imagine participating in the ceremonies. I'd had more than enough. I just wanted to be at home.

I didn't have a grand plan when I got home from the Olympics. I knew that my first goal was to work on rebuilding my relationship with Tom. I realize now that I was wrong about wanting to go on with Tom. To anyone looking in from the outside, the only solution was to get out of that relationship as fast as possible.

The way I saw it, there had been no way for us to build a relationship when we were separated by a continent for months at a time. Now that I was finished with my diving career, I would be home most of the time and we could focus on solving our problems. We had talked about couples therapy before, and I thought we might get into therapy now.

I also wanted to get focused on my acting, which had taken a backseat to diving. In the weeks immediately after the Olympics, there wasn't a lot of time for anything because of all the public appearances and speaking engagements that Tom had scheduled for me. He had me running around everywhere talking about the Olympics, from colleges and universities to corporate groups and organizations of all kinds.

After the first few appearances, I started complaining to Tom that I was getting tired of rehashing the Olympics. It was especially difficult because I couldn't tell the whole story about what had really happened. Tom insisted that I do just about everything that came along, or at least everything where the money was right. He figured we'd better earn the money while we could, and it didn't matter to him what it was or what any particular group or company stood for. As long as it paid, that's all that mattered.

During the times I was at home, the adjustment turned out to be difficult for both of us. Tom complained that I was always underfoot, and he gave me little projects to do, trying to keep me busy while he did the important things, like answering the phone, paying the bills, keeping up with the mail, and arranging appearances for me.

It wasn't a lot of fun for me either, because Tom was more controlling than ever. I knew that a lot of this had to do with the fact he was sick: He couldn't control his health, so he wanted to control me. If I tried to go out on my own, I had to face a barrage of questions: "Who'd you see?" "Where'd you go?" "What'd you do?" If I went out with a male friend, he'd ask, "Did you sleep with him, too?" All those years later he was still throwing it in my face that I'd "cheated" on him.

It wasn't even as if I went out a lot. There weren't many people I was friendly with anymore. Tom had been my go-between for so long that he'd chased off almost everyone. He drove away my friends. He cut me off from my family. There was hardly anyone left except for Tom and me. I was very isolated, and I was beginning to feel like a prisoner in my own home.

The only place I felt really comfortable was in Debbie Shon's law office in Los Angeles. I would go there to make phone calls without getting the barrage of questions from Tom. If I called Megan, for example, when I got off the phone, Tom would say, "Oh, so you've talked to that bitch. What are you talking to her for? She can't do anything for us." It didn't much matter who it was—he'd lay into anyone I talked to.

Tom didn't even have to be home to challenge me over who I was talking to, because he would go over the phone bill to see who I'd been calling.

There had been a time in my life when I didn't mind Tom's being controlling. I was content for him to be my eyes and ears to the world. I didn't want to be bothered by anyone or anything, and I was happy for him to be my buffer. But now it was too much. For one thing, after training in Florida for so many months, I'd gotten more used to being on my own and making a lot of my own decisions. I no longer liked having Tom tell me what to do all the time. Now that he wanted total control of everything, it was becoming impossible. I began to realize that I had to make a change. And I began to see that I could.

Things got to be so bad with Tom that I started sharing with Megan how unhappy I was. I'd call her when he was out of the house and ask, "Am I crazy? Am I losing my mind?" Megan tried to tell me that I wasn't going crazy, and I started to open up to her about what Tom was doing. She reassured me that I was okay and explained how Tom was being manipulative.

My relationship with Tom was hardly a new subject with Megan, but I'd never been willing to acknowledge in the past that there was anything wrong. Two years earlier, Megan had hinted strongly that Tom was taking advantage of me, and she asked me if I knew where my money was and whose name was on what. Megan knew that Tom had power of attorney, so he was able to do whatever he wanted with my business interests.

Megan was pretty persistent, but she couldn't come on too strong because I was still very defensive. One time, she said, "Just to entertain me, please find out about the finances." I listened, but I wasn't ready to follow through.

In the months leading up to the '88 Olympics, Megan got more and more blunt, sharing with me what other people thought of Tom and how they thought he was destroying my career by the way he represented me to the press and companies that might hire me. Sometimes she tried to give me feedback about how she saw Tom treating me, but

I still defended him. I still didn't want to believe that he was the way Megan was describing him.

It's not as if Megan was the only one telling me things about Tom. I had other people who came to me and told me that Tom was going to bars and making out with guys. Or they would say he was at bars handing out his business card, trying to make a pickup. His card stated in bold print under his name, MANAGER OF GREG LOUGANIS, OLYMPIC DIVER.

Megan told me several times to confront Tom about these things, and on the few occasions when I raised the subject of him going out at night, he always made it sound like he was out there working for me, promoting my interests.

In the late fall of 1988, I mentioned to Megan for the first time that maybe I should break up with Tom. We were on a plane together going to an exhibition in Wyoming. She said that before I did anything, I needed to call my attorney and have her find out whatever she could about Tom, to get back my power of attorney, and to keep it all as quiet as possible. She knew as well as I did that if Tom got wind of this, it would be hell. She told me that if I didn't call my attorney, she was going to do it. Her concern was that I'd be making a lot of money during the coming months, and unless I did something, I'd wind up without a penny.

Megan was very insistent. While I was finally ready to listen to what she was saying, I wasn't yet ready to call my attorney. I thought I'd do some snooping around myself first, just to see if there was anything that didn't look right. I was still hoping I wouldn't find anything to worry about.

After I got home from that trip, I started poking around the office, looking in files. Tom caught me a couple of times and he got extremely angry. Suddenly I was forbidden to set foot in the office, which made me very suspicious. He was acting as if he had something to hide. I figured he was trying to hide a boyfriend. So I waited until he was out of the house, and I started going through the files, the checkbooks, and the phone logs. I was always on guard, because I was afraid that he'd catch me. Usually, I waited until he went to the grocery store, because then I could time how long he'd be away.

The first thing I came across left me a little puzzled. I found several letters from young gay men who had written to me after the publication of the GQ magazine profile of me earlier that year. In the letters, they told me about their lives and what a positive role model I'd been for them. Some of the letters had pictures with them. I wondered why Tom hadn't shown them to me. In fact, I'd never seen *any* letters in response to the article.

I looked through a few of the letters and noticed they were all from kids who lived in places where I'd done appearances or was about to do appearances. They seemed to be set aside for a reason. Tom often came along with me on my trips. Suddenly, I started to worry that he had been calling them up and having sex with them.

But the letters were nothing compared to what I discovered about my finances: I had only $2,000 in my personal checking account. Everything else—all my investments, all of my savings—was either in Tom's name alone or in both our names. Since the Olympics, I'd been making a lot of money, but none of it was in my name. I couldn't understand what was going on.

I wanted to say something to Tom as soon as he came back from the grocery store, but I waited a little while so he wouldn't think I'd been playing detective. That evening, I mentioned that I'd written a check from my personal account and my balance was a lot smaller than I'd expected. I asked him in the most nonconfrontational way I could what had happened to all the checks that had come in for my endorsements, appearances, and speaking engagements. Tom explained that he hadn't had a chance to get to the bank, so he had sent the checks in to his own account.

I may have been stupid when it came to finances, but I wasn't *that* stupid. I decided to take Megan's advice and talk to Debbie Shon, my attorney, about what I should do. I went to her office the next day and told her everything I knew up to that point. I didn't do a very good job, but however badly I explained it, Debbie understood enough to be concerned. She said that we had to handle the situation very delicately and suggested that she arrange a meeting at her office with Tom and some of the other attorneys to talk in general about my finances and taxes.

Debbie gave Tom the impression that it was her office that initiated the meeting, not me. She decided not to run the meeting, because she knew he would take it as a personal attack. One of her senior partners presented their concerns about the way Tom had structured our holdings. He explained that it could look as if we were doing it to avoid paying taxes, which could lead to charges of fraud. He laid it all out very logically, so it was hard for Tom to argue with.

The result of the meeting was that my finances were restructured in a way that protected my interests and prevented Tom from walking off with everything. One of the first things they did was rescind his power of attorney so that he couldn't do anything with any of my personal finances or our joint finances without my approval.

I could tell during the meeting that Tom was furious. He had been outmaneuvered by his little dummy. If things at home had been cool up to that point, they were cold from then on. Tom didn't know for sure that I had initiated the meeting, but he had an idea, because I'd been spending so much time with Debbie. After that meeting, Tom started calling Debbie a "meddling bitch."

The first thing Tom did after we got home from that meeting was draw up a letter outlining my relationship with him and send it to anyone I had business dealings with, from Speedo to the banks. In it he said something to the effect that when you were dealing with him, you were virtually dealing with Greg Louganis. He intended the letter to give him free reign to do whatever he wished regarding my business and financial matters. I'm embarrassed to admit it now, but I signed the letter. He was furious over the confrontation with our attorney regarding the power of attorney, and I thought I could placate him by signing the letter. Now I see that I was still trying to keep the peace and still trying to make things okay. I was still afraid to say no.

Megan couldn't understand why I was still with Tom. I explained to Megan that despite everything, and no matter how irrational it was, I still loved him. And I told her that Tom had AIDS. Then she asked me how I was. I told her that I was HIV-positive. None of that was a surprise to her, because she knew all about Tom's being sick. I went on to explain that the main reason I was so reluctant to leave Tom was that we'd each promised that we wouldn't let the other die alone. She understood, but she still urged me to talk to my attorney about having Tom investigated to see if there was anything else to be found out.

I didn't like the idea of hiring a private investigator to look into Tom's past, but I called Debbie anyway. I talked to Debbie about the private investigator, and she thought it was a good idea. I was still reluctant, and I told her that after six years I already knew everything there was to know about Tom, including his criminal record. Why hire an investigator?

Early on in my relationship with Tom, he told me that he'd been convicted of disturbing the peace following his arrest at a gay rights protest. I respected that. Just to appease Debbie and Megan, I said it was okay to hire a private detective.

Well, I couldn't believe what the investigator found. Tom's actual record showed that he'd been charged with both petty theft and grand theft. I shouldn't have been surprised, given what Tom had done with my finances, but I was. There was more: Tom was involved in insurance fraud. When we got together he'd told me that he had a Mercedes that had been vandalized and was in the shop being fixed. The investigator turned up that Tom was the one who had done the vandalizing, but not of a Mercedes-Benz. Tom did have a Mercedes, but the car he'd vandalized was his Volkswagen. Tom would never have harmed his precious Mercedes, which he kept parked in the garage on an Oriental rug.

That wasn't the end of it, and it certainly wasn't the worst of it. Tom had been arrested for solicitation. He pleaded guilty to a lesser charge of disturbing the peace. He hadn't been arrested at a gay rights protest. He'd been arrested for hustling. It was so hard to believe, but the investigator talked to people who knew Tom, who confirmed that he'd been a hustler on Santa Monica Boulevard.

I had a terrible time believing that Tom had lied to me, and even though there was no way to explain away his record, I couldn't really believe it was true. That night, I slept with him as I always did. I couldn't let on what I'd learned. I had to be careful, because I had no idea what he would do if I confronted him. So until I decided what to believe and what to do, I pretended that everything was normal. It was an incredibly difficult acting job.

≈

AROUND THIS TIME, I met a man who turned out to be very instrumental in helping me realize that I deserved better than Tom. He was someone I came to lean on as I tried to figure out what to do. I can't use his real name, because he's an extremely private man. So I'll call him Steven.

I met Steven in late 1988, when I was driving home from San Diego after visiting my father, who was in the hospital. He'd gone in to have his heart checked and they found a spot on his lung, which turned out to be cancer.

I was driving in pretty heavy traffic. I looked over to the next car and saw an attractive man staring back at me. We continued driving, and we kind of played cat and mouse with each other. At one point, when we were stopped in traffic, he passed his phone number over to me. I didn't know it then, but at first he didn't know who I was, which was very appealing to me, because that meant he wasn't interested in me just because I was famous.

The next time I went to San Diego to see my father, I took Steven's phone number with me and called him. If Tom had found out, he would have made my life a living hell. But I needed the attention and I needed to talk to someone so desperately that I was willing to risk it.

When I spoke with Steven, I thanked him for making my day. I felt comfortable talking to him, so I shared with him a bit of what had been going on in my life and how unhappy I was. I told him that he'd made me feel attractive, which I hadn't felt in a long time. Of course, here I was saying I didn't feel attractive, yet I was photographed for magazine covers and calendars and plenty of people told me how attractive I was. It always felt like they were talking about somebody else, and I just never allowed myself to believe what seemed to be obvious to everyone but me.

At the end of the conversation, Steven and I agreed to meet in the morning for breakfast. I knew that would be safe, because I was leaving right from there to go home. I needed to make sure there was no opportunity for me to go home with him, because I didn't trust myself. If we'd made plans to get together the night before, I feared I'd end up staying over with him. I wanted to, but given that I was still with Tom, I knew I shouldn't.

During breakfast, I told him I was HIV-positive. Steven was a wonderful listener. He reassured me that I was right to be upset about what I was going through with Tom, that I was better than Tom had made me believe I was.

Steven made me realize that my life wouldn't be over if I left Tom. Here was someone who was attractive and kind, who liked me. He was a relative stranger who didn't have to like me but did. My mind raced ahead, and I thought, If I leave Tom, maybe I can have a relationship with Steven.

Knowing that Steven was out there made it possible for me to face the truth for the first time. I couldn't do it before, because if I looked at the truth, I'd *have* to leave Tom. But I couldn't leave Tom as long as I thought that no one else would want me. But now that someone did, I could look at the truth and look at myself.

Steven gave me something that none of my friends and family or the gold medals ever could. He gave me hope that there could be life after Tom. I didn't know for sure that we'd wind up in a relationship together, but there was the possibility, and that was enough.

The truth was pretty harsh. Tom was using me, and had been for a long time. He had never looked out for my best interests. And more than all of that, he had made me feel unwanted and unloved, which is one of the worst things one person can do to another. I had to face the fact that there was no salvaging the relationship, because there was no relationship to salvage. I had only one choice.

It was shortly after that breakfast with Steven that I decided to tell Tom I wanted us to go our separate ways. The decision came from a combination of things—my having experienced a sense of independence in Florida, my finding out that Tom had been mishandling my finances, his continuing verbal abuse, my discovery that he had lied about his record. Tom himself had finally pushed me to the point where I had to push back. With the love of my friends and family, and knowing I could depend on Steven, I finally felt strong enough to challenge Tom and break free.

Once I decided to break up with Tom, I had to figure out how and where to do it. I couldn't do it at home when we were alone, because I was afraid of what he might do to me—I knew what he was capable of. I couldn't have the conversation in a public place, for obvious reasons. So I decided that I'd do it in a limousine on the way to the airport. I figured that was the safest place to confront Tom, because if anything happened, at least there would be a driver up front if I needed help.

Tom and I were scheduled to go to New York that weekend, where I was booked to do an appearance at a department store or a convention. I don't remember which, because that whole time is such a blur, but I do remember that we were going to fly out on a Saturday, do the appearance on Sunday, and fly home on Tuesday.

My plan was to tell him that I wanted us to go our separate ways and then make a very generous settlement offer. I hoped he'd be reasonable, but I also knew that he might get angry and hit me. I imagined myself showing up for my appearance with a fat lip or a black eye and having to explain how I got it.

Steven was the only one I confided in about my intention. I wanted to be sure I could go through with it before I said anything to anyone else. At first, I wasn't sure I *could* actually do it. Once we were in the limousine, it took me a while to get up my courage to say anything. In general, I'm unsure of myself when I have to talk to anyone, and here I was about to confront Tom, who still frightened me. The truth is, part of me still loved him. So I felt very ambivalent.

Here we were in the back of the limousine, and Tom put in one of his tapes and turned the volume way up. I said, "Tom." I was trying to get his attention, but he didn't hear me. He always teased me that I mumbled, that I didn't articulate. So I did what he always told me to do—I raised my voice above the music. Almost shouting, I said, *"Tom!"* and asked him to turn off the music. He turned it down, and I said, "You might want to put up the partition. I don't think you're going to want the driver to hear this." He put it up.

I already knew what I was going to say, having gone over it a hundred times in my mind, but I was having a very difficult time initiating the conversation. In that one moment, just to say the first few words, I had to overcome every name I'd ever been called by my father, by kids in school, by Dr. Lee, by *myself*.

Tom, impatient as always, turned to me and said, "Do you have something to say, or are you just going to waste my time like you always do?" Somehow I managed to ignore his nastiness, and I blurted out, "Tom, you've done a lot of good things for me, but I don't trust you, you don't trust me, so I think it's best that we split everything and go our separate ways."

I don't know who was more surprised, Tom or me, but I'd done it: I'd confronted him. Tom looked at me and said, "What? You made this decision without me?"—which struck me as funny, because this wasn't exactly something I could have discussed with him. I didn't say anything.

It took a few seconds more before what I had said sank in. Then Tom warned me that I'd signed a contract with him and that he wasn't going to let me off so easily. "If you try to get rid of me," he said, "I'm going to destroy you. I'm going to take you to hell with me." That frightened me, because I felt that he could. He told me he'd call a press conference and tell everyone how it really was: that he had AIDS, that I'd infected him, that now after all these years and his hard work, I was throwing him out on the street. He said that people would see me for the selfish, uncaring slut that I was. "After that press conference, you can kiss your contracts goodbye, because you'll never work again," he said.

There was enough truth in what Tom said to make me wonder for a second if I was doing the right thing, but only for a second. I said, "I've thought about it, and I'll buy your half of the house from you," which was a substantial amount of money. Mind you, I had paid for the house with my own money, but I didn't care. I just wanted to divide everything in half and be done with it. I felt I was buying my freedom.

I must have been naive to think that Tom would consider this a generous offer. The way he saw it, he had made me, and if he couldn't have me and the life we had together, he simply wanted to destroy me. He actually believed that he had made me.

My approach at this point was to be totally calm and rational. I tried to reason with him, repeating that we needed to go our separate ways because we no longer trusted each other. I again offered to split things down the middle, offering to buy his half of the house so he could find someplace else to live and get on with his life.

While I was explaining this to him, it dawned on me that Tom was blackmailing me. He didn't want to hear about any kind of settlement. Tom wanted things to stay just the way they were, with him in complete control of my life and my finances. He was blackmailing me to get me to back down. That made me sick to my stomach, because I had thought he would take the money and run. It had never occurred to me that he would blackmail me. So I said to him, to confirm what I thought he was doing, "You're trying to blackmail me." He just kept repeating, "I made you, I can destroy you." I realized then that this was going to be worse than anything I'd imagined. Money wasn't going to take care of it, because money wasn't the issue. If Tom couldn't have me, then he'd destroy what he saw as his creation.

What I didn't realize then was that Tom was terrified of losing me because without me he had very little identity of his own. As much contempt as he had for me, Tom was probably counting on my taking care of him through his illness. He was going to do whatever he could to hang on, and if he couldn't change my mind, then he wasn't the only one whose life would be destroyed. He was going to take me with him.

When we pulled up to the departures area at the airport, I got out and took my bags out of the trunk. I started getting his bags out, and he said, "No, don't. I'm not going. I have to take care of business here." I had to go because I had an appearance that I couldn't miss. I left his bags in the limousine.

As soon as I got into the terminal, I called Debbie. I was worried, because I didn't know what Tom was going to do. I told her, "Debbie, I did it!" Her greatest concern was that I was okay, and I reassured her

that I was. My biggest concern was what Tom would do with my finances, but Debbie reassured me that the way we had restructured
things, I was protected and there wasn't much Tom could do. She was,
however, very concerned for my safety.

I wasn't on the phone long with Debbie, because I had to catch my
plane. I don't remember anything from that flight except that during
the movie I went into the rest room and sobbed. After I went back to
my seat, I tried to keep my mind occupied with the movie, but I was
overwhelmed by my emotions. It was a combination of amazing relief
that it was finally over and sheer terror because I didn't know what
Tom was going to do. I didn't know what he was capable of. He didn't
have power of attorney any longer, but they knew him at the bank, and
I doubt they even knew he no longer had power of attorney. Debbie
had already reassured me that she would take care of things, yet I
couldn't help but worry. So many conflicting emotions were racing
through me at the same time, from relief to joy to sorrow, that worrying
about the finances was the easiest thing for me to latch on to.

Somehow I got to the hotel—I don't remember how. I don't remember which hotel I stayed at. I was completely exhausted by the
time I got to my room, but I couldn't sleep. I called Debbie again, and
then I called Megan to tell her what had happened.

I did my appearance the next day, totally numb. I don't remember
anything about it, but people who were there told me later that I
seemed upbeat and very friendly. I'd learned a long time ago how to put
on a happy face no matter what was going on, to do what I was supposed to do and to say the right things.

Usually at appearances I had little dialogues with myself. Someone
would say, "You went through so much at the '88 Olympics, hitting
your head and coming back and winning the gold medal," and I'd nod
and think to myself, Oh, if you only knew the half of it. Or when
women would say, "Oh, I have a daughter I want you to meet," I'd
think, I don't think you *really* want me to marry your daughter. Sometimes I'd actually say what I was thinking. Like one time when someone asked who the woman in my life was and I said, "Maile." "Oh,
that's an interesting name. Where does it come from?" I explained that

it was Hawaiian, but I never mentioned that Maile was covered from head to toe with black hair, walked on all fours, and had pointy ears.

That day at my appearance I was on autopilot, and when people asked me how I was doing, I'd say I was fine and tell them about my acting classes. The whole time I was thinking, Oh, everything's okay other than the fact my lover just threatened my life and he's trying to take everything away from me.

As soon as I was done, I headed for the airport and took the first flight home. Debbie met me at the airport and brought me back to the house she shared with her sister. We talked a lot that day, and that was when I told her about Tom raping me.

Tom was expecting me back on Tuesday and this was Sunday, so I had a couple of days to pull myself together and to plan out a strategy with Debbie. At that point I was more excited than scared. Telling Tom that I wanted to break up was one of the most difficult things I'd done in my life, a lot more difficult than winning four gold medals. Diving was easy by comparison. It was physical. Breaking up with Tom, telling him what I wanted, meant that I had to verbalize what I was feeling. I had to stand up to somebody I felt inferior to.

I called Tom from Debbie's house, pretending I was in New York. Debbie listened to the conversation on another line. I wanted to find out his thoughts on what we'd discussed. Was he going to leave? Would he agree to what I'd offered him? He was furious, and he threatened me. He told me again that he was going to take me to hell with him, that he would go public with everything and destroy me, that I could kiss my acting career goodbye. He said he'd hold a press conference and tell it the way it *really* is, the way that I *really* am. He was going to tell the "true" story, that he was being thrown out on the street with full-blown AIDS. And he was going to blame me for giving him AIDS, putting me on the defensive, trying to dispute his story.

I asked Tom what he wanted and he said that he'd already told me what he wanted. I thought that meant he was going to make me live up to my contract, which had another year or two to run. But then he simply repeated all his threats about destroying me, and it was clear that what Tom wanted went beyond the contract: He wanted me back under his control, or he wanted to see me destroyed. This time, though, Debbie heard the whole thing, so she knew I wasn't crazy, that Tom had really said these things.

I told Debbie that I thought one way to deal with Tom's threats was to go public, hold a press conference ourselves, put it all out on the table. The thought that kept running through my head was, The truth shall set you free. My thinking was that if I took the upper hand and was aggressive and held a press conference, it would be out there and he would have nothing to blackmail me with. I would be taking control of my life, and I wouldn't have to worry about being on the defensive. With the truth out there, people could draw their own conclusions. They might have faulted me for getting involved with Tom and staying with him for as long as I did, but they couldn't fault me for telling the truth and getting out of an abusive relationship or trying to get on with my life.

Debbie thought that, in this case, going public with the truth was a bad idea. There was no way of knowing how the public would react, and she didn't want to see me get hurt. She thought the best tactic was to reach a settlement out of court.

Deep down I wanted to come clean with my whole situation, but I had no support among my small circle of friends and family for doing that. I think the overriding concern for everyone was that it would be impossible for me to make any kind of living once this was all out on the table, that I would be sabotaging my own future. I don't think their concern was unreasonable or unwarranted at the time. For one thing, most of my contracts have a morals clause, so any of the companies I already worked for would have had a pretty easy time getting out of its contract. If I couldn't make a living doing appearances, exhibitions, and endorsements, what would I do?

Even if I'd had support, I doubt I would have followed through with my thought to go public. The truth is, I didn't want to close the door on my acting career, and I really wasn't ready to deal with going public about being gay and HIV-positive. Part of me wanted to, but I was afraid of the consequences and I just didn't have enough confidence. So for the time being, going public wasn't an option. Looking back, it was the right thing to do. I needed a lot more time to get comfortable with being gay and having HIV. Everyone moves at his or her own pace, and I wasn't rushing anywhere.

The day after I talked to Tom by phone, I went back to my house with Debbie, her sister, and a colleague of Debbie's to get some clothes and some of my other things. We'd talked about bringing the police with us for protection, but we were concerned that the neighbors would notice and that people would start asking questions. We figured the best thing to do was surprise Tom, and with other people along with us, he wasn't likely to do anything.

I was terrified as we pulled up to the house. It wasn't as if I was afraid of what he might say. I knew he wasn't rational. And I was with a group of people, so it was safe. But I was afraid. I knew he was going to be angry, so I guess that's what I was afraid of, his anger. I guess that's what I've been afraid of all my life: anger.

Before we got to the door, Sherrie, a major fan of mine from Kentucky, came out of the house. I knew he wouldn't dare do anything with her there, but I had no idea what she was doing there. I found out later that she had been doing secretarial work for Tom. She was upset with me and said that she was disappointed in me, that all she wanted was a thank you for all the work she'd done. I had no idea that she'd been doing work for me.

Tom always told me that he handled all the mail. I thought he did everything, so how could I have known to thank her? I think Tom didn't even pay Sherrie. He just used her. He must have told her, "We need some help here, and Greg would really appreciate it if you did this."

When Tom came out of the house, he said he was going to call the police. I told him that this was my house too and that these people were my guests. In fact, it was my house period, but that didn't even occur to me. My voice was shaking as I talked. I was terrified, and I was trembling. Tom let us go in. As we started packing some of my things, Tom hovered over us and took Polaroid pictures to make sure that we didn't take any of his stuff. It reminded me of how Kevin had made sure I didn't take his painting.

I took mostly clothes, and since Tom couldn't fit into my clothes, there was nothing to fight over. I also took my Olympic medals and a number of my awards. I was afraid he'd destroy them if I didn't take them. It's not as if he could object to my taking the awards. He could try to claim that without him I would never have earned the money I did, but he could never claim he won my Olympic medals for me. They were mine. I didn't care about anything else. I just wanted to get out of there.

As we drove down the hill to the Pacific Coast Highway, I kept thinking to myself, I did it. I really did it. I don't think anyone was more surprised than I was.

25

SETTLEMENT

LOOKING BACK, I realize that this wasn't the first time I had fled the home I shared with a man I loved. It was the third time. But I had no interest in looking back and even less interest in trying to figure out how I got myself into those situations.

The day I went to the house to get some of my things, I figured it wouldn't be long before Tom and I came to some sort of settlement and I got the house back. I figured wrong. Tom wasn't going anywhere fast, and he wasn't in a negotiating mood. The one time I tried talking to him, he told me that he had a gun and that if I ever showed up at the house again he'd "blow my fucking head off." That's when Debbie decided it was time to file for a restraining order, which we did on March 28, 1989. In my statement to the Los Angeles court, I wrote that I feared for my life, and I asked the judge to bar my fired "business manager" from having any contact with me. I went on to state, "After being held hostage for over four months since my retirement from diving and my return home from the 1988 Seoul Olympics, I felt that I could no longer tolerate the abuse and threats . . . I believe that [Tom] is unstable and capable of violent acts of aggression. I sincerely believe that he intends to harm me."

By then, Tom had his own attorney and, in a sworn statement, said that he was willing not to threaten or harass me because he had never done so. He stated, "I have never threatened his personal safety in any way." The judge ordered Tom to stay away from me.

Despite the restraining order, Debbie was very concerned about my safety, and she advised me to take a different route every time I drove back to her place, which was where I'd been staying. She also told me not to keep a regular schedule. It was very frightening.

Once it looked like I wasn't going home anytime soon, I decided I couldn't sit around waiting for the lawyers to work out a settlement. I had to get on with my life. That meant finding a new place to live, getting started with acting classes again, and getting a dog. The first thing I did was get a dog.

As soon as I broke up with Tom, I started looking for ads in the newspaper for Great Dane puppies. By this point, Maile, the Great Dane Kevin had given me for my birthday, was long gone. Tom had convinced me several years earlier to give her away. I was out of town so much that he thought she'd be better off living with a family that could give her the attention she needed. I was heartbroken, but I gave in, and a family in Las Vegas adopted her.

Now that I was on my own, I could do whatever I wanted. Well, not quite, because I was staying with Debbie. There was no way she was going to let me keep a puppy in her house, and I didn't even ask. But while I was looking for a new place to live, I could at least look at puppies.

I found an ad in the paper for Boston and Harlequin Great Danes, so I went and met the woman who had placed the ad. I fell in love with the mother of the puppies, Dolly. She reminded me so much of Maile, the way she pressed her head into my stomach. She had a great personality, and I thought that if her puppies had half the personality she did, I'd be very happy.

There were two puppies left. The smaller of the two was getting beat up a lot by his bigger brother. I felt bad for him and I identified with him. I knew he was the one I wanted, and I later named him Freeway. Freeway had the kind of markings that meant I could show him in conformation, which is basically a beauty contest for dogs where they're judged for how closely they match the standards for the breed set by the American Kennel Club. I thought that might be something fun we could do together down the line.

I arranged with the breeder to keep Freeway until I moved into a new house. She said that was fine, but I had to come visit, which I did. That's how I came up with his name. I knew I'd be spending a lot of time driving back and forth on the 405 freeway to see him. I would go by and pick Freeway up, and we'd go for a drive and I took him for walks. A couple of times I took him to Debbie's house, but I never told her. We had a great time together and really bonded.

Freeway gave me added incentive to find a new place, and I quickly settled on a small house in Venice, not far from where Debbie lived. Being nearby made me feel safe and secure. The house needed some work, but not a lot. Steven came up from San Diego to Venice to do some of the work. Not surprisingly, we became boyfriends.

I probably should have stopped at one dog, but not long after I moved into the house in Venice, I got a second Great Dane, Leilani. I'd been feeling really down, and I was just looking through the newspaper at ads for dog litters. I came across an ad for a litter of Harlequins and Bostons in Riverside. So three and a half hours later, I brought home Leilani. She's a lovable and very strong dog. Before I was done collecting dogs, I had five Great Danes and a corgi.

Even though I wanted to get on with my life, I didn't really know where I was going. When I was diving, there was always a rhythm to my life. My training and competition schedule gave me structure, and diving gave me goals. I also had the satisfaction of winning year after year and performing in front of the crowds.

Now I had acting, but it wasn't nearly the same thing. There wasn't the same sort of intensive training, although I did go to classes. No one was exactly knocking down my door offering me roles. I could count on one hand the number of acting jobs I had in the years immediately following the Olympics. I wouldn't say I was lost, but I probably had too much time on my hands and not enough to distract me from my moods, which were getting pretty bad again.

The good thing about having free time was that I got to spend some of it with my father. That may sound strange given our bad relationship, but following his cancer diagnosis in early 1989, things began to change, and we grew a lot closer. My father had been pretty much on his own since the divorce. Now that he was sick, he needed me.

During one of my father's hospital stays, when he was undergoing a series of radiation and chemotherapy treatments, I told him that I was HIV-positive. Part of the reason I told him was practical. He was going to start doing my taxes again, and he would have been able to tell from my medical expenses that I was sick. But it was also something I wanted to share with him—in some ways we were in the same boat. It wasn't clear how much time either of us had, so I thought it was better to tell him sooner rather than later.

My dad and I had never even talked about the fact that I was gay, let alone HIV-positive, but I assumed my mom had talked to him about it when I broke up with Kevin, as I'd asked her to do. So I started by saying, "Well, Mom had that conversation with you about my sexuality when I broke up with Kevin. . . ." And he said, "No, she didn't." I was stunned, but Dad said he'd figured it out for himself a long time ago, after I first started living with Tom. He was upset about it back then, but by this time in his life, my father didn't get really upset about much. He seemed calm about the whole gay issue. Given that he was fighting for his life, the fact I was gay must have seemed minor by comparison.

We talked a little about the gay issue, and then I broke the news that I was HIV-positive. His first reaction was to get angry with Tom, because he blamed Tom for giving it to me. He didn't know much about HIV and didn't realize that I could have been infected even before Tom. But even if he knew, it was just easier for him to be angry at Tom than to think about what the future held for me.

At this point, I brought my dad up to speed on what was going on with Tom. He knew we'd broken up, and now I told him the details and explained that Tom was going to sue me. He said, "Let me contact some of my fisherman friends and they'll take care of him." It was a nice thought, but I told him not to. For the first time in my memory my father was trying to be protective of me, and I appreciated that.

The negotiations with Tom's attorneys went on for months. Neither side really wanted to have this wind up in court, so the goal was to reach some kind of settlement. I'm sure my lawyers thought I was a terrible client, because I wasn't great at returning phone calls or reviewing the papers they sent me. The relationship was over, and I didn't want to think about it. By the summer of 1989, I didn't have a choice, because the lawyers were working out the final details of the settlement, and this time I was determined to know what kind of deal I was getting myself into.

Basically, what I agreed to do was take care of Tom for the rest of his life, whether that was a year, five years, or longer. That included my buying a place of his choosing for him to live in, with a limit on how much the property would cost, and the house would remain in my name. Tom was given a specific amount of time to find a place, because we were concerned that if no limit was given, he'd try to stay in the Malibu house forever. I also had to give Tom a lump-sum cash settlement and a generous monthly stipend.

As part of the agreement, I would continue paying for Tom's life insurance. Upon his death, I was to be the beneficiary of one of his two policies. Half of the other was to go to his niece and nephew, which I was happy to agree to, because I knew how much it meant to Tom to leave them something.

I felt awkward about being the beneficiary of Tom's life insurance, because it was upsetting to think that I would benefit from Tom's passing. But it was the right thing to do financially: The insurance money was meant to reimburse me for the cost of supporting Tom after our breakup and to make up for some of the personal and financial hell he'd put me through. The money would also provide extra financial padding for me when I got sick and couldn't work again. That was a major concern of my attorneys. In coming up with a settlement, they wanted to make sure that I could manage financially when my own health failed.

The final meeting was very businesslike and cordial. We were all resigned to it by this point, so there was nothing to be gained from being difficult. I'm also sure that Tom's attorneys had advised him to be polite, at least until we got all the papers signed.

With the settlement signed, the only thing left to do was go through the contents of the house. That was cordial, too, except that we didn't always agree on how we should divide things up. Tom tried to claim half ownership of everything. His belief was that we had a common-law marriage and we should split everything fifty-fifty, including things that I'd paid for, gifts that had been given specifically to me, and things I'd owned before we met. For example, my mother had given me a gold coin that had been given to her by her father. It was a family heirloom, but Tom claimed that he owned half of it. There were posters of me. He wanted half of those. I had a stack of T-shirts that I designed in Korea. He wanted half of those. He wanted a piece of everything.

I really don't think it was the money at this point that motivated Tom. He was mad at me, and the only way he could get back at me was to fight over property. He thought he could hurt me, but most of the things didn't mean very much to me. I just wanted to get it over with, and I was very willing to compromise.

A few months after we signed the settlement, Tom moved into the new place I'd bought for him. He'd picked out a condo in Dana Point, around two hours south of my house in Malibu. As soon as he was out of the Malibu house, I drove up to see what kind of condition he'd left it in. It was strange walking into the house. Other than a lot of dust and some new stains on the carpeting, everything looked okay. But it felt so empty. It wasn't the blank spaces where Tom's furniture had been that made it feel that way—it just felt like a sad and empty place. Standing in the middle of the living room, I felt terrible that this was what had become of my relationship with Tom. I also felt a twinge of guilt for forcing him to move out. Tom was sick. How could I have forced him out of his home?

I went downstairs and walked, through the bedroom, out to the pool. I walked around the deck, and something wasn't right. At first I couldn't figure it out, and then I realized something was missing. On the steps down into the pool there had been a ceramic tile that read "Especially designed for Greg Louganis by California Pools and Spas." It had the company logo on it, and it had been put in by the people who built the pool. The tile was gone. Tom had chipped it out. And then I glanced up and noticed there was toilet paper in the pool, and something in the water. Tom had defecated in the pool.

≈

NOT LONG AFTER I moved back into the house, Tom asked to come by with his sister to pick up a few large plants that he'd left behind. I was terrified of seeing him, but Steven was at the house doing some remodeling work, so at least I wouldn't have to face Tom alone.

He didn't say what time he was coming by, so of course the moment I made a quick run to the grocery, he drove up. When I pulled into the driveway and saw his truck, my heart started racing. It wasn't even a truck I recognized, but I knew it had to be Tom's. When I got down the hill, I saw Tom and his sister loading his plants into the truck. I drove right past them and pulled up in front of the house.

I walked into the house and asked Steven what had happened. He told me that Tom had pushed his way in, demanding to be allowed inside. Steven tried to keep him from getting in, but Tom just pushed him aside. Steven thought it best to let him get his plants and go. I know how Tom bullied people, so I imagined that he'd been really awful to Steven.

I was very angry and went right to Tom and said, "I need to talk to you." He asked me what I wanted, and I said, "This is my house. Don't go barging in yelling at people. If you need something, talk to them and treat them with respect." I sounded pretty confident, but my heart was pounding outside my chest. Tom still scared me, even though he looked awful.

I said what I had to and went back into the house with Steven, who had followed me out. As soon as we were inside, I sank to the floor and wept. Mostly, I cried because it hurt me to see Tom that way. After all

I'd been through with him, I still cared about Tom and he was clearly sick. He'd lost a lot of weight and was gaunt. It also looked like he'd been having some kind of infusion. I could tell from the Band-Aid on his arm and the black-and-blue marks.

What was especially upsetting about seeing Tom was that I could see myself in him. Tom was clearly dying, and my turn was next. I was crying for what had happened to us, for everything that went so wrong.

I never saw Tom again after that, but I got notes from him periodically. Most of them were just cards with one of his nasty pet names for me written on it. One time he sent a pack of cigarettes, knowing full well how hard it was for me to stay away from them. The last note I got from him was over a payment he hadn't received on time. It was a sort of "Dear Moron" card where he took a slap at me for writing in my own zip code on the address instead of his, which was why the payment got there late. He told me that I needed to get my act together.

My knee-jerk reaction when I read that note was to feel bad, as if I'd done something stupid again. But then I realized that I wasn't so stupid. I'd left him, hadn't I? It was probably the smartest thing I'd ever done.

26

FORGIVING

BECOMING FRIENDS WITH my father wasn't something that happened overnight, and it took a lot of work on my part. I really had to push myself on him. I would hug and kiss him when we said hello or goodbye, which is something we never did before. He was a little reserved at first, but he came around. After a while, he'd occasionally come up to me and give *me* a big hug and a kiss. I'd pull away thinking, Is this my father?

It wasn't just that I pushed the relationship. The fact that we were both at similar points in our lives, facing our mortality, not really knowing how much longer we had to live, gave us some very powerful common ground. In the past, diving was the one thing we could talk about. There wasn't much to say about diving anymore, but now we could talk about his cancer and my HIV. We became sort of like two old men sitting on a park bench talking about their aches and pains, but a lot more serious.

Because we knew that our time was limited, the hours we shared seemed much more precious. We talked on the phone at least twice a week, and if he was going in for chemotherapy or some other kind of treatment, we talked more often than that. I went down to see him, especially when he was in the hospital, and on occasion he would come up to Malibu and stay at the house with Steven and me, which was great. He'd hang out at the house and he'd go to Oxnard to visit his sisters. We'd talk about the dogs—he was very impressed with my dogs—we talked about what was going on with U.S. Diving, and he'd share with me what was going on at the National Boat Owners Association, which he was involved with.

Throughout 1990 he got progressively worse, and by Easter he was talking about how it was time to start getting his ducks in a row. One of the things he told me was that he was setting aside $20,000 to go specifically toward my medical expenses, which he knew I'd been paying out of pocket. He said, "I've put a Keogh-IRA in your name. I know how much money you have going out for your medications, and this is the least I can do." My father was always a good provider; that was the one way he felt comfortable being there for me. I was moved by his concern and his desire to take care of me.

Dad managed to keep a pretty good attitude through the summer, but by the fall, all the doctor visits and the chemotherapy were beginning to wear him down. He got very negative about the whole thing. I tried to get him to see how important the treatments were, to have a more positive attitude and to get more involved in decisions about his care. But my father wasn't interested. He left it all up to the doctors, which was frustrating for me, because I was much more active in my treatment. To get through the Olympics, I had had to be. There was no way I could passively let the doctors make all the decisions for me. I had to be aware of the impact each of the drugs had on me, and we adjusted my medications so they didn't hurt my performance. Even after the Olympics, I stayed involved with my treatment.

Studies show that patients who are involved with their treatment and things like support groups live longer and with a better quality of life. But my father didn't really care. After he came back from seeing his doctors, I'd ask him, "What did they say? What do they want to do? What are your options?" My questions only upset him and made him even more anxious when he realized how much he hadn't listened to what they'd said. I wanted to go with him to the doctor so that there would be two sets of ears listening, but he didn't want me to interfere. As he got weaker, our roles began to reverse and I became the parent. It was an odd feeling for both of us. At first he resisted, but over time, he gave in and just accepted that he would have to let me care for him.

I think part of why my father didn't take a greater interest in his treatment was that he felt he'd already lived his life. He'd reared his kids and achieved a certain amount of financial success. It wasn't like my situation, where I was facing HIV before I was even thirty. He was ready to toss in the towel, but I was just starting to fight.

As his cancer spread, it started affecting his memory, and occasionally he'd get confused. One time, my cousin Paul called me, very upset. He said, "Where the hell are you? Why aren't you down here? You told your father you were coming down to see him." I had just gotten back from a trip, which my father knew about, but he was confused.

As Dad's condition got worse, we had a conversation about how if things got really bad, I wanted him to move up to Malibu to stay with me. He would be closer to his sisters and to his nephews, and Steven and I could look after him. My father wasn't enthusiastic about that idea. He didn't want to be a burden. My sister told me that Dad told her he didn't want to move in because I was living with a man, but he never said that to me. I'd like to think my sister misunderstood him.

By November he was doing pretty badly and he had to go into the hospital again. It turned out that he had something seriously wrong with his intestines and he had to have a colostomy. Recovering from the surgery wasn't the worst of it. Before he went in, he'd already been having trouble with his leg, and they did an X ray of his left femur. The cancer had spread to his bones and the femur was very thin. He had radiation treatments, but he wasn't able to put any weight on the leg because they were afraid the bone would fracture, which meant he had to be in bed most of the time.

In the middle of all of this, I got a call from one of Tom's friends saying that Tom wasn't doing well and that it looked bad. I decided to send him flowers, and in the note I wrote, "I forgive you. Love, Greg." By that time I'd gotten over the anger and rage I felt for Tom. I'd found a sense of peace and I wished that for him. I could have been extremely angry and bitter, but I wasn't. Some of what Tom did to me was evil, but that didn't mean he was an evil person. It was just unfortunate that I was the recipient of Tom's anger and evil behavior.

I heard from friends that Tom was touched by the gesture. He died a few days later. I debated whether or not to go to Tom's memorial service. Would it be a slap in the face to him if I went? Would it be a slap in the face if I didn't go? Finally, I decided not to go. I didn't feel that it was appropriate.

When I told my dad that Tom had died, he said that he deserved it. I told him that nobody deserved that. Tom did some terrible things, but that didn't mean he deserved to die.

Soon after Tom died, my father was transferred to a convalescent home, where he was able to get the round-the-clock care that he needed. He was really sick, and there was no way he could take care of himself at home. The doctors were saying that he would probably die there, but I wanted to bring him up to Malibu. Between his sisters and nephews and Steven and me, there were plenty of people to look after him.

My father didn't like that idea. He decided that he wanted to go to my condo in Dana Point, which was empty now that Tom was gone. Dana Point is north of San Diego, which meant he would be a little closer to Oxnard, where his sisters lived. So his friends and family from both places could see him. It was especially important to him that he be near his grandchildren—Despina was married with three kids by this time—and they were near San Diego.

It turned out to be very complicated to get my father out of the home, not because they wouldn't let him go, but because there were all kinds of family disagreements over what to do with him. There were battles over everything, from whether or not he was going to be cremated to the specifics of his will. All I cared about was getting him out of the home and to a place where he could comfortably spend the last days of his life.

The convalescent home was not at all comfortable. The first room they had him in was for three people. One man was on a respirator. The other had emphysema and was hacking up a storm. It was awful. I went down there and got him moved—one of those times that my celebrity status came in handy. I don't like using my celebrity, but this was for my father and it worked. I brought along pictures and autographed them for the nurses and spent time talking to the staff. I got my father moved to a double room. He wasn't there very long before the guy next to him went into cardiac arrest. As they were trying to resuscitate him, my father pulled back the curtain and said to the nurse, "If there's anything I can do, let me know." He'd become a very different person from the man I knew as a child.

The double room was better, but it was still a nightmare. So when Dad suggested going to Dana Point, I was all for it. My sister consulted with a couple of doctors and one suggested that it was fine to move him even though he was very ill, but the second doctor said that my father would not survive the trip up to Dana Point. My sister went to my dad's sisters in tears, telling them that he wanted to go to Dana Point but that it was going to kill him. They came rushing down to San Diego along with my cousins. None of them wanted to go along with what my dad wanted and suggested moving him to a private room.

I was very frustrated and told all of them, "Look, if he's making his last request to go to Dana Point, you have to honor that. He's told us that he's thought about it and he's fully aware of the possible consequences. If he wants to take that risk, then we have to let him." If he died in the process of getting there, at least we would know that we tried to honor his last wish.

I was so upset at this point that I told them that I was going home and they could do what they wanted. The family tension was too much for me to handle. I said goodbye to my dad, but I didn't tell him about the battle that had been raging just outside his door. I didn't think it was fair to get him mixed up in it given how sick he was.

The next day, my dad called me up at home and he was crying. He wanted to know what was going on and pleaded, "Why aren't we at Dana Point?" I had no choice but to tell him that the family didn't want him going to Dana Point, that they were afraid he'd die getting there. I also told him that I had decided to remove myself from the whole thing because I was afraid of a lawsuit from my relatives if anything went wrong, although no one ever made any such threat. He said, "How do we get to Dana Point?" I told him that getting there wasn't the problem, that the first thing he had to do was call his sisters and tell them what he wanted.

A few hours later, I was getting frantic phone calls from his sisters and my cousins. They were yelling at me, "This is your idea, what are you trying to pull?" I explained that Dad had called me, that I wasn't going to lie to him and tell him that the doctor said he couldn't go. The doctor I talked to said he could go to Dana Point if he wanted to.

What finally convinced them was my father. He insisted that he wanted to go. I got on the phone and found out how to rent a hospital bed, how to get all the things we needed to take care of Dad at the house. The next day, Steven and I went to the house in Dana Point, cleaned it up, and started getting everything set up for him.

By Friday we'd made all of the arrangements to have him moved. Dad had already taken care of getting a twenty-four-hour-a-day nurse. He hired a wonderful woman from the Philippines named Esther. She spoke with a beautiful British accent, and sometimes it was hard to understand everything she said. But she was very sweet, and she and my dad had fun teasing each other. He smiled a lot when she was around.

On Friday, Esther and I took Dad by ambulance up to Dana Point. When we got to the house and got Dad settled in, we had a big celebration. My Aunt Rose, who was really a family friend, and my dad's sisters, Aunt Mary and Aunt Virginia, were there along with my Uncle Press. My cousins Peter and Paul were there. Aunt Rose danced around my father's bed. We were all very happy that he'd gotten there safely, and he seemed so happy to be there.

Esther had plenty to do once everybody left. Dad could feed himself, but that was about it. And it didn't always stay down, so there was lots of cleaning up to do. He couldn't get from the bed to a chair, so I would lift him out of bed. It was so odd, because I remembered him being so strong and now here I was carrying him. I also gave him back rubs, which he needed for his circulation.

Esther was at the house full-time, so between the two of us, we managed to take care of my dad around the clock. At first, Esther slept in a chair next to Dad's bed, but I didn't think that was fair. She worked all day and needed to get some rest. We rearranged things, and after that, Esther stayed with Dad until two or three o'clock in the morning and then I would wake her up to go to bed. Then I slept in the chair next to Dad's bed in case he woke up and needed something. All of that was the easy part. Watching his deterioration was hard.

Sometimes I think it was a shame that it took illness—my father's and my own—for us to have a relationship and to make peace with each other. But at least we found some common ground and developed a relationship before he passed away. It was a very special time for us. He needed me and I was able to be there for him, and he was able to accept my help. The way I looked at it, I was just doing for him what I would have wanted him to do for me. If I had gotten sick first, he might not have been able to do the same for me, but that wasn't important. It made me feel good to be there for him, the way I had once promised I would be there for Tom and the way I hope someone will be there for me.

It wasn't until after I got my dad moved into the Dana Point house that I had a chance to think about how sad it was being in the house that Tom had died in. Now this was where my father was going to die. I wondered if I was going to be the next one to die in that house.

Shortly after we got Dad moved to Dana Point, I had to go to Florida. I had a prior commitment to be a part of a five-day study for U.S. Diving, a modeling study where they take you through the diving process and ask you what you're thinking as you go through the dive. I was nervous about leaving my dad for so long, but my friend Margo, who was also a friend of Dad's, volunteered to stay with him and Esther.

That Thursday, I got a call from Margo that Dad had taken a turn for the worse, that he was having hallucinations and not making sense. I called Despina to let her know what was going on and asked her if she could go over to see Dad because I couldn't get there until the next day. It was about an hour's drive from her home in El Cajon. Her response to me was that she might be able to drive up on Sunday. I told her not to bother and hung up. I quickly arranged for a flight home and left the next morning. By the time I got there, they'd figured out it was a reaction to a sleeping pill, and within a couple of days he was pretty much himself again.

After that I was very reluctant to leave him, but he encouraged me to continue with my acting and voice classes. So a few days each week, I left Esther alone with Dad and went to Los Angeles. When I came back to the house, we would talk about what I was working on. He'd look forward to the conversations and seemed really interested in hearing about my day. That was during the Gulf War, and Dad kept the television on all the time. When I got home, he'd tell me all about the latest news. He also liked talking about the stock market.

My own health remained basically stable, although I'd developed resistance to the AZT, and my doctors put me on ddI, another antiviral drug. As a cautionary measure, Debbie Shon arranged for me and my doctors, Kathy and John, to meet with the director of the National Institute of Allergy and Infectious Diseases, Dr. Anthony Fauci, to discuss my case. She explained to me that he had coordinated AIDS research there since the beginning of the epidemic, in the early 1980s. Debbie said that when she first talked to Dr. Fauci about me, he told her, "He's a national treasure and we should help him as much as we can." I was very flattered. Dr. Fauci was careful to explain to Debbie that they could provide no special treatment for me, but he agreed to meet with me and my doctor to review my records.

A short while later, I flew to Washington to meet with Debbie, Kathy, John, and Dr. Fauci. At the time I didn't realize how extraordinary that meeting was—that not many HIV patients got to meet personally with Dr. Fauci. The purpose of the meeting was to make sure we were on the right track. Kathy and John brought my records along. The meeting was very good-natured. At first, we talked about the Olympics and we talked about Dr. Fauci's interest in running. He's a bit of a jock, and he told me about his sports regimen, which was very challenging.

Things got more serious when Dr. Fauci reviewed my records and he and Kathy and John discussed my case. Dr. Fauci agreed that ddI was the best alternative to AZT, and he encouraged me to keep taking my medication and to keep doing whatever I was doing, because I was in relatively good shape. He and my doctors talked a while longer about my treatment, and then the meeting was over.

When I got home, Kathy wanted me to come in to her office to have a gamma globulin infusion. But I didn't want to take even more time away from my father to go to her office, so I convinced her to send me everything I needed so I could do it myself.

In the middle of the night, after both Esther and my father had fallen asleep, I locked myself in the bathroom and set up the whole thing. I hung the bottle containing the fluid from the shower rack, hooked up the plastic tube, and inserted the needle in my arm. I have great veins, but I discovered that it's not easy putting a needle into your own arm. A few minutes later, there was a knock at the bathroom door. Dad had awakened and wanted to be moved—Esther needed my help. I was in a panic. I quickly clamped the tube, pulled the needle out of my arm, put everything in the cabinet under the sink, and went to help Esther. Afterward, I went back into the bathroom and started all over again.

Ironically, I had a nurse in the house who could have helped me with the infusion, but I couldn't ask for her help because I couldn't tell her why I needed the infusion in the first place. That whole experience made me feel very alone, especially since I couldn't tell my father what had happened. I could have, but I didn't want him to worry about me.

≈

ON MY FATHER'S good days, Esther and I got him into a wheelchair and we moved him onto the back porch. He'd sit out there with his Ray Ban sunglasses on, looking like one of the Blues Brothers. One time I rolled him around the neighborhood in his wheelchair. I had Freeway with me, and he stayed right by the wheelchair with Dad.

Every time we stopped, Freeway put his head on my father's arm. Dogs can be so sweet, especially around sick people.

We talked about all kinds of things during those few weeks at the house—our lives, what we'd accomplished, his illness, my illness. He talked about how proud he was of me; he called me his "champ." We really never talked about death much beyond the fact that my father didn't want to live if he was going to be a vegetable or in a lot of pain. We'd already talked a lot in the months before about the quality of life versus the quantity. Dad made it clear that when it came time, he just wanted it to be over. He didn't want any machines or anything like that.

We both talked about how we didn't really fear death as much as we feared being sick. We talked about wanting to die with dignity and how if things got really bad we'd be there for each other. I told him, "If the time comes and I'm not able to care for myself and the quality of life is gone, then if I need assistance, I want you to help me die in peace." Dad wasn't as specific as I was, but he said that he wanted me to put him out of his misery when he got really sick. He said that when the time came, I should do whatever was necessary to allow him to die in peace. I promised I would do that and I know it gave him peace of mind.

My dad's decline was pretty gradual, and toward the end he was on a morphine pump to keep the pain in check. Despite the morphine, he was still thinking clearly up until four or five days before he died. On the Friday before he died, he called Steven and me into his room and started going on about how he had floated up to the ceiling, then pushed off the wall and pushed off the ceiling and landed back in bed. I repeated back to him what he had just said, and he got very alarmed. He said, "Now I've lost it." Then he started muttering about wanting to go to the hospital. I tried to find out from him if he was feeling sick, but he kept saying, "No, they'll give me a shot. They'll put me out of my misery. That's what I want." We calmed him down and assured him that everything was okay, and he drifted off to sleep. He never regained consciousness, and on Sunday, he died.

Shortly after he died, I sold the Dana Point house.

27

REBIRTH

MY FATHER'S DEATH was a huge blow. On top of that loss, I was still dealing with Tom's death. Several college classmates and other friends had died of AIDS as well, including the roommate who had first introduced me to Tom. And Kevin, my lover before Tom, died around the same time Tom did.

Shortly after my father passed away, one of my old friends who was sick came to visit me at the house. Ken and I had dated off and on during and after college, but we hadn't talked in a few years. He called out of the blue one day to tell me that he had AIDS and hadn't been doing very well. From then on, we stayed in touch by phone, and we made a date for him to come visit.

When Ken got out of his car, I could see that he'd lost a lot of weight, but he was still handsome. We sat in the kitchen and talked a lot about my relationship with Tom and how it had ended. He'd been friends with Tom, so when I talked about Tom, he knew what I was saying. We had a lot of laughs about Tom and all of his claims, like his three college degrees from U.C. Irvine and being on the 1980 Olympic rowing team. It was all made up. What could I do but laugh?

I told Ken about my HIV status. I wanted him to know that I really understood what he was going through, that he wasn't alone. It also made me feel better to tell someone I cared about, so I didn't feel so alone. We talked about his treatment and what he'd been through, including the medications he was taking, the bad reactions he'd had. I was very curious, because I knew it was something I would likely have to face. I figured that the more I knew, the less fearful it would be for me. I also thought I'd better ask Ken while he was still around to talk to. He'd been in the hospital several times because of various complications related to AIDS, and I knew from experience that I shouldn't count on seeing him or talking to him again, especially since he talked about being tired of fighting. He also talked about his good days and going to the movies. Unfortunately, his eyesight was failing.

Ken left the next morning around nine o'clock. When I said goodbye to him in the driveway, I thought it might be the last time I would see him. Even if it was, I believed that it would only be a temporary separation anyway. It didn't surprise me when I got a call from Ken's mom shortly after that visit saying that he'd passed away.

With so many people close to me either dead or dying, I couldn't help but feel like it was my turn next. The whole thing was overwhelming, and I got terribly depressed and withdrew into my shell. Looking back, I can see that I started losing the will to live.

AFTER MY FATHER died, I had kept his morphine. There were two kinds: injectable morphine and pills. I had kept it because I thought I might need it to end my life in the event I got really sick, but I didn't save it. I got so depressed that I decided to use the morphine to see if it helped. The morphine did exactly what I needed it to do: It numbed the pain and left me feeling mildly euphoric. It's very embarrassing to admit I did this. It makes me feel very weak. It's also illegal.

For the next few months, I injected the morphine two or three times a week, until I had used it up. Then I took the morphine pills until I used those up. Some days I didn't take any, and on a bad day, when I was feeling depressed or I'd had an argument with Steven, I'd take two. I don't think Steven had any idea what I was doing.

In all, I was on morphine for about a year before the pills ran out. I thought I would have withdrawal problems, but the pills weren't that potent, and I didn't have any bad symptoms. But I missed that mild euphoria that kept me from getting upset about things. On morphine, nothing seemed worth getting upset about. I could still function, but everything seemed okay. Without it, I started feeling overwhelmed again and the depression got really bad.

That summer, I was up in Canada at a dog show and I found another narcotic that helped take the edge off. In Canada, Tylenol with codeine is sold over-the-counter, and I bought a few bottles. I took that pretty regularly, three pills on a bad day, but usually less. I knew it was wrong and that I needed help, but my only goal at that point was to make myself numb.

I was in a real fog from the narcotics during that time. I don't remember doing much other than taking care of the dogs. I'd quit my acting classes. I did an occasional appearance for Speedo, I did some work for the 1992 Winter Olympics, but that was about it. I spent most of my time at the house in Malibu with Steven. Instead of building a life together, Steven and I were hiding out, and I was waiting to die. As if the HIV needed any help, I stopped taking my medications regularly and started smoking again.

Megan tried very hard to keep me informed about the latest developments regarding HIV and how I could stay healthy. She did lots of research, but I didn't pay any attention to the material she sent me and most of it is still sitting on my desk. She talked to me about visualization as a way to enhance my immune system. She talked to me about developing a sense of purpose in my life, but I stopped caring all that much about living. She got very upset with me when I started smoking again. It was frustrating for her to watch me give up.

Toward the end of 1992, what I was waiting for started to happen: I began getting sick. I developed chronic diarrhea. I was tired all the time. I was sleeping a lot. I started dropping weight. I couldn't get motivated to work out, so I began losing muscle tone, which made me even more depressed. The doctor put me on an antidepressant, but it didn't seem to do any good. I really should have been in therapy, but I didn't care enough about living to go to the trouble. I could barely get myself motivated to take care of the dogs, and Steven wound up doing that most of the time.

By Christmas 1992, I began to think that this would be my last Christmas and that my thirty-third birthday, coming up in January, would be my last. So I told Steven that I wanted a big birthday party. He knew why, and I could tell he was sad, but he was also excited because this was something he wanted to do for me. It turned out that he'd already been talking with my mother about giving me a surprise party. When he told me that, I said, "I don't want to be involved with the planning. Just surprise me." I gave Steven my phone book, and he took it from there, although I pretended to forget about it.

The party was to be on January 29, 1993. My mother came in early that day from San Diego, and I went to pick her up at the airport. It was her responsibility to get me out of the house for the day while Steven got everything set up. I figured this would be a good time to tell her that I was HIV-positive. I'd held back telling her in the past, because I didn't want to worry her. But now that I was already having symptoms, I thought it was better to tell her than to wait until I was really ill. I wanted her to hear about it from me before it wound up in the newspaper.

I met my mom at the airport, and our plan was to go shopping for her Christmas present. I'd told her that the next time she visited, we'd go get her a coat. Before we went shopping I took her out to lunch at the Ivy restaurant. Afterward, as we were driving to a store, I told her I was HIV-positive. I didn't tell her that I was already having symptoms, because I didn't want to overwhelm her.

When I told her, I felt pretty certain that the news didn't come as a total shock, because my mother knew that Tom had died of AIDS. I explained to her that I didn't yet have full-blown AIDS. She understood the distinction between being HIV-positive and having AIDS. Then she told me that two years earlier, my sister had told her that I had AIDS. My sister had been doing some secretarial work for me, and she came across some paper that had led her to think I had AIDS.

My mother said that even before my sister told her, she had known for a long time that something was up. She didn't know if what my sister said was true, but whatever it was, she knew I'd tell her when I was ready, because I always did. She told me it put her mind at ease to know what the problem was. Recently, she told me that it broke her heart to know I was HIV-positive and that she thinks about it every day, but that day in the car, she put up a good front.

By the time we finished shopping, I was totally exhausted. It didn't take much to get me tired, so I was really wiped out on the drive home. As we made the turn onto my street, there were cars parked everywhere. I pulled up to the driveway and there was a VALET PARKING sign right in my driveway. I couldn't believe that this was really happening. I was nervous and excited driving down the driveway because I didn't know who was going to be there.

Brutus, one of my dogs, was with us in my van. We all got out of the van and walked up to the front door, and Steven came out and said, "Get in there." But I wasn't rushing. I told him that I had to walk Brutus, that he needed to be fed. I was stalling because I was afraid to go in. But Steven told me to get my butt in the house.

I walked in the door with my mom and everyone yelled, "Surprise! Happy Birthday!" Megan was the first person to come up to me and she gave me a big hug. She'd flown in from Colorado just to be there. She was one of the very few people at the house who knew why I'd wanted this party. I'm sure some of my friends suspected I was HIV-positive, but I don't think they realized that I thought this was my last birthday.

The house was filled with people from all corners of my life: diving friends, acting friends, gay friends, and straight friends. My cousin and doctor, John Christakis, was there. And Kathy Shon was there, too. Ron O'Brien couldn't be there, but Mary Jane came from Florida along with one of my diving friends, Kent Ferguson. Linda Provenzale, my baby-sitter from when I was a kid. Billy Day, a diver I worked out with when I was training with Dr. Lee. People from my acting classes. Grover Dale and Anita Morris, whom I met when we did *Circus of the Stars* together. Friends I had met through dog breeding, like Kathleen Mallery, from Idaho, and Doug and Ann Toomey—Doug is one of the top handlers of Great Danes. Leigh Benson, who was assistant manager at Chess King, the clothing store I'd worked at as a salesperson. Juliet Lambert, who was my Cinderella and who's gone on to Broadway in *Meet Me in St. Louis* and *Passion*. And, of course, Aunt Geri came up from San Diego. My friend Michael Feinstein couldn't make it, but he sent a gift basket filled with all kinds of wonderful things.

I never imagined that all of these people would meet. My life had been so compartmentalized that most of them had never even heard of each other. And here they all were mixed together, thirty-three years of my life under one roof. Remarkably, everybody had a great time, especially me. There were so many loving faces that I didn't know which way to turn.

The whole party was very emotional because, looking around the house, I had such a sense of accomplishment that I'd done so many different things in my life. I thought of my dad and how after he passed away everybody got together but he wasn't there. Now here were all the important people in my life in one place and I was still alive to enjoy it. It was like I got to go to my own memorial, but I was there to see everybody one last time and everybody was happy, not sad.

My family was so funny, especially Aunt Geri. She couldn't believe who was there. She totally flipped over Dawnn Lewis, who used to be on *A Different World* and then moved to *Hangin' with Mr. Cooper*. As soon as Dawnn walked in, Aunt Geri got so excited. "That's Dawnn Lewis," she kept saying. I said, "Yes, I know. We went to school together." She said, "No, you don't understand, that's Dawnn Lewis!" When she finally calmed down, I introduced them.

The birthday cake was beautiful. I had designed it. I wasn't supposed to get involved in the planning of the party, but Steven had asked what kind of cake I wanted and I drew up a design. It was a big rectangular cake, and on top, drawn in icing, was a picture of me with one of my dogs, a drawing of Cinderella's slipper, a splash in blue icing, and written underneath were three 10's and a 9.5, and the words *Where'd he go?* Before I blew out the candles, Rita Coolidge, whom I had met through Joanne Carson, sang "Happy Birthday," and then everyone went back to having a good time.

Besides dancing, there was karaoke, a roving magician, and a woman reading tarot cards downstairs in the workout room. With all of the people and so much going on, I should have been exhausted, but being there with all of them was invigorating.

≈

THE ENERGIZED FEELING I got from the party didn't last. Within a few days I sank back into my usual deep depression, and over the next few months, as my health got worse, so did the depression.

Kathy had me take multiple lab tests to find out why I was losing weight. Everything came back negative, and she suggested that I needed to have a sigmoidoscopy and possibly a colonoscopy. Kathy wanted me to have the tests done in Florida, where John practiced, because in Florida it would be easier to keep the whole thing confidential. But I didn't want to go for any more tests. I didn't care enough to make the effort, and I wasn't all that sick.

A couple of times they put me on a drug called Flagyl for intestinal parasites. It's the same drug that's sometimes prescribed for people who pick up a persistent intestinal bug from drinking the water in countries like Mexico. Flagyl is disgusting. It makes everything taste metallic, so nothing tastes good. Even a glass of water tastes like liquefied tin. It's disgusting on your teeth. It's disgusting going down. It's just disgusting. I lost even more weight at a time when I was supposed to be trying to put weight on.

The one thing you absolutely have to stay away from when you are on Flagyl is alcohol. You can't have anything that has even a hint of alcohol in it, because it can make you vomit. One time, just a couple of days after I stopped taking Flagyl, I was in Florida at dinner with John and his wife, Stephanie. John asked me if I wanted a glass of wine with dinner and I said that I'd better not, because I didn't want to take a chance. Then I went and ordered spaghetti with clam sauce. It didn't occur to me that the sauce had wine in it.

I'd only eaten about half of my dinner before I started sweating profusely and salivating. I was very nauseated. I excused myself from the table, went to the rest room, and had the dry heaves. I splashed some water on my face, took a few deep breaths, and made my way back to the table. That seemed to help, so I sat down and pretended that I was okay. It was one of those situations where you think you can get through it if you just stay focused on keeping your food down.

We got back to John's house and talked for a while before I had to excuse myself. I still wasn't feeling great when I got into bed. As soon as I put my head on the pillow, the room started spinning. I started salivating and sweating. I barely made it to the bathroom. It was awful.

Unfortunately, the Flagyl didn't do any good and the symptoms got much worse. By late spring, I was getting diarrhea four to six times a day. But I still had an appetite, so I wasn't losing that much weight. And I had this incredible craving for milk. I couldn't seem to get enough of it. I didn't think to tell my doctors about that, because it hadn't occurred to me that might be a symptom of something. I also didn't tell them that Megan thought I had systemic candida, which is a yeast infection.

By July, my appetite was gone, I'd dropped twenty pounds, and I'd started vomiting frequently. Around the same time I started developing fevers, which got as high as 104 degrees. Something was definitely going on and I was scared. The fevers started on a Thursday, and we had a wedding reception planned at the house for Saturday.

I talked with John, in Florida, and Kathy, and we decided that I'd fly to Florida and check in to a hospital down there for more tests. I agreed with Kathy that it would be much easier to keep my diagnosis secret in a Florida hospital than it would be in L.A., where privacy is hard to come by. My goal was to hold on through the wedding reception and then leave on Sunday for Florida.

I flew down by myself and stayed briefly with John and his wife before checking in to a hospital in Boca Raton under the name Peter Cicero. I dressed up in humongous baggy pants and a very large T-shirt, hoping that people wouldn't be gawking, "Oh, that's Greg Louganis." The whole effort was a little silly, especially because we didn't go nearly far enough with the disguise. The nurses and the nursing staff knew who I was right away, but they were wonderful and maintained my privacy. The head nurse was very concerned and told me she wanted to know if anybody was out of line and how my treatment was going.

Even though my attitude wasn't very positive when I first checked in, it was pretty clear to me that I wasn't ready to die. It's one thing to think about wanting to die and a whole other thing to be faced with the real possibility. With the attention I was getting from the nurses and the doctors, I began to think there was hope. But I was worried. The diarrhea was really bad, I had a lot of abdominal pain, and the fevers were pretty high. I wasn't delirious, but I wasn't dealing with a full deck, either. I was sweating a lot and getting the chills. First I would throw off the blankets, then I'd pull them back up, then I'd throw them off again.

Right away they hooked me up to an IV, because I was really dehydrated. John had arranged for two different specialists to see me. One was a gastroenterologist. The other was an immunologist. After examining me, they arranged for a colonoscopy. They wanted to have a look around my intestinal tract—apparently, around a lot of it: The tube was about six feet long.

Before they performed the test, they sedated me. I'm terrible under a sedative. I get very happy and romantic. I thought the doctor was kind of cute, so I looked at him goo-goo-eyed, grabbed his hand, and thanked him for being there. I really embarrassed myself.

The test showed that I didn't have a systemic yeast infection, which had been Megan's guess, I had intestinal histoplasmosis, a fungal infection. The doctors prescribed a course of intravenous treatment that was just awful. The medication was toxic, and I reacted badly to it. The infusions had to go in very slowly and took four hours or longer.

The first time they gave me the infusion, I went into shock. My temperature shot up and I was shivering violently and uncontrollably. They had to give me Demerol. This happened the second day, and the third day as well. After that, they figured out how to administer the drug without the bad side effects. They gave me Tylenol a half hour before the infusion, and halfway through the infusion I got a second dose.

This all sounds even more terrifying than it actually was, because the doctors did a good job keeping the pain in check with Percocet. I was in a relatively drugged and dreamy state despite everything.

After a week they discharged me from the hospital, by which time I was basically symptom-free. I was grateful to be out of the hospital. The whole experience had been frightening, both because I'd been sick and because it gave me a sense of what was likely to happen to me at some point in the future. I hope that's the distant future, but HIV isn't all that predictable, so you never know.

Once I got out of the hospital, I stayed with John and his family for another week and went for a few more treatments at his office. Then he gave me instructions to continue getting infusions of the medication on a periodic basis, which I was going to do at my doctor's office in Los Angeles. I was also given a restricted diet designed to keep the infection under control. John also told me to drink lots of Ensure, which is a high-protein and high-calorie drink, to put some weight back on. He also told me to take it easy for a while.

From Florida I went up to New York to see a play that my manager wanted me to audition for. I started to realize that I wasn't going to die right away after all, so I figured it couldn't hurt to start thinking about working again.

28

I FLEW TO New York and went to see *Tony 'n' Tina's Wedding*, an improvisational play in which the audience is part of the show. It wasn't for me.

But while I was in New York, I got to see a lot of other theater. One of the plays I liked the most was *Jeffrey*, a comedy by Paul Rudnick, about a gay man and his struggles finding a boyfriend in the age of AIDS. At the time I saw the show, the New York company was preparing to leave to mount a Los Angeles production. That meant they would be recasting the New York show, so I told my manager that if there was an opportunity to do it, I wanted to try out for the role of Darius. He's a gay chorus boy who dances in *Cats*, the Broadway musical.

There was a lot about Darius that appealed to me: He's an uncomplicated guy who's very wise about life. He has a solid relationship with an older, well-to-do lover whom he's devoted to, and he has AIDS.

Darius gets to deliver what I think is the most important message of the play: "Hate AIDS, not life."

I thought that playing Darius would give me the chance to face my own fears about AIDS and my own mortality. Onstage I would get to experience what it was like to have AIDS and have everyone know about it. In contrast to what I'd been doing hiding out in Malibu, I'd get to see what it was like to live life to its fullest to the very last minute. Five days before Darius dies, he's marching on Fifth Avenue in the annual gay pride parade. I'd always wanted to march in one. Darius wasn't afraid to live, which struck a very deep chord in me, because after my HIV diagnosis and after I stopped diving, I think I did become afraid to live.

My manager wanted me to try out for one of the two leads, but I didn't want to. First of all, I didn't think I was appropriate to play either of those roles. And second, I didn't want to have to carry the show. Darius was the ideal part for me. And it turned out that Darius was exactly the role that the director, Christopher Ashley, wanted me to try out for.

They got me the script well in advance of the audition, and I worked on it and worked on it and worked on it. I flew to New York for the audition and worked with the director. Chris really challenged me. The one thing that I will say for myself is that I've always been coachable. I may not have good instincts initially, but I'm coachable.

It didn't take them long to decide to give me the part. I had about a week and a half before I started, and in between I had to go home for a small role in *Mighty Ducks II*. So I went back to California, and the day after we finished shooting, I was back in New York to start work. I was both excited and nervous, especially because I was still recovering from my stay at the hospital. I'd lost about twenty-five pounds by that point, and I had to go out onstage in my underwear in the opening scene of the show. I drank as many cans of Ensure as I could, which wasn't easy, because I didn't have any appetite. As soon as I got to New York, I started going to the gym to try to build myself back up.

Not everyone thought it was such a great idea for me to do *Jeffrey*. Some of my friends were concerned that I would be so closely linked to a gay character that sponsors and potential sponsors would interpret it as a statement about my own sexuality. After what I'd just been through, I really didn't care how being in *Jeffrey* would affect my marketability. Playing Darius was very important to me, and if that meant losing my contracts or hurting my prospects for future sponsors, I didn't care. Who knew how much of a future I had anyway? All I knew was that this was a role I wanted to play and needed to play now. I'd deal with the future later.

My doctor had the loudest objections, because he was concerned about my health. He advised me against doing the show, and from where I sit now, that seems like very reasonable advice. But John also knew how important work was for me, so he didn't forbid me from doing it. He knew that I'd do what I wanted anyway.

I was pretty scared getting ready to go onstage for the first time as Darius. It wasn't that I was afraid of being onstage performing in front of an audience—that didn't bother me—I was worried that I wouldn't be worthy of the role, that I wouldn't do justice to Paul Rudnick's wonderful lines, that I wouldn't be able to convey Darius's message. It's a very difficult subject—I had to die every night!—and I wasn't confident that I was good enough to pull it off. As it turns out I really didn't need to worry, because the reviews were wonderful.

Playing Darius turned out to be even more therapeutic for me than I thought it would be, in part because Darius's life is in so many ways close to my own. I remember talking with a reporter who asked me if I could relate to the character I was playing. I said, "Yeah, right, a chorus boy with an eighth-grade education." I was sidestepping, because we do have a lot in common. He may have been a chorus boy with an eighth-grade education, but he was gay, he had AIDS, and he was facing the end of his life.

For me, playing Darius was like a dry run of what I thought my life might be like down the line. I got the chance to wear an ACT UP button onstage, and I died every night of the disease that will probably kill me. I got to be publicly gay without being self-conscious. Darius was totally out and proud, not at all afraid of being himself. I got to experience what that was like as Darius, in preparation for doing those things as Greg. That's one of the reasons I fell in love with acting in the first place. You can be anyone you want and do anything you want.

I came to envy Darius as if he were a real person or a friend of mine. I admired his zest for life, which was something I was still struggling with. I know that no one is up all the time, but Darius did a good job of enjoying life and conveying that joy to those around him. All of his down moments were offstage, which was exactly when I had to be up. Offstage I had to put on a happy face for the other cast members, because I didn't want anyone to know what was going on in my head. I had to "play" Greg the character, who is a lot happier than Greg the real person. At the time, I was lucky if I could just stay afloat and not get overwhelmed by my emotions.

In some ways, I can't quite believe that I put myself in the position of playing a role in a show that was dealing with what I was living with every day. Twice during the time I was in *Jeffrey*, I had to get infusions to keep my fungal infection under control. One time I did it in Florida, and the next time in California. I couldn't say anything to anyone about what I was going through. Sometimes I wanted to scream.

One of the great benefits of doing *Jeffrey* was the opportunity to work with a group of gay men who were comfortable with their sexuality and felt good about themselves. The men in *Jeffrey* became my role models. They didn't have advisers telling them what to say or what not to say. They just lived life on their own terms, which impressed me.

With the cast, I never made any secret of the fact I was gay. I didn't formally come out and say I was gay, but when we talked, I didn't hide the truth about my life. Unfortunately, I didn't feel I could be open about my HIV status. The cast was wonderfully supportive of me, onstage and off, but I wanted to be treated like any other actor, which was already difficult given what I'd done as an Olympic athlete. If they knew my status, I think it would have been even more difficult for them to treat me like everyone else. Also, I wasn't ready to go public about being HIV-positive, so I was still being very careful about whom I told. That part was frustrating. My whole life I couldn't fit in, because I was stupid, because I had dark skin, because I was adopted, because I was gay, and now because I was HIV-positive—even though I was in the midst of a group of proud, openly gay men in a play about AIDS.

Hiding my HIV status forced me to keep my distance from everybody in the cast. Pretending that everything was okay was very exhausting, so a lot of the time, rather than hang out with the rest of the cast in the green room, I stayed in my dressing room under the stage, which I shared with one other actor. The excuse I used was that I wanted to smoke, and the only place where I could smoke was in my dressing room. Sometimes, especially on the weekends, when we had matinees, the cast went out for dinner between performances. I usually made up some excuse and went off by myself, afraid that if I spent time with them, they'd see through my facade.

When it came to the press, there was never any question about what I would and would not talk about. I'd already taken a huge step just by being in *Jeffrey* and playing a gay character who had AIDS. Talking to the press about being gay was a whole other level of being public about my sexual orientation that I wasn't ready for. Talking about my HIV status was absolutely out of the question.

You would think that at this stage of my life, playing a gay character in a show about gay dating, I could handle talking publicly about being gay. But I couldn't. I told myself that it was simply nobody's business, that my personal life was my personal life. The truth is, I was still terrified that if people knew I was gay that they'd think badly of me. On top of that, after so many years of being in the closet, I'd gotten used to it. I really didn't know how to live any other way. From spending time with the actors in *Jeffrey*, I could see there was another way to live, but I'd had a very isolated life, and it was still all new to me.

There were a few occasions while I was in New York for *Jeffrey* when I found myself stunned by how casually people talked about and dealt with homosexuality. The first time, I was at dinner with a former diving teammate and his mother and sister. They came to see me in *Jeffrey*, and we went out after the show. At some point in the conversation, I asked my friend what he was up to, and I don't know how we got onto the subject, but he said something about his lover. Then he caught himself and said ex-lover. I was startled. I looked at his mom and I looked at him, and I felt like saying, "Should we really be discussing this in front of your mother?" But his mother looked just fine, so apparently his family knew.

I was kind of embarrassed. For one thing, even though I had assumed my friend was gay from when we trained together, it wasn't something we'd ever talked about. Also, I wasn't accustomed to talking that way in front of anyone's mother. I was so uncomfortable with the whole subject that I never used the word *lover* in front of my mom. It wasn't the kind of thing I would have talked about with people I didn't know very well, and he and I didn't know each other that well. But his mother seemed perfectly comfortable, and before we said good night, she told me to give her a call anytime I needed a good home-cooked meal. I thought it was incredible how they all treated being gay as the most normal thing in the world. It was a revelation to me.

The second time that happened, I was at lunch with another friend and his mother. He and I had talked about being gay, but I'd never met his mother before. My friend had to make a phone call and left me alone with his mom for a few minutes. She asked me about my dogs. I told her a little about them, and then she asked who was taking care of them. I told her that I had a friend taking care of the dogs, and she said, "Oh, is that your lover?" I almost fell off my chair. My friend had told me that his mother was very comfortable with gay people, but I wasn't used to hearing that kind of question from someone's mother. When I got over the shock, I said yes, that the man taking care of my dogs was my lover. Then she wanted to know how long we'd been together. This was going to take some getting used to.

It turned out that the reporters also took some getting used to, because they weren't at all shy asking me about my personal life. When I first started out in diving, I would hedge when reporters asked about girlfriends, and I'd say that I was too busy or too shy, or I'd just let them think what they liked. Over time, as reporters realized I was gay and discovered that I never answered personal questions, they generally stopped asking. In a way, they protected me by not stating the obvious, like the fact that Tom was not only my manager but my lover, too. I was grateful to the press for protecting me during those years when I wasn't yet ready to talk about it.

But a lot had changed in recent years, and even sportswriters were no longer reluctant to ask pointed questions about homosexuality or to write about it. And, after all, I *was* playing a gay character in a play about gay men, so it shouldn't have surprised me that the subject of my sexuality came up a lot.

Robert Lipsyte, of *The New York Times,* was one of the most persistent of all the reporters. I was delighted when Robert told me he liked the show, especially when he explained that he had come to see it knowing that he'd only write about it if he liked my performance. So he didn't tell me in advance that he would be there. After the show, he came backstage, and the first thing he said was, "Darius, you were fabulous," which was a line from the show. Then he told me that he thought I was terrific and that in many ways I *was* Darius. He didn't realize how close to the truth he was. Right after that, he asked me, "So does this mean you're out?" After a long pause, I asked, "Out?" I'll let Robert describe what follows. He wrote:

He became, briefly, zoned, as if he were on the edge of the diving board, gathering himself for that leap into space. "Didn't we have this discussion before?"

"Five years ago in a Sizzler restaurant outside L.A.," I said. "You said then that your sexuality was a totally private matter."

"I still sort of feel the same," he said, stretching out the sentence, inflecting words, as if it were the three seconds from board to water. There was no suggestion that the topic was taboo or even discomforting; in fact, he seemed to enjoy confronting it, playing with it, as I took notes for the next 25 minutes.

"It's different now. I asked the question then because there were so many rumors, and I didn't include the answer in my report because it ultimately had nothing to do with the story of you preparing for Seoul.

"But now," I gestured at the empty stage, "you are in a gay

role, in a gay play. It's so New York, the way you seem to be saying
'Drop dead' to anyone who ever called you a name."

Louganis laughed and squirmed and nodded . . .

The article went on for quite a bit after that, but I never acknowledged being gay. I feel a little silly now, but I wasn't yet ready to cross
that line.

Plenty of other sports reporters and people from the diving world
came to see me in *Jeffrey*. I didn't anticipate any of the sports people
coming around and supporting my efforts. I didn't make any attempt to
let them know what I was doing. *Jeffrey* is a very gay play, and I didn't
think that the two worlds would mix.

Whatever my feelings, they came, including the administrator of
U.S. Diving and a woman from U.S. Diving whom I'd worked with.
After the show, they wanted to talk to me about the play. I thought
they would just say hello and go, but they wanted to talk about Darius,
the rest of the cast, and the message of the play.

My mother came to New York to see the show on a Saturday, and
she saw both the 7:00 P.M. and 10:00 P.M. performances. I told my mom
that she didn't need to see both shows, but she wanted to. She said that
she wouldn't be able to enjoy it the first time through because the only
thing she would see was me.

At seven o'clock, we generally had rather reserved audiences.
When the show was over that night, I told my mom it was a good thing
she was staying for the ten o'clock show, that it would be a better
house. She said, "No, they wanted to hear every word you said, that's
the reason they were quiet."

When I asked her what she thought of the play she said, "The only
criticism I have is that you aren't onstage enough." That's Mom. She
sat through the ten o'clock show, and we had a pretty raucous crowd.
They enjoyed the show and they were very vocal about it, laughing in
all the right places.

After the show, I introduced my mom to the cast, and they loved
her. They couldn't believe she had sat through two shows in a row.
Then I told them that she'd been to another Off Broadway show for a

matinee earlier in the day. They were dumbfounded, because it's so exhausting sitting through that many shows. Later, several of the cast members came up to me and said, "We know why you're so nice. You'd have to be, with a mother who's so supportive and nonjudgmental."

≈

THE MONTHS I was in *Jeffrey* flew by. Before I knew it, I was waiting to go onstage for my final performance, which proved to be extremely difficult and emotional for me. Saying goodbye is never easy, but it's grown increasingly difficult, because I don't know what the future will bring. That last performance was also difficult because the sense of isolation I felt was so intense. I couldn't share with anyone what I was feeling and experiencing, because I couldn't tell anyone the whole story. Some of the other cast members noticed I was melancholy, and I imagine they figured it was just because I was leaving.

What also made me sad was knowing I was unlikely to get another chance to play a role that was meaningful. All of the acting I had done up to that point was relatively meaningless. *Jeffrey* was that rare opportunity for an actor to do important work, to deliver a message, to say something noteworthy.

In some ways, playing Darius was more satisfying than winning a gold medal at the Olympics, because it was so much more challenging than diving. With *Jeffrey*, I had to convey emotions and thoughts through spoken and unspoken language—which was never easy for me. I had to engage the audience in a much more direct way than I did when I was diving.

I held it together until the final scene, which was always a difficult one. That's when Darius comes back as an angel and asks Jeffrey to look after his lover, Sterling. Darius says, "Be nice to Sterling." Peter Bartlett, the actor who played Sterling, looked down at the floor, because he knew if he looked at me he would lose it, too.

The curtain call was terribly emotional. I had tears streaming down my face. The audience didn't know that this was my last performance, so they were probably wondering what was wrong with me. The whole experience had been so emotional for me that I had no energy left to keep up the happy face. I went to my dressing room, packed up my things, and headed home.

The experience of performing in *Jeffrey* really opened up my life. It gave me new hope and it also gave me a hint that maybe I could still make a difference in this lifetime. That renewed hope gave me just what I needed to make a couple of big decisions, both of which I made in November of 1993, toward the end of my run in *Jeffrey*. One was to get off the painkillers I depended on to get me through the day.

The other was getting started on this autobiography.

29

GAY

GAMES

1994

IF I WAS going to take an honest look back at my life, which I had to do in order to tell my story, my mind had to be clear. I decided to get sober. I had to face my emotional pain, not deaden it. But that wasn't the only incentive to stop taking the painkillers. I was ashamed that I was dependent on drugs, and I didn't want that hanging over me anymore.

By the time I decided to quit, Tylenol with codeine was no longer my drug of choice. When I was in the hospital being treated for the fungal infection, my doctor prescribed Percocet for the severe abdominal pain I was experiencing. I was only supposed to take the Percocet for a short time, but I quickly grew dependent on it and went right on taking it.

Getting off Percocet was the most uncomfortable thing I'd ever experienced. I had to wean myself off, because I didn't know how functional I'd be if I tried to quit cold turkey. I was onstage every night, so I had to be functional. First, I cut back to half a tablet a day. That was okay. Then I did quarters, which also didn't seem to be a problem. But when I tried to go off it entirely for a day or two, my skin felt itchy to the core and I couldn't sleep.

With that kind of reaction, there was no way I could stop the Percocet entirely while I was still performing. I decided to finish up the prescription on quarter-doses, which I figured would last me until I went home to California for Thanksgiving. I hoped the long weekend would be enough time to get over the withdrawal symptoms. I also thought that if I had to, I'd check myself into the hospital and delay my return to New York.

The first three days at home were pretty bad. Between the itchy, crawling skin, not being able to sleep, and terrible anxiety, I was miserable the whole time. It wasn't as if I could tell anyone what I was going through. No one knew that I'd been taking the pills, not even Steven. By the end of the holiday, the symptoms began to subside, and knowing that I was going back to New York to start work again gave me something to focus on other than how rotten I was feeling.

I'm still embarrassed and ashamed that I depended on drugs to get me through some rough times. It wasn't as if I didn't have choices. I could have gone to a counselor, which I did briefly, but I didn't stay with it. Killing the pain just seemed so much easier than dealing with it.

Once I was off the Percocet, I began thinking more seriously about doing my autobiography. I realized that the bottom-line reason I wanted to do it was because I didn't know how much longer I had to live, and I wanted to tell my story in my own words while I was still alive. I'd had a pretty good scare over the summer, and I didn't want to wind up like Rock Hudson or Liberace. Rock Hudson only came forward with the truth at the very end of his life, long after he was in a position to tell the public himself. Liberace died hoping to take his secret with him. I want to be able to do this with dignity, to stand up with a sense of pride in who I am, to say, "This is who I am and this is what I have and this is what I've done."

Part of the motivation behind doing this book was the sense that maybe my story could make a difference in other people's lives. I knew it would make a big difference in my life by letting me get out from under all the lies and half truths. Of course, I didn't need to write a book to do that. I could have held a press conference or arranged for an in-depth interview with a magazine or gone on a television talk show. But at the time I decided to do the book, I didn't have nearly the confidence to do that. I wasn't at all sure of myself when it came to talking about everyday things, let alone subjects as complex and emotional as homosexuality and HIV. Also, I wanted to put my sexual orientation and my HIV diagnosis in the context of my entire life. I thought the best way to do that was in a book.

I didn't really know where to start when it came to figuring out how I'd do my autobiography. I knew nothing about the publishing business, so I started talking to some of the new acquaintances I'd met since coming to New York for *Jeffrey.* One of those people, Robby Browne, who is also a diver—and a four-time gold medalist in the Gay Games—put me in touch with my co-author, and within several weeks we had a proposal, an agent, and a contract. That turned out to be the easy part. Going through my life was even more painful than I'd imagined it would be.

From the very first day that I sat down with my co-author it was an emotional roller coaster. Without the Percocet to blunt the bad feelings, I had a really hard time. The more we talked, the more depressed I got. It was clear that I needed to get professional help. I asked around and got a referral to a psychologist, and after procrastinating for several weeks, I called and made an appointment. What a blessing that turned out to be. How could I have waited so long?

After the first several sessions with the psychologist, and in consultation with a psychiatrist, I was put on an antidepressant. I've suffered from depression all my life, and I've always assumed it was something I had to battle. After a few weeks, the depression began to lift. It wasn't like taking a painkiller, which only took the edge off and left me feeling like I was in a fog. This time, I started feeling normal for the first time in my life. Not that life was perfect. There was—and is—plenty to deal with in therapy, but at least I'm no longer overwhelmed by incredibly dark and paralyzing moods.

Many of the people closest to me were not that supportive of my decision to do my autobiography. Several friends and family members were very concerned about the impact telling the truth would have. Even Steven, whom I'd been with for nearly four years by this point, was against the book. His objection to the project contributed in a big way to my decision to end our relationship. I also came to realize that I got involved with Steven in the first place because I thought he wouldn't hurt me, not because I thought we had a lot to offer each other. We've gone our separate ways, and for a change, I didn't have to pack my things and move.

Those who objected to the book had a hard time understanding why I didn't want to just go on living the way I had been. They didn't understand that hiding out in semi-retirement in Malibu wasn't living. Unless you're living in the kind of isolation I was, having to keep secret something as profound as an HIV diagnosis, it's hard to understand how crushing that can be. It's like you're on an island all by yourself. I had to get off that island, and working on the book was my way of doing it. I didn't see where I had a lot to lose by telling my story. I thought I had a lot to gain.

My original plan had been to wait until after the book's publication to talk about being both gay and HIV-positive. But a number of things happened that led me to step forward a little earlier than I expected to talk about being gay.

Soon after I started working on the book, it became clear that the whole gay issue might not be nearly as big a deal as I had once thought it was. The first time I got that sense was when Liz Smith, the gossip columnist, published an item about my signing to do the book with Random House. The item mentioned that I would be talking about my homosexuality in the book. Strange as it may seem, that was the first time it was ever stated in the press that I was gay. I held my breath for a few days after that, but nothing much happened other than phone calls from talk-show producers who wanted me to appear as a guest. The sky didn't fall. I didn't get any hate mail. The lack of reaction was almost disappointing.

A month later, I was visiting with Ron and Mary Jane in Fort Lauderdale. I was at the Swimming Hall of Fame pool doing some practice dives, and this guy kept coming over to ask me questions, which was annoying. Finally, he asked something about my acting, and I told him that I'd recently been in an Off Broadway play called *Jeffrey*, which was about gay dating in the nineties. I thought that would scare him away. But I was wrong. He wasn't at all put off.

I was pleased with myself that I'd been that bold—even if my intentions were less than honorable—and I learned an important lesson. The whole gay issue might be much larger in my head than it was in the minds of the general public. Maybe it wasn't so shocking after all. That helped me feel a little more comfortable being myself and speaking honestly.

At the same time, Robby Browne started encouraging me to think about getting involved in Gay Games IV, which was scheduled to take place in June 1994 in New York City. The Gay Games is an Olympic-style event that brings together mostly gay and lesbian athletes from around the world. More than ten thousand athletes were expected to attend, a larger number than came to the '88 Olympics. At first I was a little hesitant, because that would be very public. I didn't know if I was ready. But after thinking about it, I eventually decided that I'd participate in the opening ceremonies and do at least one diving exhibition prior to the diving competition.

I got to New York the Thursday before the opening ceremonies of the Gay Games to join the other gay and lesbian divers at practice. Everyone was wonderfully supportive and welcoming. I don't know exactly what I expected, but I had no trouble fitting in. In the diving world, I'd always been something of an outsider because I was gay. Now here I was with a group of divers who were gay and I didn't have to feel at all self-conscious. I could be myself and not worry about being judged. That was incredibly liberating.

Because of a schedule conflict, I couldn't be at the opening ceremonies, which were set for Saturday, so they arranged for me to tape a video. I figured that would be easier than actually speaking in front of a large crowd. I was also a little worried about how I'd be received by the fifteen thousand mostly gay and lesbian people in the audience. Over the years I'd gotten an occasional note from gay people who knew I was gay but were disappointed that I hadn't been more public about my sexual orientation. I wasn't sure if this was a widespread feeling or not, but it did make me wonder about how welcome I'd be.

The script for my videotaped welcome was very simple. This would be the first time I publicly acknowledged being gay. I didn't want to make a big deal of it. The video starts with me doing a dive, and then I swim to the side of the pool and say:

> Hi! I'm Greg Louganis. Sorry I'm not with you tonight in person to celebrate the start of Gay Games IV, but I'll be there in a couple of days, back on the diving board joining other gay and lesbian athletes from around the world.
>
> I'm real excited to be part of an event that's all about true Olympic ideals. This is our chance to show ourselves *and* the world how strong we are as individuals and as a community.
>
> Welcome to the Games! It's great to be out and proud.

I wish I could have been in the stadium to hear the reaction when the video was shown, but several people called to tell me that the audience erupted in cheers as soon as my video was introduced, and everyone went wild when I said that final sentence. I said it so casually that you would never guess what it took to get to the point in my life where I felt comfortable enough to publicly acknowledge something so fundamental about myself.

As promised, I got back to New York a couple of days later, in time to do an exhibition between rounds in the diving competition. I just about melted from the way I was welcomed. The audience gave me a standing ovation when I was introduced for my exhibition. They cheered and cheered. In that moment, I knew everything would be okay. With that kind of support from gay and lesbian people, I figured I could handle any kind of criticism I got for coming forward. I've never felt so warmly embraced in my life, and for the first time, I felt like a complete person.

I had such a good time being at the diving event that I volunteered to do the announcing. I came back a couple of days later for the second night of the diving competition to do the announcing again and to do another exhibition. On that second night, I also got to present a gold medal to Robby Browne. I placed the medal around his neck and I gave him a big kiss and a hug. Later that evening, I was in a cab with Robby and I said, "I wonder where that kiss will wind up?" The place had been filled with television cameras and photographers. Robby said, "What kiss?" It might not have been memorable for him, but that Friday night, CBS Evening News did a story on the Gay Games, and there we were, kiss and all.

When I got home to California, I began thinking about what my next step would be. I felt incredibly inspired by my experiences at the Gay Games, and thought there might be an opportunity to take that inspiration and throw my support behind something I had started reading about while I was in New York.

For several months, a controversy had been brewing over the planned venue of the 1996 Olympic volleyball preliminaries, which were set to be held in Cobb County, Georgia, which is outside Atlanta. In August 1993, Cobb County's commissioners passed an anti-gay resolution, which stated that "lifestyles advocated by the gay community" are "incompatible with the standards to which this community subscribes." A number of organizations had been lobbying the Atlanta organizing committee to move the volleyball venue because of that resolution. The Atlanta committee was not exactly rushing to make a decision, and the U.S. Olympic Committee was keeping a very safe distance from the whole controversy.

Two weeks after the Gay Games ended, I had a perfect opportunity to say something directly to the U.S. Olympic Committee about what I thought should be done. Several months earlier, I'd been invited to go to St. Louis on July 7 to accept the Robert J. Kane Award, which is given annually to an "American athlete who achieved success at the U.S. Olympic Festival, who continues to give back to his or her sport, and who exemplifies the spirit and ideals of Bob Kane, including fairness, a commitment to excellence, and a dedication to sport and athletics." Robert Kane was the founder of the U.S. Olympic Festival, and the award this year was sponsored by the Xerox Corporation.

So I decided that I'd talk about Cobb County in my acceptance speech. I also wanted to talk about my experience at the Gay Games and what it meant to me. But I decided to start my speech by dedicating my award to Dr. Tom Waddell, who founded the Gay Games. He was a former Olympian, and he died of AIDS. Dr. Waddell had originally wanted to call the Gay Games the Gay Olympics, but the U.S. Olympic Committee sued him to prevent him from using the word *Olympics*. To pay his legal bills, Dr. Waddell had to mortgage his home. The U.S.O.C. won its case, and I thought that Dr. Waddell deserved some recognition for his dedication to Olympic ideals and for giving gay and lesbian athletes around the world a place to compete without the fear of being judged or condemned for who they are.

I have the bad habit of not paying attention to the specifics of an event until I get there. In this case, it was a good thing I didn't, because I'm not sure I would have had the guts to deliver the speech I'd prepared. When I got to the hotel that night, I looked through the materials that had been left for me and discovered that this was not going to be a small awards breakfast. This was being held at the U.S. Olympic Festival, an annual event that brings together young athletes from around the country and U.S. Olympics officials. A thousand people were expected at the breakfast. I didn't sleep very well that night.

The next morning, I went over my speech several times more before I left my room for the banquet hall. I knew I could get through it okay, but I was nervous. I was about to bring the issue of homosexuality to the Olympic realm in a very public way. In a confident moment, I thought, "It's about time!"

When I was introduced, everyone in the hall stood up and applauded. It was a wonderful welcome, but I wondered how enthusiastic they were going to be once I finished my acceptance speech. Before I started talking I had an awful sense of terror, unlike anything I'd ever experienced on the diving board. Sitting in the audience not far from where I was standing were officials from the U.S. Olympic Committee, a table full of officials from U.S. Diving, and a table full of people from the Atlanta organizing committee. I was already sweating by the time I finished thanking the U.S. Olympic Committee, Xerox, and all the appropriate people. I took a deep breath and said:

> I accept the Robert J. Kane Award with humble gratitude, and I'd like to dedicate it to the memory of Dr. Tom Waddell, an Olympic athlete who died of AIDS on July 11, 1987. Tom was a college football player, a gymnast, and a track-and-field star. He was thirty when he made the U.S. Olympic team and finished sixth in the 1968 Olympic decathlon. I was only twenty-eight when I *retired* from diving. Tom was also a physician, a paratrooper, and a father. He was also gay, and in 1982, Tom founded the Gay Games, an Olympic-style event that embraces many of the same ideals that the Olympics and the Robert J. Kane Award are intended to celebrate.
>
> As many of you know, I was in New York City two weeks ago to be part of Gay Games IV. I wasn't there to compete, but I had the chance to work out with divers from around the world, including a couple of former Olympians. I also volunteered to announce the diving competitions and I gave two diving exhibitions. I did pretty well, but I was glad there weren't any judges scoring my dives.
>
> During my time in New York, I was welcomed as warmly as I've ever been, and for the first time, I was welcomed as an openly gay athlete. It was a real thrill for me, and that experience made me realize how important it is for athletes to feel welcome for who they are. It made me think about the Olympics when I was a competitor, and how challenging it was to do my best. The physical and psychological pressures of competition at that level are enormous, even when you feel you have the support of the nation or the community in which you're competing.
>
> That's why I'm concerned about some of the athletes who are scheduled to compete in the volleyball preliminaries at the 1996 Olympics in Atlanta. I remember my last Olympic preliminaries very well. I still have a dent in my head as a souvenir. The volleyball preliminaries are set to be held in Cobb County, Georgia,

just outside Atlanta. Last year, Cobb County adopted a resolution condemning gay people. It's the first and only anti-gay resolution of its kind to be adopted by a local government in the United States.

So now, added to the normal pressures of competition, the gay men and women who will participate in the volleyball preliminaries will have the pressure of knowing they're not wanted in Cobb County. No athlete should need to worry about feeling judged or unwelcome, especially at the Olympics. What should matter is doing your best.

I guess the people of Cobb County have every right to pass whatever resolutions they like. But by passing this anti-gay resolution they have made clear that some of our athletes are unwelcome.

The U.S. Olympic Committee has already sent an important message to all Olympic athletes by giving the Robert J. Kane Award to an openly gay athlete. You've made it clear that sexual orientation is not a barrier to full participation in the Olympic movement. Now you can reinforce that message by encouraging the Atlanta Committee for the Olympic Games to move the volleyball preliminaries to a venue that welcomes all athletes, including gay and lesbian Olympians.

This is not a political issue. It's an issue of fairness. It's about demonstrating our commitment to the Olympic spirit and the very ideals that motivated Robert J. Kane to establish the first National Sports Festival.

Before closing, I just wanted to tell you how impressed I was to find out that Xerox has made a considerable effort to make its gay employees feel welcome by including sexual orientation in its nondiscrimination clause and by supporting its very active gay and lesbian employee organization.

Again, thank you to the U.S. Olympic Committee and Xerox for this great honor. I promise to do my best to live up to the ideals of the Robert J. Kane Award.

When I finished, there was a pause before people started applauding, mostly polite applause this time, nothing like the rousing ovation I'd gotten when I was first introduced. I looked out at the banquet hall, and only about a dozen people were standing to applaud me. That really didn't matter, because all I cared about was whether or not they were listening. From their reaction, I could tell they had heard me.

As I stepped down from the podium, Jackie Joyner-Kersee was there to greet me with a high five. Jackie and I were named the 1987 sportspeople of the year by the U.S. Olympic Committee. Before I had a chance to say anything to her, I was surrounded by reporters and young athletes. It was an absolute whirlwind, with reporters asking questions, photographers wanting to take pictures, and athletes wanting to talk to me and get my autograph.

The most memorable moment was when a group of deaf girls came up to me and talked to me through an interpreter. First they told me that what I did was the bravest thing they'd ever seen, and that in my diving it must have been extremely lonely. They asked how my parents reacted to my sexuality, and they said they hoped my parents were supportive, because they knew how lonely it could be when you were different. It made me feel so good to know that there were people in the audience who empathized with what I'd experienced, that I wasn't all alone. When they were saying goodbye, one of the girls threw her arms around me and gave me a big hug, and I hugged her back.

Almost every article about that event described me mopping the sweat from my brow after I finished the speech. I was soaked, but I was very proud that I'd done it. It was worth it, because clearly what I said had some sort of impact. The day before the event, the U.S. Olympic Committee's official position on Cobb County was that it was up to the Atlanta organizing committee. After my speech, when reporters asked U.S.O.C. president LeRoy Walker for his comments, he said that the issue would be dealt with soon. He said, "I don't think this is something that can simmer. I think the committee will look at it now and do something quickly. We're going to either have to say we're going to leave it there, or we're going to move it." He added, "But it's strictly up to the local organizing committee."

If I had any doubt that my message got across, it evaporated three weeks later, when the Atlanta organizing committee announced that it was moving the volleyball competition out of Cobb County. A lot of people had been working very hard for several months to get the venue changed, and I was thrilled that I was able to help bring the issue to a head.

I came away from my experience in St. Louis with a new sense of pride in myself as a gay man and in my ability to speak my mind. In the past, I'd always let my diving speak for me, because I had no confidence that I could communicate in any other way. That worked for a long time. But in St. Louis I'd had something important to say, something that couldn't be said through my diving. I had to speak, and people listened.

≈

I DON'T THINK of my experiences in New York and in St. Louis as the end of my story. I really feel like I'm starting life all over again.

The past year has been challenging, but it's also been exciting, rich, and expansive. I've been learning a lot about what it means to be gay, meeting with and talking to many different gay and lesbian people, including author Paul Monette, whose book *Becoming a Man* has inspired me to take a closer look at my own life. I've also met with Terry DeCrescenzo, who runs an organization for gay and lesbian youth in Los Angeles. Given the difficult time I had growing up as a gay man, I'm very interested in exploring ways that I can be of help to young gay and lesbian people today.

In recent months, I've gotten more involved in AIDS work. Besides participating in fund-raisers, which I've done for several years, I've been doing volunteer dog grooming for an organization called PAWS—Pets Are Wonderful Support. PAWS volunteers take care of the pets of people living with AIDS and HIV so they can keep their pets at home with them. The organization also places pets in new homes if a client passes away. In the future, I'm planning to devote even more of my time to AIDS education and fund-raising efforts.

I don't know what direction my professional life will take, but this is a great time for me to explore my various interests. I love my dogs, and most likely I'll continue to be involved in breeding and showing them. Another thing I've enjoyed doing in the past is teaching dance, and for the first time this past fall, I began teaching a theater-movement class at the University of Southern California. I have twenty-eight students and we meet twice a week. I'm enjoying being a teacher, and I think I'm learning as much from my students—mostly about communication—as they are from me.

I still have a lot to figure out about healthy relationships, and I'm trying. One important lesson I've finally learned is not to jump from one relationship into the next. For the first time in my adult life, I've been single for an extended period. And I'm dating, which is, I'm sure, as much fun and as awkward as it would be for any other retired Olympic champion diver in his mid-thirties with HIV. I've discovered that there are indeed very kind and loving gay men out in the world, but I imagine it will be a while before I'm ready to get involved in a serious relationship. I still have a few things to sort out.

One thing that has helped me begin to sort out my past experiences and my life is professional counseling. Therapy is helping me learn how to live again, and maybe for the first time learn how to live as a full person proud of who he is and tolerant of what he's not. Perhaps most important, it's helped me understand my ongoing problems with depression and why I've always felt so bad about myself. I've been off antidepressant medication for a couple of months now, and I've been feeling good. I still have ups and downs, but not like I used to.

My health, thank goodness, has been stable. Over the past six years, I've taken the whole range of available HIV antiviral drugs, and now I'm back on AZT, but at a lower dosage. I'm still on daily medication to keep my fungal infection in check, and I take the usual prophylactic drugs HIV patients take to stay healthy.

As I look back over 1994, I can see that one of the most important lessons I've learned is that while diving may be my true gift, that doesn't mean it's the only way I'm able to communicate. My experience in St. Louis taught me that. And now that I don't have to hide the fact that I'm both gay and HIV-positive, I have a lot more that I want to say. I just hope I have enough time to make a difference.

Wish me luck. I'll need it.

EPILOGUE

~~~~~~

LIVING FREE:

LIFE WITHOUT SECRETS

OVER THE PAST YEAR, many people have written to
me asking what it's been like for me since the publication of my story.
In a word, it's been *incredible*, the most incredible year of my life. I
thought I'd share with you some of what happened just before publication and in the year since.

When I finished work on the final chapter of *Breaking the Surface*,
I still had five months to go before publication, five months before I
could leave my self-made prison. You'd think that after keeping silent
about so much for so long that five months would be nothing, but it
felt like forever. Honestly, though, after so many years in hiding, I
had a lot of work to do before I was ready to talk publicly about
things I never even talked about in private. I needed every one of
those months to prepare psychologically and emotionally for what I
knew was going to be one of the biggest challenges of my life.

In some ways, getting ready to tell the truth about my life was
like preparing for the Olympics. I had to train. I had a coach. And I
had specific events to get ready for. My coach was Dr. Stan Ziegler,

a wonderful psychologist, and we worked together three hours a week for the better part of a year. The goal was for me to be ready by the time of my first major event, which turned out to be an interview with Barbara Walters, for ABC's 20/20 in late January. The interview was scheduled to air less than a month later, on the Friday before the book was set to arrive in stores.

Part of me wondered if I'd ever be ready, if I'd ever be fully prepared to go public. And, of course, I couldn't be. Just like diving off the ten-meter platform, you can prepare as much as you want beforehand, but once your feet leave the platform, it's still a free fall. In diving, you hope you land on your head, with virtually no splash. In this case I knew that no matter what, I'd make some waves, but I at least needed to land on my feet, and I wasn't sure I could do that.

Stan and I talked about everything from my bad self-esteem and past relationships to growing up and my thoughts about the future. There was never any expectation that we could possibly deal with everything in the short time we had, but we covered as much ground as we could. One of the major subjects we put off discussing was how I felt about my change in status from being HIV-positive to having AIDS. Although I had no symptoms, my T-cell count had fallen below 200, which, according to the Centers for Disease Control definition, meant that I was classified as having AIDS.

At the end of our second-to-last session before the Barbara Walters interview, Stan said, "Well, we didn't get to the question of what happens if Barbara asks you if you have AIDS. I know that we've neglected this, but we'll discuss it on Friday."

At that point, my thinking was that I'd talk about being HIV-positive but not say anything about my T-cell count and AIDS. I felt fine. I didn't feel sick or look sick, so I was having a hard time accepting my official diagnosis. It was overwhelming to think about it, because in my mind AIDS meant that the end was near. And I knew that would be the public perception as well. I could imagine the headlines—"Greg Louganis Has AIDS"—and everybody would be thinking I was on my deathbed. I couldn't deal with it, but at least there was still time to talk it out with Stan.

On Friday, when I went to Stan's office, there was a note on his door saying that his associate was taking his appointments. I assumed that Stan's friend, Paul Monette, the writer, had passed away. Paul had been gravely ill with AIDS, and I knew that Stan had been helping take care of him. I figured I'd talk to Stan later in the day, and that we'd do my session by phone. This was an important session, so I knew Stan would find the time for us to talk.

Shortly after I got home, Mitchell Ivers, my editor, called and asked me if I'd heard the news. I told him that I'd gone to Stan's office and there was a note on the door, so I figured Paul had passed away and that Stan was helping Paul's lover with the arrangements. Mitchell said, "No, Stan died."

Stan was forty-four years old. He didn't have AIDS. He hadn't been sick. This was completely out of the blue. I couldn't speak. All I could say to Mitchell was, "I've got to go," and I hung up the phone. I thought to myself, "Isn't life supposed to be easier than this?" I learned some days later that Stan had died from unusual complications of Crohn's disease, which he had battled for many years.

≈

THE DAY AFTER Stan died, I was still in shock, but I had to drive down to the diving pool at Belmont Plaza in Long Beach to meet Barbara Walters and the 20/20 crew. The actual interview wasn't scheduled until Monday, but they wanted me to do some dives, which they planned to videotape for the story. I cried the whole way down the coast, but by the time I got to the pool I'd managed to pull myself together. I was okay when I met Barbara.

Once we started taping, there was so much down time between dives that my mind started wandering. I thought about how this was what Stan and I had worked so hard to prepare for, and Stan wasn't there. I was standing up on the diving board, feeling very alone, and tears started streaming down my face. Someone must have noticed, because Barbara came over and asked me what was up. I came down off the board and told her that my therapist had just passed away, and I started crying. She was wonderful and held me as I cried. I was very grateful to Barbara for her compassion and genuine concern. I got through the rest of the taping, and I drove home.

Two days later, I met with Barbara for the formal interview. After it aired four weeks later, many people asked me if I was upset with

Barbara, because they thought she was harsh in questioning me. I never thought that. Off camera, Barbara was warm and loving. Of course, when the cameras rolled, sometimes the questions sounded as though they had a hard edge to them, but she was just doing her job. I didn't feel in any way that she was trying to judge me or catch me off guard.

I was pretty nervous during the interview itself. This was the first time I was talking so publicly about a lot of difficult things. It helped that everybody was so nice to me. I'd already spent time with the crew, so I felt comfortable. And during the actual interview there were a lot of tears from them. They'd had no way of knowing what they were going to be hearing.

None of Barbara's questions surprised me, including the one about whether I had AIDS. What came as a surprise to me was my own response. I hadn't really thought through what I was going to say, but saying I had AIDS never crossed my mind. As I started explaining that according to the CDC definition I had AIDS, it was almost as if I was in a dreamlike state. I couldn't believe what was coming out of my mouth. It was information that I had in my head, and it just came out.

After the interview was over, I told Barbara that I wasn't sure I was comfortable with the response I'd given about having AIDS versus being HIV-positive. She explained that I had until the morning of the air date to let her know if I wanted it cut from the interview. She told me, "If you're not comfortable with what you said, we don't want to go with it." But I didn't really want to take back what I had said. It was something that I had to start dealing with, and I figured I might as well come clean from the start. It was a relief now that I had nothing left to hide.

≈

I HAD TWO primary goals for the weeks following the taping of the 20/20 interview, a period that I knew would be the quiet before the media storm. First, I had to find someone to take care of my dogs during the several weeks I was going to be away promoting the book. The other thing I needed to do was talk to several of my friends about my HIV status. I had waited this long to tell anyone because the last thing I wanted to have happen was for the news to accidentally leak before the book was out there to explain the whole story and before I was ready to talk about everything.

The plan was to have the 20/20 interview air on Friday, and the following Monday, the day the book arrived in stores, People magazine was scheduled to publish an excerpt of the book. That same day, with everything already out there in print and having told at least the big news to Barbara Walters, I was going to speak at a student-sponsored event at Columbia University, to which the press had been invited. It was all meant to be very orderly and dignified.

Well, it didn't exactly work out the way we had planned. Six days before the 20/20 interview was set to air, one of the national tabloids ran an article about me being HIV-positive and that I was going to announce this news, among other things, in an interview with Barbara Walters. My editor had heard a rumor that this was going to be a cover story, so we were relieved when we found it was buried way in the back. We hoped no one noticed, and I just went about my business as if nothing had happened. Of course, it was noticed, and on Wednesday a gossip columnist in Chicago ran with the story. By that afternoon it was out on all the wire services that I was HIV-positive and had been when I hit my head on the diving board in Korea and "bled in the pool." I never bled in the pool, but that was what just about every reporter seemed to accept as fact for the next few days as my story played out in the news media around the world.

By three in the afternoon, a half dozen reporters and television news crews were camped out in front of my house, and the phone was ringing off the hook. Some of the messages were from friends, people close to me, including Jeanne White, Ryan's mom, whom I hadn't yet had a chance to talk to. I'd planned to call all of them that night and the next day. One of the calls was from Dawnn Lewis. She'd heard the news on the radio and was really upset. She just assumed that I was coming forward because I'd gotten very sick, and she thought I was on my deathbed. I quickly reassured her that I was okay.

As I was trying to talk to people on the phone, the news people were calling to me through the front door, telling me that they wanted to hear my side of the story. Some of them slipped notes under the door. There was no way I was going to talk to them. My agreement with *20/20* and *People* was that I not talk to the media until after the Barbara Walters interview aired and *People* magazine hit the stands. I had every intention of honoring those agreements even though my initial instinct was to open the door and say, "You've got the story wrong, and you obviously don't know how people contract the AIDS virus."

It really upset me that there was all this misinformation. Fortunately, over the next few days, as doctors and AIDS experts were interviewed by the media, they explained that I had posed no danger to the other divers and that only the doctor who had sewed up my head was even remotely at risk of being infected, and then only if he had punctured himself with the needle. I was grateful that it was the experts who got to explain things, and not me, because I'm not a doctor or a scientist. They were far better at explaining everything than I was. By the time I talked to the press on Monday, most people were pretty clear about the fact that you can't catch HIV from pool water, even if someone has gotten a cut and bled into the pool.

As the number of reporters on my doorstep grew, I finally decided to call the local security force. They removed everyone from my property, so now the news crews were all camped out on the road above my driveway and were shining bright lights on the house. The whole thing was kind of funny. Here I was on the phone trying to explain to friends that I wasn't dead yet, fielding calls from the publicist at Random House, who was trying to make arrangements for me to fly out that night to Chicago to be interviewed on *Oprah* the next day, and in the background I had the television on and I could see they were doing live reports from outside my house and showing video clips of me hitting my head on the diving board.

When the driver arrived to take me to the airport, the reporters were still up on the road. I wanted to avoid them, so he put my bags in the car, and I told the driver to go down the hill to my neighbor's house and I'd meet him there. I turned out all the lights and went out the back entrance of the house and started making my way down the hill behind my house to my neighbor's. I hadn't gone very far when this guy with a television camera started chasing me. It was a very dark night, and I could hear him stumbling along the path. I felt sorry for him, trying to run with that heavy camera on his shoulder, but I wasn't about to stop to show him the way. I got down the hill, but he was right on my heels. I jumped in the car, and there he was shining the light of his camera in the car window. As we drove off, I couldn't help but laugh, thinking that this is what it must be like to be Michael Jackson.

At the airport a woman who worked for American Airlines, whom I'd seen a number of times before, came up to me and said in the most concerned way, "Are you okay? Are you feeling all right? Do you need help?" It was such an overt show of concern. I tried to reassure her that I was fine. And not only was I fine, I was really, really fine. In fact, I couldn't have been better. I was free. My secret was out there, and now I was free.

≈

THE INTERVIEW WITH Oprah, which had been very hastily arranged the night before, following a call from her producers, was so much easier for me than the interview with Barbara Walters. When I had talked with Barbara, I wasn't fully prepared for the questions about HIV-positive versus AIDS, and my responsibility in 1988. Now I'd had three more weeks to think and talk about these things, so I felt confident saying I had AIDS and didn't hesitate to take responsibility for my decisions back in 1988. It also helped having such an overwhelmingly supportive audience. They were incredible. I'm a gay man who didn't get AIDS from a transfusion, and they were still on their feet applauding and cheering. I was really touched by their response. And Oprah was right there with me. She'd read every word of the book, and I could tell that she really understood some of what I'd been through.

The one thing that I was upset about before going on *Oprah* was that I still hadn't had a chance to talk to a number of people about my HIV status. One of those people was Jeanne White, so the first thing I did after getting to Chicago was to call her. I got her answering machine. It never occurred to me that she was in Chicago. Oprah had flown her in that night to surprise me on the show. During the interview, when Oprah started asking me about Ryan White and what he and Jeanne had meant to me, I said how upset I was that I hadn't had a chance to talk to her. Oprah said, "You can tell her right now," and out walked Jeanne. I'm emotional to start with, and that was an emotional time. Of course I burst into tears as Jeanne and I hugged each other. It was wonderful. I told Jeanne, "I wanted Ryan to know." She said to me, "He knows, Greg, and he loves you just like I love you." Ryan is my guardian angel.

≈

THE AUDIENCE RESPONSE in Chicago was the first hint I got that people were going to respond to me more positively than I had thought. But it was in New York the next day, on the subway of all places, that I started to fully realize what kind of impact my story was having on people.

On Friday afternoon, my agent, Jed Mattes, took me to meet with a group of gay, lesbian, and bisexual teenagers at the Hetrick-Martin Institute, an organization that, among other things, runs a high school for sexual minority youth. The kids were incredibly insightful and asked me all sorts of questions about whether I had experienced homophobia in my sports career, and they wanted to know if I'd had the support of my parents once I told them I was gay. The kids were amazing.

When we left Hetrick-Martin to go back to the hotel, it was around five o'clock, rush hour. There weren't any cabs, so we got on the subway at Broadway and Eighth Street. As we were waiting for the N train, a guy in his twenties came up to me, excused himself for interrupting, and said, "I wanted you to know that I started diving when I was twelve years old because of you. You've always been a hero of mine. And now I'm fighting the same battle you are. It means so much to me that you're talking about it publicly." I was really choked up. I thanked him, and he walked away. On the train, which was fairly crowded, I noticed a conservative-looking middle-aged man, dressed in a business suit, several feet from us. I had a sense he was trying to come up to talk to me. After a few attempts he finally came over, and from his first word I could tell he was about to cry. All he managed to say was, "I admire you so much." He was really emotional. I knew there was a story there, and I wanted to throw my arms around him and give him a hug, but before I could even say anything, he walked away.

That night I watched the Barbara Walters interview in my hotel room with a handful of other people. What struck me more than anything while watching the story was my diving. I was watching beautiful dives, and I was the one doing them. That was the first time I realized I was a beautiful diver. I know that must seem ridiculous, but I'd allowed myself to think of myself as a beautiful diver.

By the time I got to bed that night I was emotionally and physically wiped out. I just wanted to be home with my dogs in my own bed, but there was no going home now. This was just the beginning of a nationwide adventure.

≈

WHEN I WAS an Olympic athlete, I got a lot of attention from the public and the press, but it was never as emotionally intense and rewarding as it was traveling across the country promoting *Breaking the Surface*. Everywhere I went, people offered their support, shared their stories, and wanted to take pictures with me. Before the book came out, I had been afraid that parents wouldn't want their kids to come near me once they knew the truth about my life, but over and over again parents wanted to take pictures of me with their kids at my side. I guess I overestimated people's prejudices and underestimated their compassion and love.

The first stop on the media tour following New York City was Fort Lauderdale, where I was scheduled to do a press conference and a book signing at the Swimming Hall of Fame. The signing was run by Outbooks, a local gay and lesbian bookstore.

Going to the Swimming Hall of Fame was like going home for me. It was where I'd spent a lot of time training and where Ron O'Brien and his son Tim still coached, and I knew the people who worked there. Before I got there, I'd heard there was a problem with the executive director, who was apparently less than enthusiastic about having the press conference and book signing there. In the end, he simply didn't come to either event. I was grateful that he stepped aside and let his staff handle the whole thing because they were great, especially Holly, who did everything she possibly could do to make the event a success. I'm just sorry the executive director didn't get to be there to see the outpouring of support.

I don't know what I expected, but I never thought that so many people and so many different kinds of people would come to meet me. The line snaked back and forth through the museum, past the big exhibit about my diving career, down the steps and out on to the street. I'm told there were between 1,200 and 1,500 people there to get books signed. And people didn't just want their books signed. They brought gifts for me. They wanted to give hugs and get hugs. They wanted their pictures taken with me. It was unbelievable. We had a whole team of people keeping everything running smoothly, and even then it was more than three hours before everyone got through the line.

Two people really stood out for me that evening. One was a man who was clearly very ill with AIDS. I could tell he was suffering from dementia and wasn't completely aware of what was going on. I was sitting up on a platform, and I could see that there was no way he could climb the steps to reach me. So I came down off the platform. He had a friend with him, and I signed the book that his friend had brought. I asked if he thought it would be okay if I gave the man a hug. He said, "He'd love that. Before we got here, we talked all about how much he wanted to meet you, but he fades in and out." I put my arms around him and gently hugged him. He hugged me back. I couldn't help but cry, because that could have been me. I could have been looking in the mirror, and if that had been me, I would have hoped that someone would have done that for me. I pulled myself back together and went back to meeting people and signing books.

At the very end of the line was a six-year-old boy with his sister and mother and father. I learned later that they came to the signing because the little boy had seen me on television and he wanted to tell me something. He kept asking his father all day to take him to meet me, and finally he gave in. They all got in their car and drove over. They were the last people to get in line before the line was cut off.

This little boy climbed up the stairs to the platform, got on his tiptoes, and reached across the table. He leaned on his elbows, and said, "I hope you feel better." I melted. By this time I was completely exhausted, but that little boy left me feeling incredible.

From Florida I traveled all over the country, and everywhere I went, people offered me encouragement and told me their stories. It was overwhelming. Hundreds and thousands of people came to meet me, from young divers and deaf kids to grandparents and HIV-positive gay men. They said things like, "I've been HIV-positive for ten years. You can make it." "I haven't had T-cells for three years. I still feel great. Hang in there." The hardest were the people who had been newly diagnosed with HIV. A number of them said, "You've given me the courage to continue on." "Whenever I need encouragement, I reread your book."

There was a young man who came to one of my signings whose father had died of AIDS just the night before. He told me that his father had made him promise to come meet me to lend his support. Someone else brought a cellular phone so I could speak with his friend who was in the hospital with an AIDS-related illness. I got on the phone and told the friend that I was sorry he couldn't make it to the book signing, but I was signing his book as we spoke.

A lot of women told me the book gave them the courage to stay away from their abusive spouse, that by talking about my abusive relationship they felt better about themselves.

People brought all kinds of things for me at every book signing. After each event I'd have to send at least two or three boxes of things back to my house in California. People brought teddy bears, hundreds of teddy bears, healing crystals, T-shirts, earrings of all kinds. I've sent most of the teddy bears to the children with AIDS at a hospital in Los Angeles, and a lot of the T-shirts and clothes I've given to one of the local AIDS hospices. Everything has gone to good use.

I wear a number of the earrings, although not all at once. I'm still wearing a pink triangle earring that a man gave me in Atlanta. I'm still signing books with the pen another man gave me at La-Guardia Airport when I first left on the tour. It's a good pen. I was given scores of Bibles, many with my name inscribed on them.

People also brought food of all kinds and herbal teas that are supposed to be good for people with HIV. My favorite was the peanut butter cookies that a woman named Helen brought to give out to people at my signing in San Francisco. Helen had this warm, loving smile. She had originally planned to bake chocolate chip cookies, but she didn't want the chocolate to get all over the books. When she got to the front of the line, she told me about her son who was HIV-positive. At some point while she was telling me how wonderful he is, I realized that she may have been trying to make a match. Mothers are amazing. They just want their children to be happy.

People have also sent me scores of audio and video cassettes, mostly concerning alternative treatments for people with AIDS. Then there are the letters. Thousands of letters. One of the most frustrating things is that I can't possibly answer all the letters personally. At first I thought that I'd be able to answer every letter, but it's simply not possible. I'm only one person. I know there are people who are upset with me for not personally responding to their letters, but I hope they'll understand.

There is one letter that I carry with me wherever I go. And I'm hoping the young woman who wrote it will contact Tom Perry, the publicist at Random House, so I can talk to her. She came to my book signing in Capitola, California. Because there were so many people at each stop, only those who had books were permitted to stand in line. She told the people at the bookstore that she just wanted to see me because I'd been such an inspiration. She left a note for me, but I never got to meet her and there was no return address on the letter or even a last name. Her letter said:

Dear Greg,
I just wanted to thank you for being a positive influence in my life. I was homeless and living in a homeless shelter during the [1988] Olympics and I saw you dive. You are the best. It made me think, "What am I doing here? What am I doing with my life?" Your victory was my victory, for it gave me the strength and courage for doing something good for myself and to society. I am currently going to school and I hope someday to be a positive influence on someone as much as you were with me. God bless you. Love, Sophia. Age 23.

Sophia, you're an inspiration to me. I hope I hear from you.

≈

BEFORE I CAME out about being gay and HIV-positive, one of the things that really scared me was the potential negative response of right-wing reactionaries. What if they picketed my events or yelled at me or sent hate mail? Well, I got fewer than a half dozen pieces of hate mail, and it really wasn't so bad. I just filed them away. The one time I encountered anti-gay protesters, I dealt with it. This was in Lawrence, Kansas, and I knew before going that this anti-gay radical was going to be picketing the event with his family. They were there with signs in their hands, standing outside the building where I was scheduled to speak. The signs said: "Die AIDS Faggot, You'll Burn in Hell." One of the placards had my picture on it with "666" across my forehead. They had drawn in fangs and I had horns growing from my head.

During the question-and-answer period after I gave my speech, someone in the audience asked what I thought about the people standing outside the building. I said that I thought I should hand the leader of this group a teddy bear and tell him he needed lots of hugs. I explained that if you meet hate and anger with hate and anger, then you turn your power over to them and they win. If you meet them with love and compassion, they don't know what to do. I learned later that the gay-lesbian-bisexual student organization sent scores of teddy bears to this man. I really do think he needs hugs.

Now I know I can deal with the anti-gay radicals, whatever they have to say. I'm glad I didn't let my fear of them keep me in the closet forever.

One thing that kept me in the closet for as long as I stayed there was my fear that my acting career—however limited it was—would be over if I came out. As an HIV-positive gay man I assumed I'd be a liability. Who would hire me if they knew the truth? Obviously, I reached the point where I felt it was worth that sacrifice. Surprisingly, I've had more opportunities to work as an actor now than ever before.

Over the summer I was in New York for a few days, and my friend Robby Browne suggested I go see The Only Thing Worse You Could Have Told Me . . . , which was a one-man show written by and starring Dan Butler from Frasier, the television show. Dan is openly gay, and a lot of the show was autobiographical. Robby arranged for the producer, Scott Allyn, to take me to see it. On the way there, Scott started talking about the possibility of me replacing Dan when he went back to Los Angeles to work on Frasier. I thought to myself, "Yeah, right, a one-man show. I don't think so." I didn't feel that I was ready for a lead role, let alone the only role in a play. But I decided not to say no right away. I figured I'd watch the show and think about it later.

It turned out that the show consists of more than a dozen different characters. There are all these different stories, and I thought, "Well, maybe I could do it." Scott was very persistent, so I told him that I'd audition for it. I knew that if I was going to be able to do the role, I'd have to convince the director that I could. I went back to California and worked with an acting coach to prepare for the audition. There were all kinds of pros and cons about doing the show, but I decided to think about that later, because I was pretty sure I wouldn't be cast.

There was only one character that I found really intimidating. He's this tough, foul-mouthed straight guy, and I thought, "I'm never going to pull this off." He was so far from who I am. But we worked at it, and I did well enough in the audition to be offered the part. Now I had to decide whether this was something I wanted to do. I wasn't really sure it was even something I could do. This was a very physically demanding part. I'd recently started on a new medication, which really wiped me out for several days with flu-like symptoms. I was fearful that I'd start the six-week run, get sick, and not be able to finish it.

I talked to my doctor and my nurse, and they thought it was an awful lot of stress to put on my body. They said they knew I would do what I wanted, but they encouraged me not to take on such a demanding show. I had to do six shows a week, and I would be on stage all by myself for a solid hour and a half.

What really helped me decide was a conversation with Dawnn Lewis. She's the greatest. We were on our way to a movie screening, and I read some of the play to her. I asked her what she thought, and she said that she thought it would be wonderful. I told her about my concerns, about my energy level, the fact it's a one-man show, that there's nobody to hide behind. She said, "Greg, as long as I've known you, you've always wanted to be an actor. This is your next challenge. You said you wanted to live your life while you were still here. This is your chance. What's to stop you?" She was challenging me with my own words. I thought to myself, "What's the worst thing that could happen? I could get sick during the middle of the run and have to drop out. Was anybody going to fault me for trying?" I didn't think so, and the next day I called to accept the part.

The first performance, I was filled with nerves. I was terrified. This was going to be the longest ten-meter dive that I'd ever done in my life. The audience was filled with friends, and they were wonderful. It may have been the longest ten-meter dive I'd ever done, but it was also the most exhilarating. When I went out for my curtain call, everyone applauded and cheered. A number of people spoke to me afterward and paid me the highest compliment: they said that after the first few minutes, they forgot it was me up there on the stage. A number of people living with HIV also told me that seeing me kick butt onstage had given them the courage to get off their butts and do something, to make the most of the time they had left. That made me feel great.

The next night, during my second preview performance, the worst happened. I got lost during the second piece. I froze. I apologized to the audience. I walked around the stage and I was thinking, "God, I know I've got the script backstage, but I can't leave the stage. What should I do?" I walked around the stage some more, and I got back on script and then continued through. I'm sure the audience forgave me before I forgave myself.

After the show, I went backstage and I cried. Getting lost is the worst thing that can happen. I apologized to the director, and the stage manager, and the crew, and everybody. After I got that over and done with, I realized that the worst thing that could happen had happened, and I was still here. It never happened again during the six-week run, and despite my fears, I never missed a performance.

GIVEN HOW INCREDIBLE this past year has been, I'm looking forward mostly with excitement toward this next year. I'm hoping to continue acting, possibly in other productions of *The Only Thing Worse You Could Have Told Me* . . . I've also gotten calls about other shows, so who knows? I expect I'll continue doing public speaking, which I've really enjoyed. It's very different now from when I gave talks years ago. Now I don't have to worry about censoring myself. I don't have to be afraid that I'll be asked something I can't talk about. I have nothing to hide, so I don't have to dance around a question. When somebody asks a question, I answer it. It's so simple, but what a struggle it was to get to this point.

I plan to continue doing fund-raisers, particularly for AIDS organizations and for PAWS. I hope to find the time to get back to doing volunteer work for PAWS. That's really important to me. Almost anybody can write a check, but it's also important to give your time, to make that kind of personal commitment.

Finding time for my dogs and my personal life has also been a challenge this past year. I'm hoping to carve out more time at home with my dogs and time with friends in the coming months. It's still hard to imagine a full-time relationship, but I've been dating, and that's been fun.

As well as everything's been going, it's impossible for me to ignore that I'm still living with HIV. I take medication every day and go for tests pretty often. And while I feel great, you never know if a cold is going to turn into something more serious. But until something happens, I plan to live my life and make the most of the time I have left, however long I have. I'd be lying if I didn't say that I hope I have a long time.

≈

JUST ONE FINAL THOUGHT. During this past year many people have asked me what they could do to help. My answer is simple. Do what feels right. For me, for the most part, that's meant doing fund-raisers for organizations and causes that are important to me. On occasion I've used both my celebrity and my status as an Olympic gold medalist to speak out on issues where I feel I can make a difference.

Each of us can make a difference, can make a positive contribution, in his or her own way, whether that means opening our checkbooks, volunteering to take care of someone with AIDS, or intervening during gym class when a kid is teased for being a sissy. I'm heartened most by a young girl I met at a book signing in Capitola, California. She was in line with her mom, her aunt, and a cousin. She said, "Mr. Louganis, I'm sorry that they called you names when you were growing up. If I hear somebody calling someone else a name, then I'm going to stop them." We should all be so brave.

APPENDIX

DIVING RECORD AND AWARDS

CAREER HIGHLIGHTS:

- 1984 and 1988 Olympic double gold medalist for 3-meter springboard and 10-meter platform
- 1976 Olympic silver medalist on 10-meter platform
- Five-time world champion: springboard 1982, 1986; platform 1978, 1982, 1986
- FINA World Cup gold medalist: springboard 1983, 1987; platform 1979, 1983
- Winner of 47 U.S. national diving titles, more than anyone in U.S. history
- Swept all three events—1-meter and 3-meter springboard and 10-meter platform at five of the eight U.S. championships between 1985 and 1988
- First diver to break 700 points on platform (and the only one

to do it at the Olympics): 710.91 at the 1984 Olympics and 717.41 at
the 1986 Mission Bay Challenge

• Swept Pan American Games gold medals in 1979, 1983, 1987,
and U.S. Olympic (National Sports) Festival titles in 1982, 1983,
1985, 1986, and 1987

• Only diver to record a perfect dive in both national and world
competition (received a score of 10 from all seven judges)

• Three-time NCAA champion

• Winner of the AAU's James E. Sullivan Award for outstand-
ing achievements in 1984

• Winner of 1987 Jesse Owens Award

• Inducted into the Olympic Hall of Fame in 1985 and the International Swimming Hall of Fame in 1993.

• Winner of the U.S. Olympic Committee's Robert J. Kane
Award 1994

NATIONAL		1-Meter	3-Meter	Platform
		-springboard-		
1988	Phillips 66 Indoor National Championships	2nd	2nd	1st
	Phillips 66 Outdoor National Championships	1st	1st	1st
	U.S. Olympic Diving Trials		1st	1st
1987	Phillips 66 Indoor National Championships	2nd	2nd	2nd
	U.S. Olympic Festival		1st	1st
	Phillips 66 Outdoor National Championships	2nd	1st	1st
1986	Phillips 66 Indoor National Championships	1st	1st	1st
	U.S. Olympic Festival		1st	1st
	Phillips 66 Outdoor National Championships	1st	1st	1st
1985	Phillips 66 Indoor National Championships	1st	1st	1st
	National Sports Festival		1st	1st
	Phillips 66 Outdoor National Championships	1st	1st	1st
1984	Phillips 66 Indoor National Championships	1st	1st	2nd
	U.S. Olympic Diving Trials		1st	1st
	Phillips 66 Outdoor National Championships	1st	1st	1st
1983	Phillips 66 Indoor National Championships	1st	1st	2nd
	National Sports Festival		1st	1st
	Phillips 66 Outdoor National Championships	2nd	1st	1st
1982	National Sports Festival		1st	1st
	Phillips 66 Outdoor National Championships	1st	1st	2nd
1981	Phillips 66 Indoor National Championships	1st	1st	2nd
	National Sports Festival		2nd	1st
	Phillips 66 Outdoor National Championships	1st	1st	2nd
1980	Phillips 66 Indoor National Championships	1st	1st	3rd
	U.S. Olympic Diving Trials		1st	1st
	Phillips 66 Outdoor National Championships	1st	1st	1st
1979	Phillips 66 Indoor National Championships	1st	1st	2nd
	National Sports Festival		1st	
	Phillips 66 Outdoor National Championships	1st	1st	1st
1978	U.S. Indoor National Championships	1st		1st
	U.S. Outdoor National Championships	1st	3rd	1st
1977	U.S. Indoor National Championships			2nd
1976	AAU Indoor National Championships		6th	2nd
	U.S. Diving Olympic Trials		1st	1st
1975	AAU Indoor National Championships		5th	5th

INTERNATIONAL		1-Meter -springboard-	3-Meter	Platform
1988	Australia Day	1st	1st	1st
	Drake International	1st	2nd	1st
	Speedo Classic		1st	2nd
	McDonald's	1st	2nd	
	Pre-Olympic Meet		1st	
	XXIV Olympic Games		1st	1st
1987	Fifth FINA Diving World Cup		1st	
	McDonald's International	1st	1st	1st
	Volksbank International		1st	2nd
	Bolzano International		1st	1st
	Tenth Pan American Games		1st	1st
1986	U.S.A. vs. U.S.S.R.		1st	1st
	McDonald's International		1st	5th
	Fifth World Championships		1st	1st
1984	New Zealand International		1st	
	Australia International		1st	1st
	McDonald's Diving Invitational		1st	1st
	U.S.A. International		1st	1st
	XXIII Olympic Games		1st	1st
1983	Third FINA Diving World Cup		1st	1st
	USA International		1st	1st
	World University Games		1st	1st
	LA 83 International Meet		1st	2nd
	Ninth Pan American Games		1st	1st
1982	Fourth World Championships		1st	1st
1981	Mexican International		2nd	
1980	U.S.A. International		2nd	2nd
	U.S.A. vs. China II		1st	1st
1979	U.S.A. International			3rd
	Eighth Pan American Games		1st	1st
	U.S.A. vs. U.S.S.R.		1st	
	First FINA World Diving Cup			1st
1978	Third World Championships			1st
1976	XXI Olympic Games			2nd

ACKNOWLEDGMENTS

Unlike diving, writing a book is a team effort. Many thanks to our editor, Mitchell Ivers, for his masterful editing and his unflagging enthusiasm; Jed Mattes, our agent, for bringing us to Mitchell and for his daily encouragement; Robby Browne, who got the ball rolling; Kathy Prata, for transcribing hours and hours of interviews; Veronica Windholz, for her sensitive copyediting; and Tanya Pérez, for her beautiful book design.

Thank you, Annie Leibovitz, and all the other photographers who contributed their wonderful work to the book. And much appreciation to Benjamin Dreyer, production editor; Elina Choung, production manager; Fred Morris, our agent's assistant; and Alexandra Fox, our editor's assistant.

Also thank you to Billy Kolber, Peggy Levine, Dr. Kathy Shon, and Maggi Stern for their helpful comments on the manuscript. And finally, thank you to those who generously shared their memories, espe-

cially Ron and Mary Jane O'Brien, Megan Neyer, and Frances Louganis.

ERIC MARCUS

It takes guts to dive off a 10-meter platform, and even more courage to
bare your soul. Thank you, Greg, for trusting me.

Thank you, also, to Daniel Levy for his advice on research; Robert
Getlan, my Mac guru, who came through in moments of desperation;
my attorney, Michael Naso, for expert advice; Joy Harris, Marian
Young, and Susan Simon, for keeping me well fed through the first ten
chapters; Brutus and Donna, who reminded me why I like small dogs;
and Barney Karpfinger, for lots of things. And thank you to my many
friends who once again offered support, encouragement, and advice,
including Mark Burstein and David Calle, Dr. Stephen Frommer, Brett
Morrow, Stuart Schear, and Phil Roselin.

GREG LOUGANIS

Boy, what a journey! Thank you to Eric Marcus for his insight, courage,
patience, and persistence in helping me dig deep into my heart and
soul to uncover my story. We both needed a lot of hugs along the way
from each other and friends.

Lots of thanks to Maggi Stern for her day-to-day help searching
through my papers and keeping me organized; Megan Neyer and Ron
and Mary Jane O'Brien, who generously offered their homes, their
time, and their encouragement; and Dr. Stan Ziegler, for helping me
understand my past and sort out my future.

And thank you, Mom and Aunt Geri, for all the newspaper clips,
photographs, and unconditional love.